Rachel Morris

Honeymoon in Purdah

HONEYMOON IN PURDAH

An Iranian Journey

ALISON WEARING

PICADOR USA
NEW YORK

Picador® is a U.S. registered trademark and is used by
St. Martin's Press under license from Pan Books Limited.

Parts of "The Small Speed Bus" and "Too Much Ridiculous"
appeared, in slightly different form, in the *Queen's Quarterly.*

Map by Stephanie Aykroyd
Text design by Gordon Robertson

ISBN 0-312-26181-0

First published in Canada by Alfred A. Knopf Canada

First Picador USA Edition: November 2000

10 9 8 7 6 5 4 3 2 1

for my mother

AUTHOR'S NOTE

This is a sketchbook, a collection of my impressions of Iran and its people. For the most part, I have painted situations as they occurred, presented voices as precisely as possible. At times, I have made collages of stories and faces, as often to protect the identities of people as to lend artistry to a scene. As is the case with many portraits, their truth is not in their detail, but their spirit.

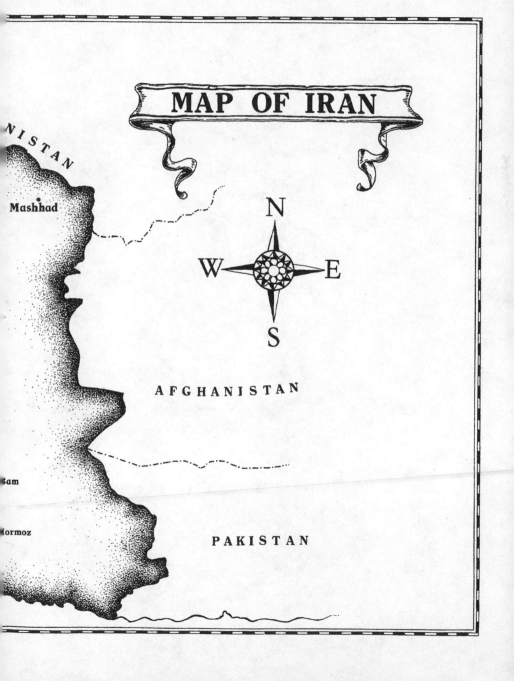

CONTENTS

THE SMALL
SPEED BUS

THIS IS THE ROOM that leads to Iran. It is oblong. A door at each end. Bare, but for two portraits, one above each doorway. General Kemal Atatürk watches over the edge of his land from the western door. The Ayatollah Ruholla Khomeini from the east. I walk to what feels like the middle of the room and stand like a flamingo, balancing between countries.

I fall back onto both feet when a group of women blows through Atatürk's door. They are ancient and wizened, tiny, all of them, and wrapped in white veils. They flutter around each other, then squat on the floor holding fistfuls of fabric under their chins. Their teeth act as an extra set of fingers, gripping and tugging their covering constantly, obsessively, as though they could work at it all day and never get it quite right. They are so skittish that the slightest thing—a door opening, someone walking too close to them, a question directed at them—sends them scurrying off in all directions. Startled chickens. They shriek and scatter, veils flapping, feet shuffling; then, gradually, they regroup, their pitch drops, the movement settles, and they return to quiet chatter and the business of covering themselves.

When we bought our bus tickets in Istanbul, we were told the trip to Tehran—approximately two thousand kilometres southeast—cost the equivalent of twenty-five US dollars and took twenty-four hours. We'd be getting off early, in Tabriz, just over the Iranian border. About eighteen hours away, by rough calculation. We ate a big meal at the nearest food stand and spent the last of our Turkish money on a bit of fruit and bread for the journey.

Eventually, somewhere in hour thirty, we asked our neighbour in the seat behind why we were still on the Anatolian plain. He smiled and explained that twenty-four hours is the "poetic" time, the time it would take, say, a good car, if it drove without stopping. Maybe a German car. But you see this is an Iranian bus, with many old parts and small speed, and we will stop for toilets and praying, and then there is the border, which can be very slow. So the real time is more like two or three nights.

Khosro befriended us the moment we got on the bus in Istanbul. "Excuse me," he said when he heard us speaking English. "Will you travel to Iran?" We nodded. He sat back and translated for his friend, Hossein. A few seconds later, Khosro sat forward again and poked his head over the tops of our seats. "Excuse me, your *choice* it is?"

We were not out of Istanbul's city limits before the first person walked to the front of the bus with a box of cookies and offered one to every passenger. A few hours later someone else offered dates, then sunflower seeds, then something that resembled candy floss. Khosro and Hossein

passed bread, cheese and vegetables up to us at regular
intervals. When I thanked them for the eggplant caviar,
which was delicious, they insisted that we take three cans.
No, four. Here's another. The old women in front of us
stuck their hands through the seats from time to time,
reached for my hands and filled them with nuts. The couple across the aisle handed us a bottle of orange soda every
time we looked in their direction.

We were also not out of Istanbul's city limits before
the bus had its first of I'm not sure how many collapses.
More than five. Each breakdown prompted men to get
off the bus, gather around the engine with one hand up to
their chin and look perplexed. Some prayed by the side of
the road. I never saw anyone but the drivers do anything
to the engine but stare.

The rest of us stood off to the side and got acquainted.

Khosro was in Istanbul to apply for a tourist visa to the
United States. He took the bus from Tehran (poetic time
24 hours; real time 75 hours), spent two days making his
visa request at the American embassy in Istanbul and
is now on his way back to Tehran. His visa request was
denied, but he plans to try again next year. Hossein came
along to keep Khosro company. Did he enjoy Istanbul?
Yes, very beautiful, though he only saw the Blue Mosque
and the American embassy.

Most of the other passengers had gone to Istanbul to
apply for visas to *Emrika* as well. No one had been successful, but most were planning to try again next year. Everyone brought at least one friend or family member along for
company; one man brought six of his cousins. There was a
family on holiday, several people on religious pilgrimages
and a young couple returning from their honeymoon.

They were proud and nervous, this couple, awkward with each other, giddy at the idea of each other. He was older, much older, and tried to look confident. She was younger, young—maybe fourteen—and in awe of the world. They kept to themselves during the trip, spent a lot of time smiling, and spoke to each other through quick, shy whispers. Occasionally touched hands in public. Prayed at every opportunity. She was the only woman on the bus in full hejab, the covering prescribed by Islam to protect female modesty: a black floor-length coat and headscarf, folded tightly around the face, covered by a chaador, the swath of black fabric draped over the head and arms. The older women wore white veils, the colour of mourning. The younger women dressed in shirts and trousers, some in dresses, one in jeans. A handful wore headscarves.

But when we neared the border, coats and scarves were pulled down from bags and the costuming began. The woman across the aisle yanked out a blue trenchcoat and donned it in the aisle, rolling her eyes as she did so. She threw on a purple scarf loosely; her teased hair held it several inches above her head.

The last stretch of Turkey was slow. A series of road-blocks had been set up by soldiers deployed in the country's eastern corner to fight the Kurdish insurrection. This was a war zone, we were told. So security had to be tight. And it was. So tight that the only way to squeeze between the tanks parked across the road was to wedge a few bills into the fist of the soldier who checked our passports. And then into the fist of the other soldier, and his friend, and the one who threatened to take us all off the bus and go through our bags one by one. An extra few for him. We were required to pass through eight of these "security checks" in the space of an hour. Some took cigarettes from passengers as they were checking them; some haggled directly with the driver. One group of soldiers dispensed with the ritual of looking at passports and simply boarded the bus saying they needed money for tea.

Forty unpoetic hours after leaving Istanbul, we reached the edge of Turkey.

Where we are now. Waiting.

ಬಬ

One of our bus drivers appears with an armload of passports and exit papers, and begins returning them to his passengers. We have been cleared and can proceed to Iranian customs.

There is a scramble at the Khomeini door, where our busmates struggle with their luggage. Some have set up an assembly line to transport their wall of boxes. The man with six cousins has each of them dragging at least ten bags. I trade winks with a woman from the front of the bus, whose hejab consists of a knee-length crimson coat with bright blue buttons and a patterned scarf. ("She's a Tehrani," Khosro explains, "so her hejab is very, hm, soft.") I gather my things and follow.

Wait—I'm forgetting something.

My husband.

Damn. I promised I wouldn't do that.

(The last time I travelled with someone, I completely forgot about him. We were in China, ate red bean pancakes for breakfast and walked to the train station together, that much I remember clearly. It was crowded, oh Mao, very crowded, and the train was delayed. It's the next bit that's fuzzy. I was in the middle of a good book—did he say something about going to find a toilet?—when there was an announcement and the train arrived at another platform. The crowd produced the standard hysteria required by such a decision: yelling, barking, tripping, kicking, squeezing, grunting, dodging, catapulting, etc. I joined the fray, was flung onto the train—book still in hand, mind still in book—squeezed onto a bench, read several chapters while eating boiled peanuts, warm beer, and a stale moon cake. Fell asleep. Awoke. Fluttered my eyes and brought the faces of the people around me into focus, looked around, gasped and cupped a hand over my mouth.

Only later did I learn that the train had not, in fact, arrived at a different platform. I had simply boarded the wrong train. To a destination six hundred miles off course, near the Laotian border.

I am quite determined not to do that again. For one, there are far fewer trains in Iran. For another, this is the only country in which I could not imagine travelling alone. Therefore the obvious destination for our honeymoon. Which this is.)

I step back from Khomeini's glare and retrace my steps, squeeze through a crowd of Afghanis, back across the point of balance, through the group of old women—scream skitter settle—and behind a pile of burlap sacks, where I left Ian sleeping an hour ago.

He looks content. Wears the beatific expression of someone resting in a bathtub. He has arranged the sacks and bags around him into a pillow and backrest. His own pack he cuddles like a teddy. I kneel beside him and touch his forehead—kissing in public isn't illegal on this side of the room, but best to get out of the habit—and he shudders awake. Starts up in a panic and checks for his pack, his money belt, his glasses. Check, check, check. Relaxes. Notices me. Smiles.

"Time to go."

He bristles. Says "Oh" in such a way that he looks like a fish, holding his mouth in an open pucker long after the sound has gone. I stick my finger into the O-shape, and he takes a deep breath through his nostrils that reinflates him so much that he jumps to his feet and stamps around a bit. Says "Whoa" and "Hokay" and "Whoohoo" and swings his pack over his shoulder.

"Let's go."

We wend our way back towards the eastern door, take an audibly deep breath and walk through.

So far, Iran is a big, square concrete room with a lot of people in it. Unlike Turkey, the room I just left, people here are standing in lines. Twelve straightish lines that lead to twelve bearded men. Behind them is a row of curtains. Behind those, presumably, is the rest of the country.

We join a line with Khosro and Hossein and wait.

Four hours later our line has moved by fifteen lengths of my feet.

Four hours after that our line has moved by twenty-two and a half lengths of my feet.

Four hours after that our line has not moved at all, but we have eaten several handfuls of sunflower seeds and some figs. Supplied by others in line.

Two hours after that we move so quickly that Ian and I are the next in line. The couple ahead of us are being asked to unpack every one of their eighteen bags. Clothes, linens, pillows (seams ripped, insides checked), canned goods, packaged foods, toys (taken out of boxes and inspected, one stuffed bear ripped open and searched), towels, breakable items (protective paper unwrapped and stacked in a heap to the side), reams of fabric, cassettes (confiscated), children's books (one, with illustrations of a blonde mother in a sleeveless dress, confiscated), cooking utensils, books (perused and approved). The couple are instructed to move to the next table to repack. Their belongings, once neatly folded and wrapped, are now littered across the inspection table and spilling onto the floor.

Without a word or a huff or a protest of any kind, the couple gather their things by the armful and transfer them to the next table. The inspector stands back. Watches. Points to a few items that have fallen on the floor by his feet. Looks away as the woman crawls under the table to retrieve them. Stares into space and tells them to hurry it up. Digs something out of his ear and flicks it onto the floor.

Once the table is cleared, the inspector motions for our bags. He asks Ian to unzip his pack and kneads through a handful of clothes, then pushes the bag away. Reaches for my bag and does the same thing. Flips through my journal as though he were fanning himself, replaces it, pushes my bag away. We zip up our bags and move towards the curtained section of the room.

"Your passports are very golden." Hossein laughs as he places his bags on the table and begins unpacking things piece by piece.

Ian and I are guided in two different directions. He to the curtains on the left, I to the curtains on the right. Behind my set are three women in full hejab. And full moustaches. Like none I have seen on any woman before. Not just a dark fringe above the mouth. The sort of moustache that would make any adolescent boy jealous. None of the women smiles. They sit slumped in their chairs, their eyes drooping down into their cheeks. The most hirsute woman beckons me and asks me to raise my arms, which allows me to survey her at close range. And she me. She does a cursory body check—shoulders, back, abdomen, legs—and asks me to explain the lump on my stomach. I unbutton my coat and shirt and show her my money belt. Fine, she nods and pushes me away. The three women continue their conversation.

I pass through the final set of curtains and move outside: a parking lot full of buses and hundreds of people either preparing for or recovering from the border. I weave around vehicles that are in various stages of being packed or unpacked, goods spilling from every orifice, but do not see our bus. Instead, I find a shack with a few tables and a samovar. I peer into the place and trade smiles with a roly-poly Mongolian-looking man in a fur hat and padded coat. He points to his thermos of tea and offers his cup. I accept. After wiping the stool next to him with his sleeve, he tosses his remaining tea onto the floor, refills the cup and passes it to me. Very smilingly.

After forty hours on the bus and fourteen on the border, this tea feels like a jacuzzi. I close my eyes and sigh. The man laughs. Pulls some leather-stale bread from a bag in his coat and rips several strips off for me. I dunk and devour, then thank him in Chinese, Russian, Farsi,

Arabic and English. I can't tell if any or all have been understood. He smiles and nods constantly whether I am speaking or not. Halfway through my second cup of tea, someone leans through the doorway and shouts. My friend sits up and responds, apologizes to me—his bus is leaving—and packs up his thermos. He leaves me with a handful of bread strips and winks with both eyes.

In his place sits a young man who offers tea he has bought at the counter. I thank him and accept. He is from Lahore. Do I know it? Well, I am welcome to visit. Very beautiful. And me? Canada! He has a brother in Canada. Maybe I know him.

"Umhm . . ." I sip my tea and accept a cookie.

"He lives in city Montreal. He is artist. Painter."

"Umhm . . ." I take another sip.

The man fumbles through his belongings and brings out his address book. Flip flip flip. Points to his brother's name.

"Umhm . . ." I take another sip of tea and glance at the book, take a deep breath through my nostrils then cough hack choke gasp cough cough choke and wipe my mouth.

He's the ex-boyfriend of an old roommate.

"He is a friend," I tell the man, who flutters his eyelashes in disbelief. Points to the name and address again to be sure I haven't made a mistake. "I lived on the same street," I tell him until he believes me. The man shakes his head and flutters some more, then leans back and explains to the men standing behind him. They come over to inspect the address book and to have the coincidence explained three or four more times. The shack owner offers us complimentary tea, but before we take our first sip, the man—Jamal, pleased to meet you—is called away by a friend. His bus is leaving too. Jamal rips a page from his address book and gives me his name and address. Invites me again to Lahore. I thank him, but tell him not to expect me soon. I write my name and address next to his brother's, turn to give the book back and see Jamal's eyes full of tears.

"My brother is happy?"

I look at Jamal and think back to the last time I saw his brother. Cold, depressed and lonely. Chain-smoking in his tiny Montreal apartment, sipping tea and staring into space. Telling me how tired he is. Tired of living in such a violent country. "Canada," he told me one day through squinted eyes and smoke rings, "is full of violent cowards. People believe they are gentle, but they attack in quiet ways. They use their intellect, their knowledge, always trying to prove they are smarter, more important. The man with no ego is the gentle man. Canada is a land of civilized barbarians."

Jamal looks pained and waits for a response.

His bus honks. It is stuffed full of people and belongings, the goods tied down to the roof increasing the height of the bus by half again. Jamal puts a hand over his heart, bows his head, then runs onto the bus. He turns around in the doorway and waves, leaving a smear of white in the air where he has left me his smile.

ରୂପ୍ୟ

I wander back to the main building and catch sight of Ian pacing outside the women's exit. Both arms fly up like a puppet when he sees me. I approach him with all sorts of *You'll never guess who I just ran into!* enthusiasm, but he cuts me off with a *Where in the hell have you been?* rancour. He is too upset to find my story the least bit interesting. I am too excited by my story to apologize convincingly. I agree to be more considerate in future—ahem—and he agrees to grant me a one-hour window of spontaneous exploration before he begins to worry.

Before we have made up completely, the sound of our English conversation has attracted the attention of two black marketeers, who offer to exchange our dollars. Ian and I lower the volume of our bickering and go in search of our bus.

It looks like a dinosaur that has just had its guts ripped out. Once the mass of boxes and bags and sacks and containers strewn across the ground are piled into and onto our bus, it will resemble the one Jamal rode away in. Until then, it is an armoured beast with open wounds. Khosro and Hossein seem to think we should be on the road again very soon. Poetically speaking.

The money-changers have followed us and continue their offers. "It is a good price," Khosro assures us. About eight times the government rate. We make the exchange just as our bus is leaving. Three and a half hours later. Just before dark.

The bus moves slowly onto the road. I hear a clinking sound and watch the man beside me pull airplane-size bottles of Johnnie Walker from his socks and stuff them into his bag. "Oh, my G—" Ian gasps. "Isn't alcohol *highly* illegal?" The man looks up and smiles, shrugs sheepishly and continues. He transfers more bottles from various pockets and stows the bag under his seat.

Not a mile along, we pull into a cordoned area and stop. A man boards the bus and asks people to get up from their seats two at a time. He checks passports, then

all seats and window curtains—finds nothing—and de-
barks. We wait. A second man appears and the bus turns
silent. So silent that I feel the air tear and crinkle as people breathe. This man is dressed entirely in black, wears
very short hair and a thick beard. He stands at the end of
the aisle and scans the bus, his eyes gouging into people's
faces with intense suspicion. He walks slowly, up and
down the aisle, stopping at random and asking questions;
sometimes demanding to see identity papers. He speaks
in a whisper. He walks past our neighbour across the
aisle, then takes steps backwards until he is beside him.
Leans down and whispers into his ear. Our neighbour
looks straight ahead and replies in a whisper. The bearded
man asks a number of whispered questions. Our neighbour fixes his gaze ahead and whispers his answers. The
bearded man straightens up and moves on. He looks Ian
up and down and asks for our passports. Squints as he
compares our pictures with our faces, then walks away
with our passports and asks something of the driver.
Again, in a whisper. The driver follows him back to our
seats and points to our luggage. The man surveys our
packs and returns our passports. Follows the driver back
down the aisle and leaves the bus. The driver closes the
door and pulls back onto the road. The air shatters into a
thousand conversations.

Khosro's face pops up behind our headrests. "Welcome to Iran," he laughs. "Do not be scared from these
men. They need for respecting, so we do not speak. It
causes that they think they are important."

A few miles into the country, we stop at a roadside
restaurant. Khosro and Hossein go back to inspect the
kitchen. "We check that it is not poisonous," Hossein

explains and hurries off behind Khosro. They return with smiles and assurances—"It is good kitchen, not dirty from old meat"—and tell us they have ordered food enough for all of us. Glasses of yogurt, plates of kebab, bread and tomatoes. Four other passengers join our table: a Kurdish couple (who join us only after I invite them and then insist), and our bus drivers.

We have two drivers. While one drives, the other stretches out at the back of the bus surrounded by pillows and tasselled curtains. (The first time I saw the relief driver lying in the resting place, hands crossed over his stomach, I thought we were transporting a dead king.) When he is rested and feels like driving again, he walks to the front of the bus. The two men wind their limbs around and through the other's, gradually passing off the pedals and the steering wheel. While the bus is in motion.

The Kurdish couple are two of the jolliest people I've ever met. People who, even if they are looking out the window saying nothing, are smiling. Nasreen sits beside me with her three-week old baby. The infant is tightly swaddled, an inanimate object that has not made a sound since we left Istanbul. It is wrapped in Nasreen's layers and layers of colour. Crimson and sapphire skirts, scarlet and ruby and indigo scarves, a ruffled plum blouse and a black shawl. Her skin is coarse and fair. She laughs like a crow. Since meeting a couple of days ago, she has taken to holding my hand at every opportunity, unless I say something she finds funny, in which case she swats me on the arm. Her husband has red hair, wears loose brown woollen trousers and a wide sash.

Nasreen has still not recovered from learning that Ian and I are taking our honeymoon in Iran. The first time it was translated for her, she squinted her entire face and said *ehhh*? After clarification and confirmation from us, she doubled over laughing and announced the news to everyone within earshot. Now, everytime there is a lull in conversation, she says *honeymoooon* and pinches my cheeks.

When the food arrives, half of it is doled out for Ian and me, the other half among the remaining six people. Protest is useless; we are the only ones at the table who are dissatisfied with the arrangement. Between bites, Khosro and Hossein are trying to talk us into going with them all the way to Tehran, but we explain our plans to get off in Tabriz, the capital of Azerbaijan province. Where we have friends, I tell them. Because I don't know the Farsi word for acquaintances.

When the bus moves back onto the road, the place breaks into song and dance. People are clapping, snapping their fingers, singing and dancing in the aisles. An old man who was asleep for most of the trip is now twisting up and down the aisle to the cheers of everyone on the bus. Nasreen giggles and ululates until the roof vibrates. Her husband gets up and dances briefly, but is quickly embarrassed and collapses his head into Nasreen's shoulder. The fiesta goes on for at least an hour; then we are pulled over again by security.

This time a simple passport/identity paper check results in Nasreen's husband being taken off the bus for questioning. "He is Kurd," explains Khosro. "They are people without country, only living in other country, for example Iran, Turkey, Iraq. Mostly they live like small citizen, without right of regular people. Some Kurdish people want own country for them, so they make little

bit war with Turkey right now. For this reason some people are afraid from them and always they have problem at
border. It is hard for them."

One of the drivers stands up at the front of the bus and
makes an announcement. Khosro strains forward to hear.
The driver speaks for ten or fifteen minutes, lays a hand
over his heart and returns to his seat. Khosro translates:

"He tell that in this time, when we must wait for this
passenger, he can share one experience from his life with
us. This driver tell that maybe it is interesting for us and
maybe we feel less long waiting when he tell story of his
hajj. Do you know what is hajj? It is special journey to
Mecca, in Saudi Arabia. Every Muslim people must make
this journey one time in life. It mean they become more
close with God and other good thing. He tell that it was
very important travelling for him, time to meet many
Muslim people from all part world. Everyone think like
brother and share. Time for seeing power of God a lot
and thinking very close about God. He tell about many
people, brothers from Syria and Iraq and many other
place. All brother in God, all—"

Nasreen's husband climbs back on the bus. Behind him
is a soldier, who waits at the front while Nasreen is woken
and told that they must take their things and get off. She is
exhausted but acquiescent. She bundles her baby in her
arms, gathers her skirts and shawls, offers tired goodbyes
to the people around her and follows her husband off
the bus.

When we pull back onto the road, the bus is quiet.
People around us speak softly. Phrases full of *tsks* and
raised eyebrows.

"What will happen to them?"

Khosro and Hossein discuss it among themselves—grumbles and lip-shrugs—then look at us with apologetic smiles. "Maybe for more question," says Khosro. "Maybe it is for war in Turkey I tell about. Kurd make big problem. Maybe soldier are afraid from these problem."

He leans back in his seat, grumbles a bit more with Hossein, leans forward again. "Excuse me. In this country has many problem. Please try enjoy. Most important you enjoy our country."

He leans back in his seat, grumbles a bit more with Hossein, leans forward again. "Excuse me. Please. Most important you enjoy your honeymoon."

ဏ

The bus driver wakes us. "Tabriz," he says and points out the window.

I am swollen with travel. My limbs are clubs, heavy and awkward. I gather my bag, my shoes, my covering, and stand. Khosro and Hossein are sitting with their heads cocked back and their mouths open. We leave them sleeping and stumble out into the night.

The driver retrieves our bags from under the bus and places them on the ground. He points to a building across the road. "Police," he says. He shakes Ian's hand, closes his eyes and bows his head to me. We thank him and say goodbye, listen to the door hiss shut and watch him leave us by the side of the road.

I have come to this place because it frightens me; because it frightens the world. And because I don't believe in fear. In giving it such power.

I am a sculptor. I walk to stone and sit with it. Walk around it and touch it, stand back from it, stare at it with my eyes closed until I see its spirit. Trapped in petrified form. Then I release its image.

I have come to release spirit from stone.

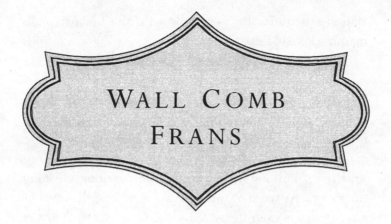

WALL COMB
FRANS

IT FEELS AS THOUGH we've been dropped into the bottom of a gorge. So hollow is the air. We watch the bus until the last trace of sound has died, then turn our heads around on our necks like owls. We have the choice of four roads, each of them leading nowhere, or the militia station across from where we are standing. It is a squat brick building with light in the windows. It houses friendly, helpful, gentle men, or xenophobic thugs; we have no idea which. Maybe we could sit here on the side of the road and wait for light—but no. Someone has seen us.

He is calling, expecting an answer, and not getting one. Walking closer. He has called several others, who accompany him across the road, where I am shuffling through my mind looking for the Farsi phrases I have spent the last few months memorizing.

"Hello. Ve-ry-pleased-to-meet-you. We-are-tou-rists."

I am sounding the words out, note by note, while staring at the air around my nose. The men take a half step back and make their faces look like puzzles. They look to each other, then to us. I repeat. They point to the militia station and motion for us to follow them. One man picks up our bags and leads.

Ian and I grip each other by the eyes and follow.

The place is very green. Green walls, green floors, green ceilings, green pipes. And it is full of green-uniformed men, all fully engaged in the act of doing nothing. There are at least thirty of them, sitting, standing, stooping, squatting, shuffling up and down the corridor, cleaning their nails. As word of our arrival circulates, the level of activity drops even further. By the time we are halfway down the hallway, all men are frozen, some in mid-stride.

We are led to a room where a couple of men are seated behind a desk and several others are leaning against walls at various points around the room. Our bags are placed by the door and our situation explained, but I don't notice the men's reactions because I am staring at the floor. We are told to sit down and surrender our passports, which we do. One of the soldiers takes our passports out of the room and down the hall.

There is silence.

The men in front of me are staring at the empty desk in front of them. The man behind me is wheezing. Three more men enter the room at different points in the silence and slump against the wall. One man sits behind the men behind the desk and begins tearing sheets of paper.

I turn to Ian and whisper that maybe we should tell them our reason for getting off here in the middle of the night like this. I pull my phrase book from my pocket and begin piecing together sentences. I whisper them to Ian, syllable by syllable, and he speaks the words in full voice to the soldiers at the desk. I am a ventriloquist.

The men look bewildered by the ritual, but they listen politely, often with strained faces, as people do when they are focusing all their effort on trying to understand. When we have finished our statement, one of the soldiers cups his hands in front of me, asking for the book. I offer it immediately. Three men lean over and begin sounding out individual words. One man shows Ian the phrase *This is my first visit to Iran* while making question marks with his voice. Ian nods. A boy appears with a tray of glasses.

"*Befarmaeed,*" he says, bowing.

"Does that mean tea?" Ian asks me out of the corner of his mouth.

"No, I think it means help yourself."

"How sure are you?"

"Fairly."

Ian reaches for a glass. He tries to follow the custom we've read about—slurping tea through a sugar cube held between the teeth—but he ends up sucking the chunk of sugar into his throat and choking, prompting all the men behind him to abandon their walls and whack him on the back. One of the men points to the tea and indicates to me. I reach for a glass and hold it close to my lips. Take slow, silent sips and fold in on myself.

My body is a shell, hard and lacquered against the air. Inside I am a tender sac. Aware of every change in the wind, every twitch.

The tea finished, we try again to explain ourselves. Ian pulls out the name and telephone number of our contact, and it is passed around and read aloud by every man in the room. One of the men puts the number in front of him and reaches for a telephone that is so large it looks like a stage prop. The receiver is of such gigantic proportions that when he holds one end to his ear, the mouthpiece juts out in front of his chest. As he begins dialling, Ian moves forward and waves him to stop. The man looks confused and rests the receiver on his shoulder. Ian points to his watch.

"It is the middle of the night," Ian says and mimes someone sleeping. "We've never met these people." He acts out someone answering a telephone and saying, *Huh??* with a sour, confused expression. The man behind the desk responds with a sour, confused expression. Listens to the interpretations of some of his colleagues, who seem to have understood. Gives Ian a not-to-worry wave. Props the receiver back against his ear. Dials again.

Ian looks to me and shrugs.

Everyone stares at the telephone.

It takes several diallings before a connection is made; an event conveyed to us by the raising of eyebrows. There follows a short conversation conducted at top volume, none of which I understand. The receiver is replaced. Our caller says a few words to his colleagues, gets up and leaves the room, thus providing us with a clearer view of the soldier seated against the wall with a stack of papers. His routine is this: he takes four or five sheets at a time and rips them into pieces. Gathers these pieces into a pile. Has been doing this since we walked into this building.

"Think he's shredding documents?" Ian whispers.

The man stops the exercise and looks at us.

"Do you speak English?" Ian asks, hesitantly.

The man gets up from his seat and walks to the corner where several men are poring over my phrase book. The shredder also peruses the book, then approaches Ian with his finger on the following sentence: *Excuse me, but do you know where I might be able to get this dry-cleaned?*

"Guess not."

The man returns to his pile.

His boss returns to his desk with a new tray, this one with a bowl of dates, a spoon and two glasses of water. *"Befarmaeed."*

It's been well over an hour and we are still here. Our passports have been returned. We've eaten all the dates and had another glass of tea. The man by the wall has finished shredding papers into squares. He has just begun ripping these squares into even smaller pieces. We have had a conversation with the men around the phrasebook—as it turns out, our shredder meant to point to the phrase *Is there a rubbish bin around here?* but had moved his finger on the walk over to us—and have just reached the chapter on family/relations.

Apparently a taxi is on its way.

There is a great fuss by the doorway, and we are led outside. The taxi driver looks as if he just rolled out of bed. Because he did. Two soldiers carry our bags to the car, others come to discuss the location of our friends' house, the best way of getting there, etc. We get into the back seat and are driven through a coil of dark streets. Several times the driver gets lost. Backs up, squints at road signs, stops and rereads our friends' address. Ian and I sit in the back seat saying nothing.

Many minutes later the driver leans back and assures us he has found the address. He slows the car and points to a man standing in the middle of the road in his pyjamas.

Our host.

The friend of a friend of a friend. Not exactly. More like an acquaintance of a friend of an acquaintance whose name was copied down on the back of a (linen) napkin one night in a smoky trattoria in Rome after homemade ravioli, rapini with garlic, thick red wine, and loud conversations about literature and masturbation.

"You travel to Iran? *Porca miseria*—I know someone there! Twenty years ago I drive to India in my Volkswagen, big van with bed, and I meet this guy, we become friends. I give you his address! You write to him! You tell him you are friend of me and come for visit!"

I folded the napkin into my pocket and wrote a letter the next day.

And now there is a man standing in the middle of the road in his pyjamas, paying for our taxi.

He introduces himself—Hamid—and invites us inside.

A woman stands in the doorway at the top of the stairs. She wears a beautiful, timid smile, a blouse and long skirt, and a headscarf. She bows her head and smiles.

"I introduce my wife, Sayeh."

I shake her hand. She nods to Ian. We take off our shoes and step inside. Sayeh asks to take my coat, then motions for me to remove my scarf, which I do, tentatively, afraid I might be misinterpreting the gesture.

"Please," says Hamid. "This is your home. You think here as your home."

Sayeh hangs my things in a closet and excuses herself. Hamid asks us to sit down.

We sit on the floor around a plastic mat and eat soup. I drown my spoon in white liquid and paint it against my tongue. The steam soothes my face, raw from exhaustion, and I blink slowly over my bowl until my eyeballs feel moist inside my skull.

It is four o'clock in the morning.

The air is taut with the politeness of a first meeting. We are all on our best behaviour. There are silences and throat-clearings. Sighs that take the place of words. I pull my face into a toady smile each time I touch the eyes of our hosts. They offer the same in return and ask me, every few minutes, if I would like some more soup.

"Na, merci."

Silence.

Smiles.

Soup.

The only sound in the room, apart from the scraping of spoons against bowls, is some dusty snoring coming from a small body on the floor in a darkened part of the room.

When my chin begins to droop against my chest, Hamid shows us to a room with thin mattresses on the floor and pillows the length of my body. We thank him and collapse.

I awaken under the gaze of a child, whose eyes widen as mine open. She stands up—still staring—and calls to her mother, who calls back to her. And begins cooking. Calls to her daughter again, then once more, before the child inches out the door backwards, still staring. Grins, giggles, skips away.

By the time Ian and I pull ourselves together, Hamid is waiting for us as anxiously as his daughter. Did we sleep?

Was it comfortable? Was there some problem with our arrangements? Did Annahita make some botherings? Are we ready for eating?

We sit on the floor—there is no furniture in the house—and Sayeh spreads a plastic mat on the floor. "Annahita like to tell something before eating," Hamid says. He speaks in a low voice to Annahita, who smiles at us. Hamid speaks to her again. She bites her lip, then smiles again.

"Wall comb," she says and giggles into her hands.

"*Well*-come," Hamid corrects. "Well-come-friends."

"Wall comb frans," Annahita repeats and giggles again.

Sayeh arrives with a tray of food. She smiles shyly and sits down next to Annahita, who is singing in that beautiful way that children do before they become self-conscious: tilting her head around and around, opening her mouth as wide as she can. Unaware that singing is embarrassing. Sayeh scolds her daughter and motions to us. Be good in front of our guests. Annahita stops.

We eat eggs and bread and white cheese in small, silent bites. Smile a lot. Compliment the food. At the end of the meal I help Sayeh carry some of the dishes back to the kitchen and pile them on the floor, but she smiles and shakes her head. Calls to Hamid to translate.

"No, thank you," he calls to me. "You are guests. This is wifely work."

Annahita is eight. She has raced home from school every day for the last month to ask whether we had arrived. This morning she awoke to the exciting news that we were sleeping in the next room and would be awake by the time she returned from school. She sits across from us now and talks to her father.

"Annahita thought that you are bigger than this. But you are of same size like Iranian people, except eyeglasses of Mr. Ian, these are not normal."

Annahita's eyes are black cherries, dark and rich. They glisten when she smiles, which is often, and are wide wide wide, full of wonder. She is bold. Speaks in full voice and asks question upon question, long after her parents tell her that is enough. Her curiosity coils her into knots, she squirms and looks determined, then asks another question—"Shhh, Annahita, that's enough"—then another and another. Finally she gets up and opens her school bag, fishes out an orange marker and dabs the tip of the marker to her nose. Looks at Ian with the most innocently inquisitive face.

"They're freckles," Ian says. (Sayeh is so embarrassed she is hiding her face behind her scarf.) "Freckles."

"Frags," Annahita parrots.

"Freckles."

"Frag holes."

"That's it."

Annahita is satisfied enough to sit down again. She sits cross-legged, is still for several seconds, then begins bouncing her knees up and down against the floor. Her mother is stern. Annahita stops. Presses her lips together and smiles with googly eyes. Her long dark hair curls around her body as she moves.

She is eight. Next year she will be a woman according to an edict of Khomeini that lowered the legal age of marriage for girls to nine. For the remainder of this year Annahita is a child. She may walk in the streets dressed as she is now: in a black-and-white minidress with white stockings and shiny red shoes, her hair loose and exposed, adorned with a ribbon. Because she is not yet tempting. But in four months she will grow into womanhood. And she must be shielded from temptation.

Sayeh whispers to Annahita and raises her eyebrows towards a closet on the other side of the room. Annahita jumps up and skips over to the closet, checks with her mother before opening it, then pulls out a fold of black fabric. She lays the miniature chaador over her head and shoulders and wraps it around her body like a cape, holds the fabric in her fists and curls them tightly under her chin. She looks out at us, coyly.

"Beautiful," Sayeh says, nodding and smiling at her daughter.

Annahita breaks out of the chaador with a burst of laughter, throws the fabric up in the air and falls into her father's lap. Sayeh scolds her daughter, demanding that she get up and put it away properly. Annahita stands up and folds the fabric, replaces it the way she found it, closes the closet door. Sits back down in her father's lap and asks another question. He whispers a short answer and stares until his seriousness has soaked into her.

"Annahita make a question, why you do not wear scarf like Sayeh," Hamid tells us. "I explain it is for Iranian woman, but for Canadian woman is differently."

ರಾಜ

I am a bit concerned that after months of teach-yourself-Farsi cassettes (played on my Walkman and recited aloud to the quizzical glances of people around me), I am unable to understand a word being spoken. Nothing in the texture and rhythm of the language is familiar.

"We speak Azeri," Hamid explains. "It is almost same like Turkey language. For Azeri people, Farsi is number two language, for example school and office, government and television, but Azeri is more homely."

Hamid shifts Annahita off his lap and stands.

"Excuse, but I must return to my work. I see you for dinner. Before that, do not worry, Sayeh meet your needies."

"We've decided to take a walk. Just a short one. Just up to the town centre. Just to take a look around. No, no, there's no need to leave work and come with us. We'll be fine, really. We'll stay on the main streets. I'm sure we won't have any difficulties. Yes, if we do, we'll call you. No, I'm sure we don't need anything, but thank you. Thank you very much. We'll be careful. Yes, I promise we'll be careful. We'll just walk up the street and turn around and come back again. Yes, it would be very nice to go walking with family after your working. Yes, good idea, let's do that. Ian and I will just take a short walk now, and then we'll all take a longer one together later. I'd better go, I think Ian is calling me. We'll see you when you finish work. Bye-bye."

I pass the telephone to Sayeh, who finishes the conversation with nodding and verbal hand-wringing. She puts down the receiver. Smiles. Gets my coat and scarf from the closet and sees us to the door.

"One hour," I tell her and point to the phrase in my Farsi dictionary to be sure she has understood.

She nods. Smiles. "Have goood time," she whispers in English and winks. Closes the door.

The houses around us are made of crumbs: grainy, rough bricks irregularly stacked. The buildings are full of cracks; second floors lean precariously.

We walk the road to its end: a paved street. I look left and right. A handful of cars. Brick buildings: square, two-storey, fewer cracks and less tilting. There is no greenery. No colour. Nothing to distinguish the road from the pavement from the walls from the buildings, except texture. Or from the sky, which holds a slate against the sun. We walk towards the sound of traffic.

At the first crossroads there is a shop with cardboard boxes of vegetables outside. Carrots and garlic. At the second and the third and the fourth intersections there is nothing. We walk past a line of grey buildings with metal grates pulled down across the entrances, past walls, endless walls, offices of one kind or another set back from the road, and a few more shops. Then a black sail billows out from a gate onto the sidewalk. Black with corners of skin. Faces. Trying to hide and peek at the same time.

They are school-aged, teenagers maybe, though it's difficult to tell. They stare—shyly, hiding one eye with a fistful of fabric—and shuffle past us in a solid black mass. Stare at me. My thin green cloak betrays me, exposes me as foreign. The girls whisper and gasp as they move past. Cowering and giggling. Giggling and cowering. I have swallowed lead balls that roll around in my stomach as I watch these girls. The way they move as a flock.

I walk as though I were not in my body; as though it were not my body; as though my body were a vehicle I had borrowed to get myself to this place. Through this place. I watch my feet scuff the dirt of this road, my fingers grip the cuffs of my coat, watch people stop what they are doing and watch us as we pass. I watch myself walking in Iran.

On the main street, tin-box cars race along like go-karts. There are no traffic lights, therefore no pattern of movement, no lulls or rushes, only a steady stream of cars moving as fast as they can without crashing. As a result, there is no opportune time to cross. The only thing to do is swallow hard and make a run for it. And not expect oncoming cars to make allowances.

The reason we are so determined to cross is that I see colour, there—*No, look: over there, no, there, in the window.* Circles of bright orange, canary yellow, two shades of green, lurid pink with black spots.

Carrots. Carrots and grapefruits and oranges and watermelons and bananas, all piled up in the window into a fruit mosaic.

Behind the counter is a young boy, looks about ten, an orange press, a blender and a juicing machine. I sound out the words from the list on the wall and am so excited by the idea of a fresh juice, I projectile-salivate when I open my mouth to order. "*Yek*—" Oops, sorry. (Wipe.) "*Yek livan ab portegal lotfan.*"

The boy blinks a hundred times as he is cutting oranges in half. Looks at us from the corner of one eye as he is pressing the fruit into juice, gives an embarrassed smile as he hands me the glass. A smile that grows as I swallow the contents in one long gulp.

I order another one each.

He looks at us face-on now, even as he is halving fruit with a knife the length of his forearm. He serves up two more pulpy juices and crosses his arms over his chest, proudly. We drink these just as quickly, replace the glasses and thank him. Move to pay.

The boy steps back. He tilts his head shyly and waves our money away. Ian tries again with a different amount, but the boy tosses his head back in refusal, raises his hand to his heart and closes his eyes.

Ian and I exchange smiles of disbelief and put the money away. We thank the boy again and again. Each time, he nods and looks embarrassed. We thank him once more before leaving. The boy smiles and shrugs. We step back onto the street.

"That was generous!" Ian and I say in unison. "What a sweet boy! So gracious! Ian checks his watch. "We should head back."

We walk back to the intersection and are gearing ourselves up to cross when the boy catches up to us, panting, eyes brimming with tears. He looks at the sidewalk, red-faced, and asks Ian, in a combination of hand gestures and humble whispers, if we could please pay for our juices.

I pull out a roll of bills and ask the boy how much. He mumbles the price out of the corner of his mouth. Seven hundred rials. Exactly what was written on the wall. The precise sum we offered him a few minutes ago. I pay. The boy bows and leaves. Ian and I watch him run back into his shop, turn, and look at each other with the dopey expression of walruses.

Hamid is beside himself with worry. He speaks for minutes at a time and has a voice like grape jelly. Did we have difficulties? Was everything enough interesting? Have we enough eating and drinking?

"Yes yes yes, just fine. Except . . . well there was this boy at the juice shop. He refused our money, then chased us down the street for it a few minutes later. We're not sure whether he——"

"——this is *taarof*." Hamid is laughing. "I think it is not Canadian *taarof*, only Iranian. A man must not take first time, no, he must not accept——" Hamid *tsks* and throws his head back, just as the boy did "——then again second time——" he closes his eyes and puts a hand over his heart "——then, third time okay for taking. It is custom."

"Custom to refuse everything twice?"

"Yes."

"Why?"

"Why?" Hamid repeats.

"Yes, why?"

Hamid pauses. Wrinkles his chin. "*Why*, it is not good question. Please make me another question."

රිංා

Ian is ill. Just a cold, but a bad one. He's been in bed the last two days. Headache, fever, chills, a cough, and a throat so sore it hurts to swallow.

Hamid is worried, terribly terribly worried. Paces and holds his head when I tell him that Ian isn't hungry. Looks teary-eyed when I tell him Ian has a cold. Shakes his head and gathers the roll of blankets in the corner of the room.

"No no, there are enough blankets. He isn't cold, he *has* a cold." I look the phrase up in my book, but it isn't there. I cough and fake the sniffles. Hamid purses his lips. Looks up a word up in his Farsi-English dictionary (bought especially for our visit) and shows me an entry translated as *Windpipe disease: infibulation of the neck and sinus holes*.

I nod.

Hamid calls a friend whose uncle is a doctor. After the examination and several glasses of tea, the doctor says he has just the thing for Ian's condition. A special medication from America, given to him by his wife's cousin, whose husband's nephew lives in Los Angeles. The doctor has only one pill left, but he is happy to give it to Ian. He reaches into his bag and passes Hamid a pill wrapped in paper and plastic. Hamid passes it to me. I take it to Ian. It is something called *Dristan*.

ريال

"Come!" Hamid calls from the doorway. "Take your money, all dollars, very importantly! Come expeditely!"

My eyes open, though I am not yet fully awake. I untangle the pile of clothes on the floor, cover all body parts and lean out of our room. "What's going on?"

"Economy very bad!" Hamid calls from the stairwell. "We must go to bazaar. Wear your manteau!"

I stare at Ian's sick, sleeping body and decide to leave him. Strap our money to my body, hide my hair and meet Hamid on the road, where a discussion is raging among a group of men, neighbours. They nod when I approach and lead us to the street to flag down a taxi. Hamid gets in next to the driver. I sit in back.

The driver and Hamid get into heavy conversation right away. Low voices, stern and serious. We get out at the main roundabout and hustle, quickly quickly, towards the bazaar.

"Dollar fall down very much," Hamid says breathlessly. "You must buy some rial before it is lately."

I scramble to keep up. "Why is it falling? Has something happened?"

Hamid leaps and skips over the garbage in the alley. "Mr. Yeltsin is not agree with Mr. Clinton. USA ask Russia for stop sell that nuclear to Iran, but Mr. Yeltsin say no. Please, we must go to bazaar. This morning dollar was 7,200 rial, but taxi driver tell to me now is 6,000. Please walk expeditely."

The money exchange hallway of the bazaar is buzzing. In the window of one office is a handwritten sign announcing today's exchange rate for the dollar (blank). In the window of another is an enlarged photocopy of a US $50 bill with the words DOWN WITH USA typed over the face. Inside a third office are three men and an abacus. It is 9:30 a.m. and the rate for one American dollar is 5,400 rials. The men seem to think it will continue dropping, so I decide to trade one hundred dollars.

"Better is change one note of hundred dollar," Hamid suggests when he notices me counting out five $20 bills. "Change rate for small note is lesser."

"What? But I only have denominations of $20. What is the rate for $100 in twenties?"

"You will get the lower rate," says a man watching our transaction.

"But that's crazy! A hundred dollars is a hundred dollars."

The man chuckles. "I know it seems crazy, but this is Iran. Unfortunately, everything is crazy. They want $100 bills because they are smaller. You can . . ." He makes a rolling motion with his fingers. "Easier for smuggling. I am sorry, but you will have the same problem in every shop."

Hamid shrugs. "Iranian way is differently."

෨෨

Ian is feeling better. Not well enough to go out, but well enough that Hamid has stopped worrying. Annahita arrives home in her school uniform—a long navy coat with trousers and a white wimple—and heads straight for her patient. She lays a hand on Ian's forehead, looks pensive as she gauges his temperature, says something scolding and pulls the blankets tighter around his chin. Her face is a round portrait of concern. She mutters to herself and heads out of the room, patting my leg as she goes by.

Sayeh catches her on the way to the kitchen and peels off the uniform. Annahita wears a pink skirt with a white sash, white tights and a white bodysuit. She squeezes out of her wimple and past her mother into the kitchen, where she begins clanging. Sayeh rolls her eyes at me and calls to Annahita, who answers in a very insistent *Don't*

bother me I know what I'm doing tone. Sayeh holds my arm
and doubles over in silent laughter.

Annahita walks past us balancing a tray of sunflower
seeds, a pot of tea and a bowl of jam. She toddles into our
room, sets the tray on the floor next to Ian and begins
talking and fussing over his blankets. She places the bowl
of sunflower seeds on his stomach and cracks the shells
between her teeth, one by one, releasing the seeds into
her palm until the entire bowl of seeds is ready to eat. She
sits cross-legged, elbows on her knees, chin in her hands,
her skirt full of shells. Waiting for Ian to wake up so she
can feed him.

Sayeh pulls me aside. She is hesitant and embarrassed.
Bites her bottom lip and speaks with her hands. She holds
Annahita's tiny coat up to my body and looks concerned.
Worried. Leans down and touches my knee. Raises her
eyebrows. Do I understand?

I don't.

Her mouth twitches. She guides me to the closet.
Points to my coat, then to my knees, to my coat and to my
breasts, to my scarf and to my neck. Do I understand?

Yes, I think I do.

When Hamid arrives home from work, Sayeh eyes me
and nods. Retreats to the kitchen and assembles lunch,
while I give Hamid an update of Ian's health. He is
pleased. Laughs when I tell him about Annahita's bedside
manner.

After lunch, Sayeh eyes me again. I tell Hamid I would
like to go shopping. I think I need a new coat—manteau,
Sayeh called it—because the one I brought with me is too
short and too thin, and my scarf is not big enough. Hamid

looks surprised, discusses my request with Sayeh, who shrugs and gathers our dishes. They continue the discussion until Hamid is nodding.

"Sayeh say it is better idea. For your travelling to holy place you need some taller cloth. We can this afternoon go for shopping because I have free from working. Please tell to Mr. Ian if it is possible."

We agree to leave Ian and Annahita behind, though I'm not sure who is supposed to be looking after whom. On the street, Sayeh links my arm in hers and smiles. Hamid walks beside us, scurries actually, a funny sort of step-hop that makes me think we aren't walking fast enough for him.

At the end of the road, we meet up with Sayeh's uncle and aunt. Ali closes his eyes and bows when we are introduced; Narghes shakes my hand. We explain our shopping plan, and Narghes begins to speak and gesture with great animation. She knows just the place, she says, and talks her idea over with Sayeh, tugging my coat every now and again to illustrate different cuts and buttons. Ali and Hamid stand on the lookout for taxis. When one finally stops, the two men sit on top of each other in the passenger seat. Narghes, Sayeh and I get into the back.

We drive to a large roundabout in the centre of the city. "We stop here and walk to shopping," Hamid croaks from his position on Ali's lap, his neck scrunched up against the roof.

The place is full of people. Full of activity. Full of the sounds of traffic and conversation and street life. Ringing the road are buildings the colour of dust. They have arched roofs and turquoise tiling and an elegance that dulls the noise.

The taxi drops us at the centre of the roundabout: a wide stretch of grass criss-crossed by sidewalks and dotted with kiosks selling newspapers and posters of religious leaders and soccer players whose bare legs have been coloured over with black marker. Billboard-sized portraits of Khomeini eye the scene at every turn. At the entrance to the park stands a painted sign depicting two women. The one on the left wears a long black manteau and wimple, dark trousers and shoes; the figure on the right wears all of this plus a chaador overtop. Both figures are faceless. The rest of the sign is in writing. I ask Hamid what it means.

"Our sign tell that this one——" Hamid points to the woman on the left "——is good, it is cloth Islamic. But our sign tells that *this*——" he taps his finger against the chaadored figure on the right "——is *very* much good dressing, most beautiful, way of God."

At the bottom of the sign there is, inexplicably, an English translation: *Veil is ornament of womens modesty. The smelling flower of chastity bush.*

We walk to the edge of the park and bolt across the roundabout like gazelles on the run. One by one, we make it to a clearing on the sidewalk. Sayeh grabs my arm and throws her chin in the direction of a young girl, teenaged, in a short red coat and white scarf. The girl eyes me—an ally in colour and style—and smiles. Sayeh *tsks* and looks disapproving. Pulls me onward.

"Maybe this girl have problem," says Hamid. "It is not good cloth as you see on sign. About yourself, do not worry. Sayeh and Narghes assist for your goodness."

We come to a shop with coats in the window. Hamid and Ali wait outside. On the walls of the shop hang cloaks in every imaginable shade of brown, some in dark blues and dark dark green, the rest in black. The walls are so dull, they practically don't exist.

The two clerks are in simple black cloaks and wimples. Sayeh explains what we are after and Narghes cuts in with details and questions. As the women discuss their wares, I walk to the full-length mirror and look at myself. Over my trousers and shirt I have on a baggy knee-length khaki coat and a rust-coloured scarf with a tattered fringe that I've knotted under my chin. I look like a tall pile of compost. The coat is formless, tent-like, but it sits snugly on my shoulders and follows the contours of my breast before falling, shapelessly, around me; when I walk, it opens at the knees. It is of thin cotton, worn and wrinkled enough that it looks dirty, as though I didn't take care of it; as though I didn't care.

On the other side of the room, the women are collecting armfuls of possibilities for me to try. I am led to a change room, where I can remove my coat and try on others. Sayeh peers in every few seconds and smiles; Narghes has not stopped giggling since this exercise began. The first manteau is the plain-Jane, no-frills, black-as-night-with-black-plastic-buttons version. And thick shoulder pads, so that the fabric sits above my frame and falls straight down to the floor, betraying nothing of my form in the process. I walk out of the dressing room and model. The clerks approve. Sayeh arranges my scarf so that the fringe falls around my shoulders evenly, then wrinkles her nose and looks uncertain. Narghes sticks her tongue out and rolls her eyes.

I try on every variety in the shop—they are all poly-ester—from the fancy-schmancy deep purple with fake gold buttons, slit up the back, a removable lining and a belt (Narghes's choice), to the pious but elegant floor-length black with silver-rimmed buttons and small silver clip at the collar. With Sayeh's encouragement, I choose this last model. I change back into my old coat and pay for my new one. Join Hamid and Ali outside.

Ali bows and apologizes—he and Narghes must leave us—but would like to invite me and my husband for din-ner when my husband has recovered from his illness. Narghes twists my coat around in her fingers and tugs at the fringe of my scarf.

"Baai-baai," she says through her laughter.

"Bye-bye," I reply through my own.

Hamid asks if I am satisfied with my purchases, and I tell him yes, all I need now is a new scarf. For this— brief consultation with Sayeh—we will go to the bazaar. We walk back towards the roundabout and attempt to cross several of its four-lane arteries. Hamid walks ahead into traffic, then waves to us behind his back, directing us either to stay behind or follow him.

"Carefully!" he shouts. "Please keep yourself!" Sayeh holds my hand and weaves me through the traffic. During the next crossing, Hamid is stranded in the middle of the road, cars racing around him on all sides. Sayeh and I are also stranded one lane behind him, and he scolds us for not waiting on the sidewalk for his signal. "*Keep yourself!*" he shouts, galloping into the next gap between cars. Sayeh mocks her husband's reproach, imitating his instructions in whiny babytalk, then takes firm hold of my hand and bolts. We run breathstoppingly close to oncoming traffic, lean back just in time to let a truck whiz past, and reach the sidewalk with our manteaux being blown across our backs. Sayeh is giggling quietly, mischievously. Hamid is flustered and full of scorn.

The two of them bicker in undertones, standing on the sidewalk, pointing back at the road occasionally to illustrate a point. In the end, Sayeh apologizes, or so it appears, but while they are arguing, I am alone on the sidewalk.

They are uniformed. The women in black, almost always huddled in groups, the men in bland unobtrusive colours, long-sleeved shirts and trousers, loose and modest Western clothing. They don't stare, the men, but they notice me standing here, sticking out, attracting attention; they glance, then twitch with shock. It is the women who stare, who leer at my covering, ratty and disrespectful as it appears. Some smile and giggle into their veils. Some go bug-eyed and race past me, then turn around to examine me from a distance.

Sayeh takes my hand, and the three of us enter the bazaar. It is a long archway lined with gold. We meander from shop to shop, looking at the trinkets that dangle behind glass under bright display lights. Sayeh points out thick bands of tri-colour gold, solid gold gumdrop earrings and piece after piece that she admires. It is only when she lifts her arm and points through the glass that I notice the line of gold bangles under her blouse.

At the end of the archway is an enormous dome. A shaft of sunlight falls from the apex and illuminates particles of dust in the air. We pass through it—the dust light dances against my face—and duck into a tiny shop. There is only room in the place for two. Hamid waits outside.

Sayeh asks the shopkeeper for a selection of head coverings. I inch into a stall just wide enough to allow me to lift my elbows and try on a wimple. It is tight, restrictive, and squeezes my face into a pucker. I make the gasping sounds of someone being choked, and Sayeh cracks open the change-room door. I blow my cheeks up like balloons and hold my breath until my skin purples, until Sayeh laughs and calls back to the shopkeeper, who passes her a simple black scarf with a clip to fasten the fabric under my chin. Knotting the scarf means that bits of my neck are visible.

The scarf fits (they are all the same size), so I buy it plus the clip. Plus, at Sayeh's insistence, a chaador to go over top of the whole outfit. I buy one in black polyester. Cotton is unavailable.

I am outfitted. I pay. We are ready to leave. Sayeh lingers. Mumbles to the shopkeeper. He rifles through a stack of scarves behind him, turns around holding a small brown box of metallic tubes and pushes it across the counter. Sayeh flicks through the tubes and folds her palm around one. Asks the price casually, scratching her neck and looking away as she is speaking. She tucks the tube of blood-red lipstick into her pocket and passes the man a roll of bills. We say good-bye and join Hamid outside.

The three of us wind through back alleys of the bazaar, past carpet shops, sacks of spices and dried legumes, rugs and stitched pillows, shopkeepers lounging on stacks of carpets drinking tea. They beckon to us, yell prices, lift corners of the rugs to show intricate handiwork, invite us in for a glass of tea. We nod and continue walking. The

further we get from the centre of the bazaar, the nar-
rower and damper it becomes. Tiled dome ceilings give
way to coarse wooden beams and alleys that trickle into
pathways flanked by mud walls.

Loudspeakers mounted on lamp-posts are broadcast-
ing a man's voice. I assume it to be prayer. Sayeh points to
one of the speakers and pats my arm reassuringly.

"This man tell that cover our women," Hamid explains.
"Do not worry. After your shopping with Sayeh, you will
cover as it is God's wish."

When we get home, Ian is sitting on the floor of the main
room with Annahita, playing cards. Sayeh leans into Hamid
and whispers. Hamid steps into the bathroom and changes
from his trousers into pyjama bottoms. Sayeh and I remove our manteaux, I my scarf.

Hamid sits down beside Ian and congratulates him on
his good health, then explains that—ahem, excuse me,
friends—card games are, actually, not permitted in Iran,
no gambling of any kind, but not to worry: "Your idea
was not teaching Annahita unkindly way." Ian apologizes
and packs up their game of memory. Annahita is confused
and disappointed, so Ian teaches her how to build card
houses instead. Sayeh returns with tea and looks relieved.

I pull out my bag and show Ian what I bought. I try
it on, piece by piece, with Sayeh's help and Annahita's
encouragement. The manteau and scarf are fine, but the
chaador is slippery, awkward, and much heavier than
I expected. It tugs at my forehead, so that the only way to
keep it from pulling my headscarf back on my hair is to
slouch or look down. And because it is a loose piece of
fabric, without a fastening of any kind, I must gather it

under my arms or hold it together with both hands. Just when I seem to have it secured, it slips off again. Off one shoulder, off the other, then off my head; first I gather too much in my arms, then too little.

Annahita finds my struggle extremely amusing. So does Sayeh, though she hides it better. Ian is laughing so hard he is wheezing. I ask him if he thinks he can do any better and he says as a matter of fact he thinks he can, so I disrobe and hand him the outfit, which he dons with great enthusiasm.

By the time he has buttoned up the manteau and clipped the scarf under his chin, Annahita is shrieking, Sayeh is burying her smile in her hands, and Hamid has laughed himself down the stairs. When he returns a few minutes later, he is still laughing so hard he can barely walk, and has several of his neighbours in tow. The men step into the room and stare—drop-jawed—at Ian, who strides across the room calling "*Salaam!*" and offers his hand in greeting. The men double back and blink. Blink blink blink blink. Cough out hesitant laughs and ask Hamid a series of giggle-filled questions. Hamid is too busy taking pictures to answer. Good idea: I take a bunch myself.

When the neighbours leave to call their family and friends, Ian decides he's had enough and strips back down to shirt and trousers. We sit down to tea. Hamid giggles every time he looks in Ian's direction. So does everyone else. Hamid collects himself and speaks to me instead.

"For visiting holy place woman must wear most respecting cloth, you must wear chaador. Also in holy city of Qom where live many mollah. For rest of your travelling you wear only manteau."

Hamid takes a sip of tea. "This way——" he convulses, giggles, then straightens up, is serious again "——this way your chaador is free that Mr. Ian can wear." Hamid's face ripples into smile, he doubles over and squirts tea-soaked laughter out his nose.

ʂʊʑ

Everyone is ready to go. Sayeh turns and mumbles to Hamid, who speaks: "You prepare now for dinner in house of uncle Sayeh?"

I nod and reach for my manteau and scarf.

Sayeh mumbles and widens her eyes. Hamid mumbles back. Sayeh mumbles again. Hamid speaks: "Excuse, please. Sayeh help you for wear your dress. Come, Mr. Ian, we wait out."

Hamid, Annahita and Ian go down the stairs to the street.

Sayeh smiles and leads me to the closet. She flicks through several hangers until she comes to a red-and-white dress, which she takes off its hanger and holds away from herself, eyeing it objectively. She looks at me, then at the dress, back at me, back at the dress. Curls her lips into her mouth. Mulls the combination over.

Yes. This is the dress for me. She points in the direction of my room and I smile, thank her. Close the door. I remove my travel clothes—trousers and an Indian cotton shirt—and squeeze into Sayeh's dress. It is made of shiny polyester with a pattern of red and white diamond shapes; there are golden sparkles across the shoulders and the skirt is cut flamenco-style, above the knee on the left side and falling to the floor on the right. A silver ruffle adorns the rising hem.

Sayeh knocks and opens the door. Smiles and beams, then flattens my chest with her hand as she zips me up the back. She helps me put on a pair of black stockings and squats on the floor to adjust them so that the seams run straight up the back of my legs. Shoes. Shoes shoes shoes. All of hers are too big, so she shreds some old rags and stuffs the toes of a pair of black high heels until they fit me.

Sayeh stands back and looks me up and down. Tilts her head to one side and squints. Is almost satisfied, but not quite. She leaves the room and returns with a hairbrush. No no no no. I wave her away. She laughs and comes closer. No no no no. She laughs and holds my arms down. Pulls out my ponytail. Begins brushing. Within the first few strokes, she recognizes the problem.

I was born with a full head of hair. So much so that when I appeared they weren't sure *what* was coming out. I've had an unruly mass of curls ever since, sometimes short, sometimes long, but always thick and always curly. I've been known to stick a pencil behind my ear and then have it swallowed up by the locks. For days. So brushing this, this nest, produces dramatic results.

By the time Sayeh is finished I look like I'm touching the static ball at the Science Centre. She seems fascinated by the spectacle, but as much in distress as amazement. She tries gathering my hair and putting it up, but it is so thick it snaps every clip. She tries pressing it into submission. Finally, she gathers a small handful from around my face, clips it to the top of my head and attaches a series of white bobbles to various points, as weights, I think, for they seem to pull enough strands down towards my shoulders that the hair at the sides of my head is no longer horizontal.

Hamid calls from the stairwell. Sayeh sighs hurriedly, retouches a few sections, winces, and hands me my covering. My new floor-length double-breasted manteau covers everything, including the ruffle. The shoes stay on only because my toes are mangled against the balled-up rags. Sayeh waves the scarf over my head, but has trouble fastening it because of the height and breadth of the hair it is intended to cover.

I hobble down the stairs and into Ian's stunned expression. "What are you hiding under your hat?"

Narghes is talking a mile a minute even before she opens the door. "Hai hai!" she shouts when she sees me.

"Hi," I answer and kiss her on the cheek. "This is my husband, Ian."

Narghes nods and smirks, then pulls me by the arm into a small room. Sayeh joins us and shuts the door. Narghes unbuttons my manteau, scorning certain bits—a poorly sewn buttonhole, a gap in the hem—as she comes across them. Her eyes glitter at the sight of my dress, but she disapproves of my hair and begins taking the bobbles out before Sayeh can explain why they are there.

There is a soft knock at the door, and two young women enter smiling. They are Narghes's daughters. They introduce themselves shyly and huddle around Sayeh, who has removed her manteau and scarf and is brushing her long brown hair. Narghes's daughters do the same: remove their scarves, brush, curl, twiddle and primp. The three women are wearing dresses similar in style to my own; Sayeh's is green with silver stars down the arms. They look at themselves in the mirror, touch up their make-up, brush and fiddle a bit more, then retie their scarves and look at me. Sayeh leaves the room when Annahita calls, leaving Narghes to attend to me.

She takes full command and uses her daughters as assistants. They pass brushes, bobby pins, barrettes, ribbons and bows, all at their mother's command. Narghes breathes heavily and uses the strength of both arms to wrestle my hair into order. My head bobs with each firm stroke of the brush; my scalp tingles and throbs. Eventually my whole wad of hair is heaved up onto the top of my head and wound up with thick red ribbon. Narghes instructs one of her daughters to make a large bow with the remaining ribbon and the other to pin it in place. Narghes snaps her fingers and asks for a pair of earrings. A set of dangly plastic white balls is produced and attached to my ears.

Sayeh comes back into the room with lipstick. The blood-red one she bought at the market the other day. It is looked at under the light, approved, smeared on my lips, then on my cheeks and massaged into my skin. The four women stand back and assess. Narghes asks for an eyebrow pencil and lines my eyelids. She jerks my chin and is about to begin colouring my eyebrows when she takes a closer look and rears back. She looks confused or annoyed. I can't quite tell which. She screws up her face and looks again, then asks something of Sayeh. Sayeh nods. Narghes asks me something about my husband. I shrug. She asks the same question again, this time more slowly. I shrug again, also more slowly. Narghes squats in front of me and speaks with every sound exaggerated and enunciated. She points to my wedding ring and asks if I am married. I nod. She smiles and looks at Sayeh. They both shrug.

Narghes goes on to explain that she, too, is married. She runs her fingernail along her carefully plucked eyebrows as if to prove her status. She does the same to Sayeh's thin sculpted eyebrows and to those of her eldest daughter. Also married, Narghes explains. Then she pulls her youngest daughter beside her and points to her thick bushy brows. Not married. Narghes pulls out a compact mirror from her purse and asks me to hold it up to my face. I stare into the tiny image of myself and watch Narghes run her finger over my bushy brows and trace the shape of eyebrows a married woman *should* have.

I am left with a sketch of eyebrow rounded into a high arch and accentuated with a charcoal pencil. The plucked section beneath is swollen up like a welt. Ian is so shocked by the sight of me, he chokes and spills his tea on the carpet. Narghes laughs and slaps me on the back. It's because I look so beautiful, she explains. My husband is very shocked.

"My God," Ian whispers. "You look like a plastic poinsettia."

What? Narghes demands to know what Ian is saying.

"Like a flower," he says. "She looks like a flower."

Hamid translates and the room gives a collective sigh. Narghes smiles proudly and fluffs out the bow on my head. Takes my hand and leads me to the kitchen.

Mina is squatting on the floor chopping onions when we are introduced. She looks up and smiles, wipes her hand on her trousers and stands to shake my hand. "I see my mother tortures you," she says, wiping some lipstick from my cheek with her thumb. "You must ask her to stop." Mina turns to her mother and speaks in an anxious voice, waving her chopping knife in the direction of the next room. Narghes follows Mina's direction and goes to begin setting up the dining mat. Mina gives me a sideways glance, adjusts her scarf and winks. "You can be comfortable," she says, and squats.

"Can I help?" I ask, and she passes me a long cucumber and an equally long knife and tells me to take off the skin.

"You must excuse my mother," Mina says as she lays the onions on a tray and sprinkles them with paprika. "She must do something." She peels garlic with the thick end of her blade. "My sisters, one is married, other one will marry next year. I am only one with something interesting."

Mina's sisters come into the kitchen and scold her for having me work for my dinner. They invite me into the living room to sit with everyone else, but I decline. Assure them I'm happy where I am. They look puzzled, but leave. Mina pulverizes the garlic with the base of her knife. I hand her my peeled cucumber and she passes me another one in its skin.

"I am only one go to university. I study electrical engineering so I must work very hard. After four years I want ready for a job"—her eyes sparkle as she says the word—"and then I want start another life kind. Here, give me your cucumber." She chops the watery green stick into cubes and passes me a mortar and pestle. "Please"—she mimes the motion.

"Grind," I tell her. "To grind."

"G-r-a-i-n-d," she sounds out the word slowly, then stores it in her mind. "To gra-ind." She sprinkles a handful of cumin seeds into the mortar. "Please graind." After approving my grinding technique, she continues, "I prefer to study at one of our bigger universities, in Isfahan or Tehran, but it is not possible. In this time I must be here in Tabriz with my family." She stretches to a small refrigerator and pulls out a plastic bowl covered with a tea towel. "What is this name in English?" she asks, removing the towel and offering me a taste of the white jelly.

"Yoghurt."

"Yo-gert." She beats the mass to a smooth cream. "Maybe my husband will be from Tehran and I will go to live there. Such a big city, but not so beautiful as Isfahan, where I used to live, with rivers and very big trees and buildings made from blue stone. Blue like this," she says pointing with the tip of her knife to a stone hanging around her neck.

Mina mixes the ground cumin, the cucumber and the garlic into the yoghurt, pinches salt and green flakes into the mixture and sets it aside. "Does your husband help with cooking?" I tell her he does, sometimes, and always does the dishes. Mina grins and shouts up into the air until Narghes comes in from the next room. Mina repeats what I've said, and her mother cackles into her hands, stomps off into the living room and announces the news. I hear a bit of grumbling, then Hamid's translation to Ian: "We discuss about your differently Canadian ways."

At dinner Mina sits beside me. Asks questions about my childhood. What games did I play with my friends, did I wear dresses or trousers, what did I want to be when I grew up, did I go to school with boys? I promise her an answer for every one she gives me. She nudges me and agrees. Serves me a plate of rice, kebab, salad and yogurt. It is simple, delicious food, spiced with the scents of the bazaar.

Ian sits on the floor on the other side of the long plastic mat. He sits with Hamid on one side and Ali on the other. Ian is spending a lot of time saying "I don't know" and running his hand across his forehead as though he were trying to concentrate. I don't understand the conversation and can't hear Hamid's translations. I ask Mina what they are talking about.

She listens and rolls her eyes. "How much costs apartment with three rooms in Canada? How much costs one litre gasoline in Canada? How much costs small car in Canada? How much earns doctor in Canada? Our conversation is more interesting." She smiles and gives me a friendly nudge.

There are two other men at the meal: the husband and fiancé of Mina's sisters. They are shy, both of them, but particularly the fiancé. He eats almost nothing and spends most of the meal exchanging long amorous glances with his future wife.

"Tell me about your Canadian life," Mina says at the end of the meal as she clears our plates from the mat. I follow her into the kitchen carrying leftover rice and kebab. "I want to know about your house and your job, what you do in your day. Tell me about your marriage." Mina grabs the scarf from her head and throws it into a corner. She sits on the floor, leans back on her arms and rests her head on her shoulder.

Mina's face is like the ocean. Pulsing and teeming with life. She laughs in bursts—waves crashing into the air—then lets her face trickle back into stillness.

We talk until Hamid comes to tell us it is time to go home. My hairstyle is dismantled and the lipstick removed with a wet towel. The scarf and manteau cover all remaining traces of the evening, of the life among family and friends; the life of adornment and fashion; private life.

Mina asks for my address, gives me hers and pleads with me to write. "I want to know everything about your travelling. Please, write to me from Isfahan. And from Turkey and Germany and Canada. Write to me from all beautiful places." She stands and holds my hand while the others say their goodbyes, then turns with a sad smile. "Don't forget." She leans to kiss me and whispers, "When I live in Tehran you will come and visit me there." I smile at her, her seashell cheeks, her warmth and energy. She pulls me closer and whispers again: "We will talk all evening and our husbands will wash our dishes." She laughs and makes a *shhhhh* gesture. Winks and waves by the door with the rest of her family.

The air is cool and dry. I smell the earth dried into dust and breathe this scent, this air; fill my lungs with it. I have been in Iran for ten days. My blood is made from the water of this place. I can feel it. How it slides through my body and shapes me.

DINNER WITH
THE SHAH

I AN TOSSES THE CAMERA into his daypack. "Oh,
wait—we should get a photo," he says and pulls the
camera back out of his bag. He puts one arm around
me, stretches the other arm out in front and points the
lens at our faces. "We'll call this *Day One Without Chaper-
one*," he says and tickles me. I shriek and giggle into his
neck. He takes the picture.

Click.

We are in Rasht, a fairly large city near the Caspian
Sea coast. We walk out of our *mosaferkhané*, a "traveller's
inn" with single beds and communal toilets, and into the
alley.

Into voices. Agitated shouting and an amplified voice
that sounds like sparks. Hundreds of people have gathered
on the sidewalks of the main street. We join the back of
the crowd and strain to see what's going on.

It is a parade. Rows and rows of men dressed in black.
They wear short hair on their heads and long hair on
their chins. And they chant. Slapping their chests with
their hands they chant, painfully, angrily. They follow the

incantation of a man standing on the bed of a pick-up truck, which crawls. The man holds a megaphone and intones: *Allahu akbar! Khomeini rahbar!* The parade of men repeats. *God is great! Khomeini is our leader!* The number of spectators grows. Ian and I are pushed apart and deeper into the crowd.

The men pass slowly and solemnly. Rows and rows of blackness. A distance behind them come eight men balancing a platform on their shoulders. It carries a coarse wooden coffin, open and brimming with flowers, white and red carnations. The flowers twitch and shift, some fall to the ground as the men move and jostle the coffin, trudging, trudging, under its weight. There is a picture on the platform of a man, bearded, with black eyes.

Surrounding the pall-bearers are mourners. Men crying, wailing into the sky, some beating their fists to their heads. All chanting. Repeating the call of the megaphone: *Margh-é Emrika! Margh-é Israel!* I don't understand the chant, though it's familiar. Something I've heard before, read before, somewhere. The coffin gets closer. I catch sight of Ian right at the front of the crowd, separated from me now by dozens of people.

My eyes fix on him, then on the chanting men. My eyes flit between the two. The chanting men and Ian. The chanting men and Ian. *Margh-é Emrika!* Ian looks captivated. Excited. *Margh-é Israel!* He reaches into his bag and pulls out the camera. *Margh-é Emrika! Margh-é Israel!* I can't reach him. Can't call to him. Can only watch as he brings the camera up to his face—*Margh-é Emrika!*—squints into the viewer—*Margh-é Israel!*—and captures the coffin as it passes in front of him. I close my eyes and let out my breath. Gasp and open my eyes. Blink my way into a moment of concentration and listen. Suddenly able to decipher the chant.

Now that the sounds have meaning, they are unbearable. I push and elbow my way to where Ian is standing and tug on his arm. He turns around and smiles.

"We have to get out of here," I say as quietly and firmly as possible.

"What?"

I yank his head towards me and shout into his ear. "They're shouting 'Death to America.' We can't stay here."

Ian's eyes snap to alert. He shoves the camera into his bag and pushes me through the crowd. We scuttle away from the parade to a stone arcade at the end of the street, and stop to catch our breath.

"Let's catch a taxi and get the hell out of here," Ian says, scanning the square. He has just stepped into the street, ready to flag down the first car that looks like a public vehicle, when a man approaches him from behind and takes his arm.

He is one of the men from the parade. Could be. Bearded and dressed in black. He wears short-short hair and a look of calm dedication to a cause. Part of his face around the right eye is missing and crudely patched. He is a war veteran. Looks to be. He has fought for Allah, would do anything to serve God. Such is the look in his eye.

He motions the clicking of a camera, then shakes his finger. Asks Ian to follow him into the alley with a nod of his head and his palm at Ian's elbow. I am whispering, *Don't go, don't go, for chrissake don't go,* but I am left behind. Left now outside a ring of black-clad bearded men who encircle Ian and walk with him, around him, off the street. I follow.

The man asks Ian for his passport. "*Say you left it at the hotel*," I hiss—but Ian pulls it out of his belt pocket and hands it over. The man flips through it upside down and holds it in one hand. Runs the other hand through his beard and stares off into space. Listening to the advice of the other men. Pondering the situation himself. It is remarkably quiet. Behind me, a tiny, apple-faced woman in a white veil is muttering insults. The men wave her away and, after giving us a good dose of the evil eye, she wraps herself up and toddles down the alley.

We stand there, the disfigured man holding Ian's passport lightly in his hand, the rest of the group murmuring to each other. I am saying all kinds of things that the group either does not understand or does not hear. Or does not acknowledge. Ian is trying to make light of the incident by telling his story like an innocent. No one is listening.

One of the men leaves and returns minutes later with a pudgy man, who takes charge. He listens to the scarred man recount the events, then takes Ian's passport, flips to the photo, matches it with the face and says in English: "Please come."

The scarred man places a hand over his heart and bows. We follow the pudgy man across the street towards a monolithic building on the main square. All the other men are left behind.

"Excuse me, where are we going?" Ian asks, innocently.

"Police."

He seems good-natured, this man. He has nothing of the expression of the other men and none of the intensity.

He wears light-coloured trousers and a sportscoat. No beard, unkempt shortish hair. And looks bored.

"Excuse me," Ian asks again. "Why are we going to the police station? What did we do?"

The man says nothing, but nods in the direction of the building and continues walking. We enter, and inside, he directs us up two flights of stairs and down a wide hallway. All doors closed. In the Shah's time, the intelligence agency known as SAVAK was known to use interrogation techniques such as the "frying pan": a metal table, with shackles, that heated up if the detainee's memory needed jogging. It is rumoured that the techniques were successful enough to survive the revolution and be adopted by the victors, though this is denied. The Islamic Republic officially imposes only punishments used in the time of the Prophet. Lashings, for example. Or stonings.

A door is opened, and three young men look up. Smiling. As though they were interrupted in the middle of a good story. They are all dressed in street clothes, one in a yellow golf shirt—an unusual sight, both colour and style—the rest in tailored shirts. None in black. The pudgy man asks them to accompany us to a room across the hall. It is an office the size of a classroom.

We are asked to sit down in two chairs on one side of the room, while the men take seats around a large wooden desk on the other. The pudgy man explains what he knows to the men, one of whom cannot stop giggling, in the way some people do when they are nervous and trying to be cool about it. The man beside him holds a toothbrush in his hand like a lollipop. The pudgy man finishes his briefing, defers to the giggly man, our translator, and leaves.

The giggly man smiles, moves to speak, but laughs instead and hides his face behind his hand while he chokes out a few words to his colleagues, who seem to bolster and encourage him. He tries again.

"Hello," he says and giggles into his hand. Straightens his face and continues. "Do you have camera?"

"Yes," says Ian and pulls it out of the bag.

"Please give to me," he says, beckoning with his fingers. Ian hands him the camera and it is placed on the desk. Exhibit A. Each man picks it up, turns it over a few times, looks into the viewer and puts it down. "Please tell," the translator says and looks to his colleagues, nodding.

Ian launches into an explanation that makes it sound as though we'd walked outside our hotel and accidentally stumbled on a circus in the middle of the road. It is a story full of surprise and wonder and innocent descriptions of a parade replete with flowers and singing, and what was in that box, was it more flowers?

The giggly man translates for the other men, who rub their fingers along their lips and look at each other out of the corners of their eyes. One of the men asks Ian to explain why he took the picture. To which Ian launches into more colourful descriptions and then recounts our adventures over the last week, explaining all of the photos he took—"I love sunsets!" he exclaims—then a complete list of our travel plans for the rest of the country, city by city.

"Thank you, it is enough," says our translator, cutting him off.

Over the next hour or so, our story is told and retold to every one of the fifteen or so men who walk into the office. All are plain-clothed, all pick up the camera, look into the viewer and put it down again. All ask a few questions of the translator and shrug. Judging by their expressions, none is particularly interested in our situation.

No one has addressed us directly for ages.

When I am sufficiently frustrated, I tell the men we'd like to leave. We had planned to travel up into the mountains today, and it is a long journey. We'd like to go before it gets too late.

The men look at me, surprised, and begin talking. They'd like the film taken out of the camera, they decide. Then we can go.

"What? But why? It has the photos of the rest of our trip. We're not going to be back to those places. They are the only photos we have."

This is translated. The men discuss. Our translator proposes just opening the camera quickly to destroy the photo of the parade.

"But opening the camera will destroy *all* the photos, not just that one."

This is translated. The men discuss. Several come and go. There is more discussion, a long exchange of ideas, then what looks like consensus. It is suggested that one of the men go and develop the whole film. That way they can all have a look, take the parade photo if necessary, and give us the remaining photos.

Ian turns to me in horror. "There are pictures of me that night at Hamid's, trying on your clothes," he mutters. "I don't particularly want these guys to see me dancing around in drag . . ."

"Thank you," I tell the men. "It's a very good idea, but this is black-and-white film, and it is difficult to develop."

This is translated.

Silence.

Pointed looks.

Raised eyebrows.

"Why film black and white?" asks our translator, no longer giggling. "It is for newspaper."

Every man stares.

"Newspaper?" Ian and I laugh. "Look at the camera! This camera couldn't take a newspaper-quality photo if it tried! Look at it . . ." Ian gets up and takes the camera from the desk. He raps it against the wood to illustrate its cheap quality. Runs his hand along the tiny lens to show the absurdity of the suggestion.

No response.

Ian keeps hold of the camera and sits back down. "Should we just open this and rip the goddamn film out?" he asks me under his breath.

I shrug. "I'm not sure we have any choice."

Ian pops the back off the camera and pulls the film out in handfuls. He looks up at the men. "There." He gets up as if to leave.

There is stone silence.

Stone. Silence.

"Please sit," says our translator. Ian sits. The men whisper to each other and to themselves.

"Is there a problem?" Ian asks. "You told us you wanted to destroy the film, so we destroyed it."

The translator listens a bit longer to his colleagues, then nods them into silence. He leans forward and looks at Ian. "Your action was not good." The men fall back into discussion.

"Now they think we've got something to hide. We're going to be here for hours." I huff and look away.

"Your wife is not happy," says the man with the toothbrush.

I look at him and fabricate. "I am unhappy because we have lost our photos. We had photos from Turkey, and of some of our friends in Tabriz, and now we have nothing."

The man looks sympathetic. "But we did not destroy. Your husband did destroy. We did ask develop . . ."

"But we don't want to sit here all day! This is our honeymoon. We came to Iran because we heard it was very beautiful and its people very kind. This morning we left our *mosaferkhané*—" the men smile to hear me use the Farsi word "—and heard noise in the street. We saw the parade, and my husband took a picture. We didn't know it was wrong, but now we do, and we have destroyed this photo, just as you asked. Now we would like to go." I take the camera from Ian's hands and walk over to the desk. "You can keep the camera. We don't need it. We're not journalists, we are tourists on our honeymoon. We will keep pictures of Iran here—" I lay the camera on the desk and point to my eye. I stay standing, ready to leave.

"Please sit."

There is plenty of discussion now. Plenty. Everyone has another look at the camera, and they agree on something. The pudgy man leaves the room. The translator assures us that everything is okay, they don't want to keep the camera and we can go very soon. *Be patient,* one of the men entreats with his hands.

The man with the toothbrush takes the camera and pulls out the rest of the film. As he is untangling the last strands and emptying them into the garbage can, the winding clip snaps off and falls on the floor. He hunches over and looks embarrassed, tries to put it back together.

No success. Several others have a go, fiddling with it to no avail. Finally Ian gets up and has a look. He brings the camera up to his eye and tries to fit the teeny clip back into place, but it slips out of his grip and falls to the floor again. He begins to laugh. More and more until he leans a hand against the desk to hold himself up and launches into this sort of gaspy-wheezy laugh. The kind of laughter that is contagious. The kind that makes people laugh even if they don't know what was so funny in the first place.

It has precisely this effect. The man with the toothbrush begins patting Ian on the back to prevent him from choking, but soon he is laughing so hard himself that someone begins slapping him the same way, and everybody is laughing.

Ian coughs and collects himself, then turns to the man. "Excuse me, but why are you holding a toothbrush?"

"For brushing," the man says, waving the toothbrush around like a baton. Then he nods, as if reminded of something, and leaves the room.

The toothbrush man returns with tea, by which time the camera has been fixed and returned to us. Ian accepts a glass and asks the men to instruct him on the art of sipping tea through a sugar cube. The men look both puzzled and excited by the invitation. Three of them actually fight to be the first to demonstrate. One man teaches Ian as he would a child, with wide eyes and encouraging nods and slow, exaggerated speech. Take a piece of sugar—see?—and put it right . . . here . . . and hold it down between

your top and bottom teeth, then sip and—*slurp!*—he
sucks in a mouthful of tea.

Ian tries and chokes, is encouraged, shown again, and
tries again. Sips, slurps, and leaks tea out the corners of
his mouth. Everyone is amused, though they conceal their
smirks in their hands. Once he's got the hang of it, he sits
back down beside me and continues drinking.

Ssccchhhllllllp

The men scratch their necks and turn away, giggling.

"How is your honeymoon?" one of the men asks
through the translator.

"It was fine until today," I laugh.

The men chortle. They talk, look vaguely ashamed,
and come up with another question: "You like hejab?"

Ssccchhhllllllp

"Pardon?"

"Do you—" the translator pauses ". . . like hejab?"

"Do I *like* wearing this?" I pull on the black polyester
that encases me.

"Yes," he says. "Is it good wearing?"

"Good wearing? Well, my husband likes it . . ."

Ian elbows and shushes me.

There are nods around the room. "It is good that you
like hejab, sir. With hejab your wife is goodness."

Ssccchhhllllllp

Questions begin coming from all sides of the room.
The translator swivels his head from voice to voice, choosing the most interesting questions from amongst the suggestions. He asks my impressions of Iranian women,
inquires about our levels of education, our jobs, our religion, our ideas about Iran, our ideas about America—"It is

very dangerous?"—then leans forward and asks with particular interest:

"Please, tell me idea of America people about Iran?"

"I don't know, but I think they are very frightened," I answer.

There is muted protest, the odd shrug, looks of resignation.

"Please," says the man with the toothbrush. "Why?"

The pudgy man returns and is welcomed by everyone in the room. He has been gone so long I'd forgotten about him. He is warm—there is sweat on his brow—and slightly out of breath.

"Please," he says and hands me a small box. He says a few words to the translator and sits down.

"This man tell, I am sorry. He could not find film black and white, but tell that maybe this is better, film colour, better for photo of honeymoon."

Ian and I are both so shocked we say nothing.

"You are angry?" the translator asks.

"No, not at all. No, thank you. *Merci. Kheylee mamnoon.* We are very grateful."

We load up the film and thank them again. Ian asks if we can have a group photo, to which everyone laughs and waves their hands. No no no. The pudgy man smiles and his face wrinkles up like one of those felt-faced dogs.

The men apologize for delaying our trip. They hope we understand, hope we enjoy the rest of our honeymoon, hope we enjoy Iran. We must be sure to visit Isfahan and Mashhad and Shiraz and Qom—Oh, do you think they should go to Qom? Yes, right, maybe not—and Tehran. Do we know where we're going now?

The translator accompanies us to the main doors and writes down directions to a beautiful village nearby that he thinks we might like to visit. Very green with many clouds. He holds the pen in his mouth as he considers further suggestions, smiles, holds a hand over his heart. "I want excuse for this trouble. Please enjoy our country."

We retrace our steps all the way back to our *mosaferkhané* and sleep for the rest of the afternoon.

"If this is the honeymoon," Ian says when he wakes up. "What's the actual marriage part going to be like?"

I pick my pounding head off the pillow and squint at him.

Click.

He smiles and puts the camera down. "I thought I'd start our new film."

ಠಠ

The juice bar huddles on the corner with its counter open to the street. Baskets of oranges, bananas, carrots, melons and grapefruits hang from the ceiling. Glass jars hold cakes and cookies. A group of men stand outside sipping milkshakes. Wide-eyed. The way milkshakes are enjoyed the world over. I approach the counter and order a banana-date-pistachio ice-cream shake for me and a carrot juice for Ian, then reach into a glass jar on the counter for a lemon cake and am just biting into it when I notice the juiceman staring at me with his knife raised.

When I shouted our order over the counter he was busy chopping, squeezing, pressing and cleaning. Now he stands still. Knife raised. Staring. His eyes twist into whirlpools. And he asks me to repeat myself. I check my pronunciation and speak again, more slowly. *One ba-na-na-date-pis-ta-chi-o-ice-cream shake and one car-rot juice for my husband. Please. Oh and this cake. (Smirk.)*

He lowers his knife. Lays it on the cutting board and wipes his hands on his apron. Comes around from behind the counter and joins me on the street. One of the milkshake men joins him in staring (not at me, at Ian), sucking his straw so hard at the bottom of his empty glass that he chokes from the exertion.

"Excuse," the young man coughs. "You are Japanese?"

Ian looks at my Anglo-Saxon face, I at his freckles and red hair.

"Uh, no," Ian replies. "We are from Canada."

The young man smiles. Extends his hand to Ian. Bows to me. The two older men beside him do the same. The juiceman slaps his forehead and ducks back behind the counter.

"Canada!" he laughs. "I go to Canada!" He chuckles as he prepares my milkshake, offers Ian a handful of cookies, chops up a handful of carrots and whizzes them through a juicer. Pulp spews out into a vat behind the counter where a tiny boy sits washing carrots in a tin pail. The concoctions are poured into tall glasses and presented across the counter to us with more offerings of cookies.

Then the fight starts. All three men want to pay for our drinks. They whisper and *tsk!* each other until the eldest man offers his money to the juiceman quietly, obsequiously, with gentle murmurings and nods of the head. The juiceman refuses the offering twice, then accepts.

"Excuse," says the young man again. "May I make a question?" We nod and slurp. "You know our Imam,

Imam Khomeini?" We nod and slurp. "Your people know Imam?" More nodding. "Please tell, what your people think about Imam?" Pause in slurping.

"What do they think?" repeats Ian. "Uh—" Ian looks to me. I shrug. Smile. Slurp. The young man stares.

"Well," says Ian. "He is very famous."

The young man's face sheds smile after smile, he shakes Ian's hand, pats the other men on the back and skips down the street grinning.

The other two men talk quietly amongst themselves, watch the young man disappear down the street and shrug with their lips.

"One of our revolution-makers," says the eldest man, chewing on his straw. "Be careful with them, careful what you say. You can know them by their beards."

"Why did he call Khomeini 'the Imam'?" I ask. "I've only ever known him as Ayatollah Khomeini, but people here always call him Imam."

The man raises his eyebrows and takes a deep breath. His friend gives him a nudge in the ribs and smiles. "Some people, like that young man, some think Khomeini is the twelfth Imam, the Hidden Imam, the one who disappeared. You know about our prophet Mohammed. And his son-in-law, Ali, the one the Shi'ites believe was Mohammed's successor, we call him Imam—it means, well, leader, religious and political leader, but normally we only use it to talk about those leaders like Ali, descendants of Mohammed. After Ali there were eleven other Imams in that line, descendants of the Prophet, but the twelfth one disappeared in the year 873. Our people always believed he would return, like a saviour, he would return to create the perfect Islamic state."

"Like Christians," says his friend.

"Yes," nods the man. "Like a messiah. The revolution-makers believe that Khomeini was the Hidden Imam. So you see, his people began to call him 'Imam' because the meaning is two-hearted: the word can mean leader, just leader, but it can also mean messiah. They were very clever, his people, they understand the power of words."

The man (who explains that he spent ten years in America as a child), translates our conversation to the juiceman, who asks to have a few questions translated for us. How much is a salary for a doctor, a teacher, an engineer, a juiceman, how much is a car, how much is an apartment, how much is a watermelon, a house, a juice bar? Each of our answers is followed by the squinting of eyes and rapid calculations.

"He wants to go to Canada," explains our translator.

The juiceman voices his agreement from behind the counter with extra loud chopping and the Farsi equivalent of *yep!*

"Everything expensive!" he shouts in English. He pulls at his clothing, points to the food on his counter, his shoes, the watch on his wrist, various items around his tiny shop. When he runs out of things to point at, he huffs and shrugs, picks up his knife and continues chopping. "All! All expensive! I go to Canada!" he says and honks a laugh into the street. All three men laugh, the way one laughs at something that isn't very funny. We slurp the remaining few drops from our glasses and say goodbye. The juiceman looks up at us and smiles. Puts down his knife and leans forward, examines my face quickly and nods a slow satisfied nod. He motions to my face, then holds the tips of his fingers together the way Italians do when they taste good food.

"Hejab good," he says.

I am covered well, in other words.

I thank him—it is a compliment—and tell him we'll see him in Canada. The other two men walk us out to the street and ask where we are headed. They flag down a taxi, exchange a few words with the driver and pass him enough money to get us there. The older man opens the door for us and says, "Please forgive our country. It is not the best time for us, but we are trapped here, for now. Maybe it is difficult for you to see the real Iran, but it is here, still." He holds his hand to his heart and clenches his shirt.

The taxi already carries two passengers: a man in the front seat and a woman in the back. I climb into the back seat beside the woman and Ian sits down beside me.

We drive on.

Less than one hundred metres later the woman passes the driver some money. We stop. All three of us climb out the right-hand door (there is moving traffic to our left), and I get back in first. Ian sits beside me in the middle of the back seat.

We drive on.

Next, an old woman hails the taxi. We stop. But she cannot get in until the man in the front seat shifts in order to make room for Ian, who gets out of the back seat and climbs in the front beside the man, who sits with one cheek on the emergency brake and the other on the lap of the (male) driver. The old woman sits beside me in the back seat, smiles, closes the door.

We drive on.

At the corner, a man flags down the taxi. We stop. But he cannot get in either. There is no room in the front seat and sitting in the back seat would mean sitting beside a woman who is not family. He waits on the sidewalk. The old woman beside me struggles out and waits on the sidewalk, beckoning me to join her. I get out, she gets back in and scrunches over to the left-hand door. I get in beside her. Ian gets out of the front seat and sits beside me (his wife) and closes the back door. The new man shares the front passenger seat with the other man.

"Getting enough exercise?" Ian laughs.

"English?" croaks the new man. He ruffles through his bag and pulls out an English exercise book. "I learn English! I will go to Canada!" The exercise book is passed around from passenger to driver to passenger. "I know many English words," squeaks the man, so beside himself with excitement that he is bouncing up and down in his seat. "Nose! Fingernail!" he shouts, pointing to the corresponding body parts. "Elbow! Earlobe!" He is so giddy his eyes are watering. "Steering wheel! Mirror!"

We drive on.

In the next block we are flagged down by another woman. "Chin!" The car is the size of a lunchbox and there are already six people in it. "Shop! Beard! Traffic jam!" We stop. The new woman waits on the sidewalk. Ian gets out. I get out. The old woman gets out. Ian gets in, I get in, the new woman gets in, the old woman climbs onto her lap. "Friends! Ha ha!"

We drive on.

The driver points out our inn at the next intersection, and Ian passes him some money. "Exit!" We stop. The two women untangle themselves and wait on the sidewalk. I get out. "Goodbye!" Ian gets out. "Goodbye!" The two women return to the back seat, smiling and waving as they do so. The men in the front seat stay seated but lean out the window to wave. The driver honks.

They drive on.

We have travelled three blocks.

ಬಬ

I like the name. I like the way it feels in my mouth, the way my mouth moves, as though a wave were rolling through it.

Caspian.

Oh to collapse into the Caspian Sea. I would do it in the same the way I dive into my first ice cream cone of the summer (tongue out, eyes closed, soft groaning), but won't. Islamic law prohibits swimming, unless I am prepared to bathe fully clothed and cloaked, which I have decided would be as uncomfortable as not swimming at all. We opt instead to rent pedal boats—after a tiff about whether they are paddle or pedal boats—more because it seems like a gorgeously absurd way to explore the sea than because either of us has a burning desire to travel in a small plastic boat.

The rates are good, one hour for three cents, so we rent for two hours but dabble around only until the novelty wears off (about twenty minutes) and return to shore perspiring like opera singers. I am so drenched with sweat that my manteau feels more like a wetsuit. At the edge of the dock, I can stand it no longer. I dive fully clothed into the brine.

Within seconds I am entangled in an octopus. The water churns as my clothing is coiled into tentacles and yanked. My scarf falls round my neck and is pulled so hard I begin to choke. The weight of the wet fabric makes it exhausting to stay afloat, but I thrash and kick until, through the clamour of yelling and screaming, I hear Ian laughing. Not just laughing: laughing so hard he is gasping for breath. Which gives me pause. Pause enough to see that the legs and arms that are entangling my clothing with such ferocity belong to the two men who own the boats coming (I realize the moment I stop trying to kill them) to my rescue. Caught between the impulse to save me from drowning and the Islamic law that prohibits contact with members of the opposite sex, the men have been attempting to drag me to shore by my cloak. But in thrashing so hard, I keep forcing them to touch me.

On the safety of shore, the men insist on refunding our money in full (after inviting us to tea, lunch, their homes for the night). Apologizing so hard they can scarcely count, the men give us a handful of soaking wet bills and bow with their hands over their hearts. Ian and I walk back towards the road to wait for a bus; we turn around to see the two men waving. They continue to wave the whole time we are waiting and when a bus finally stops (by which time I am perfectly dry), they are still waving. They wave and bow and wave and bow until we are completely out of sight.

We get off the bus several miles down the road in Ramsar, a ramshackle resort town condemned by piety and zeal. Hotels stand like skeletons. Beaches are fenced off from temptation. The wind off the sea whips a single green flag.

We have come in search of the Shah's summer palace, rumoured to rest nearby under decades of revolutionary weeds and grasses. We ask directions from a shop owner who agrees to watch our bags. He looks worried, tries to interest us in something else, but eventually points us in the direction of the hills and gives us his lunch. "You will be hungry," he explains.

Up we go into the hills. Into trees and shade and a scent so pervasive, I can taste it. Lily of the valley. Sweet white breaths. I fall to the ground drinking perfume, inhaling and sighing, I push my face through baby-bell flowers until my nose stubs against someone's toe.

Paw, rather.

Realigning my nose, I rise to meet the eyes of a leonine sculpture. It guards ornate metal gates and a palace. Wait. The word "palace" is generous. Not that it isn't impressive. But I was expecting something more along the lines of a castle. No. While constructed of colossal slabs of marble, no doubt the best that Italy could offer, the building is not obscene. It is graceful, somehow. Dignified.

Scaling the gates in three layers of clothing, one of them a black tablecloth, is an exercise I would prefer not to repeat; wading through grasses full of snakes as thick as my arm falls into the same category. And having me use his shoulders and face (he claims) as a springboard through the only broken window we can find is an exercise Ian swears he will never repeat. Even as a means of escape. But we get in—Ian shimmies up the tattered velvet curtains I toss out—and that's the main thing.

The place aches with neglect. The rooms are empty—looted—and they open to us like a smile full of broken teeth. I imagine the thrill of revolution, of storming the palace, beating down the doors of privilege and smashing the contents, feeling revenge, vindication. Throbbing

with the rage of the oppressed. The teeth-gritting desire
to right a wrong.

It has been almost twenty years since the Shah was
here. Almost twenty years since he was driven from his
country in disgrace; since the streets filled with demonstrators demanding an end to the injustices in their country: the concentration of wealth in the hands of so few,
foreign domination of oil resources, military spending
that amounted to a quarter of the national budget, cen-
sorship and the rule of fear by the Shah's security service,
persecution of religious and political figures, saturation
of the country in American values.

It has been almost twenty years since the Shah answered peaceful demonstrations by ordering his security
forces to fire on the protesters, killing dozens; since the
demonstrations grew into riots, and the Shah answered by
ordering his security forces to fire into the crowds, killing
hundreds; since a political exile by the name of Khomeini
encouraged the demonstrators not to give up their fight
against injustice, and the Shah answered by ordering his
security forces to fire into the throngs that had gathered
on the day of communal prayer, killing thousands.

We walk from room to room in silence.

Echoes of laughter—the quaint titter of the wealthy—
bleed from the ceilings. It is the sort of laughter fuelled
not by happiness, but by pride; the pride that comes
with being king, *shahanshah*, king of kings. The pride that
allows a man to rob his own people. And not think himself a criminal.

We walk through every room with our heads cocked
back, listening to the ghosts of glory. Below ground—the
stairs have been smashed, so we take a chance and jump—

are the baths: tiled rooms once home to steamy pleasures, visiting foreign dignitaries and movie stars, and fine champagne, lots of champagne. Now dry. Dusty. The graveyard of a travesty.

Upstairs we rest against the cool scribbles of marble, and I imagine what it would have been like to be a guest of the Shah. "Invited from, let's say, Italy, to have dinner at the palace. I am the wealthy daughter of someone-or-other and therefore suitable company. I made the advantageous acquaintance of the Shah and his lovely wife while on a skiing holiday in Switzerland this past winter. You remember, where I bought that Versace that never quite fit properly because my waist is a bit too small for the design—yes, that one—well, wasn't I fortunate enough to be guesting at the spa when the Shah and his lovely wife hosted a little gathering, superb caviar, some of the finest I've had this year and such delightful people, Her Majesty and I became quite chummy—such *elegance*, you'd never have known she wasn't European—and it wasn't three days later that I secured my invitation to the Shah's summer house on the Caspian Sea, oh, Mama was thrilled for me and we spent a week in Milan prepari—"

"Are you coming for dinner or aren't you?" Ian interrupts through a sigh. The way he is lying on the floor with his eyes closed and his hands across his chest, he resembles a corpse. I tell him so, but he doesn't respond. I huff and resume the story at the airport, where "I am met by a handsome driver *so exotic* who opens the door to the finest limousine one can imagine, so comfortable and full of amenities we barely notice the drive north to the seaside where the Shah and his lovely wife have their cute little summer residence—oh, the *marble*—and greet us at the door."

I give Ian a smug there-you-are glance and pass him
the story.

Which he picks up by rising from the dead and becoming the Shah incarnate by hobbling around the room
on his knees (the Shah was very short), and in an aren't-
I-splendid-much-obliged-I'm-*sho* sort of accent (which
is incongruous but fits his character nonetheless), welcomes me into his home.

"Ooh, don't mind your bags, the servants will fetch
everything. *Servants!* You may refresh yourself in this bed-
chamber. I trust everything will be to your liking. Observe the chandelier—the finest Bavarian crystal—and
the mirrors come to us from Paris, as do the sconces. And
I do hope you enjoy French cuisine, we've flown Pierre
Lepneu here to delight us this evening. Surely Maxim's
can spare him for a few days, what do you say to that?—
titter titter titter—Pity you're not staying longer. I've just
bought three hundred new tanks, one can never have
enough tanks I always say, yes, quite, and well, I thought
I'd have them paraded down the streets of Tehran when
they arrive. I can see that you're impressed. Please allow
me to excite you further: very soon—*guffaw guffaw*—
I shall have the fourth-largest army in the world! Oh, of
course the people will complain: we need running water
for the villages! they'll cry. Whiny little savages. Who can
think of water pipes when there are tanks to be bought?
And guns and ammunition and missiles—what do you say
to missiles? I think they're great fun, but *oh* the *insults*
the people threw at me the last time I bought missiles!
Vicious! Ungrateful! This country is a *paradise*, but are
my people satisfied? Oh, gracious me no. Here am I,
the leader of a Grrreat—" *pronounced with rolling "r"*

"—I say a Grrrrrreat Civilization and all the people can talk about is religion and running water. What is a king to do? There's nothing to be done. I'll just go about my business—"

Voices.

Two men.

The rattling of a padlock on the front door of the palace.

Ian and I leap to our feet and hide, instinctively, behind the one curtain in the room. Four feet sticking out beneath.

Men enter the building. We can hear them talking several rooms away.

I use Ian's thighs, shoulders and face to hoist myself back out the window we used to enter. He shimmies up the curtain, folds himself over the window ledge and thuds down beside me. Cloak hiked up around my waist, I leap over snakes and through grasses; we Spiderman up the gates and hurl ourselves back into austerity. After spinning our heads around on our necks to confirm that no one has seen us—all clear—we descend the lilied hills to the sea.

The shopkeeper seems relieved to see us. He offers us tea, which we accept, and the lunch he bought to replace the one we took, which we refuse. We ask his advice about a hotel, and he points to a yellow brick building down the street. Gives us a handful of pistachios for the journey and wishes us well.

Leaving a trail of shells behind us, we reach the yellow brick building only to discover that it is beyond our price range. We stand and look muddled—bags on the ground, heads cocked—and are approached by a man, who offers his help.

He is beautiful. Tall and lithe, soft olive skin and eyes full of grace. He swivels his hand in the gesture that asks a question. Speaks softly, says something I do not understand. I tell him that we are looking for a traveller's inn. He closes his eyes, opens them again—we're still there—and smiles. Bows. Hand over his heart. Picks up our bags and begins down the street.

He turns down an alley, checks to see that we are behind him, smiles, continues. Veers into the first open door and puts our bags down in the corridor. He spends the next ten minutes visiting rooms, checking the toilets, and negotiating prices with the owner before approaching us apologetically. "No good. Forgive me." He picks up our bags and walks back down the alley to the main road, flags down a taxi, opens the back door for us, puts our bags in the trunk, gets into the front, where he discusses our situation with the driver, quietly, with great concern. The two of them look into midair, trying to picture a more appropriate place, I assume, until the driver has an idea, and we move forward. Down the street, left onto a narrow side road to a squat brown building with a one-legged man in the doorway. The two men get out and motion to us to stay in the car. They share a few words with the one-legged proprietor and follow him up the stairs. They are gone for several minutes but return with smiles. Our door is opened, our bags taken out of the trunk, and we are escorted up the stairs and down the hall to a very clean room with two single beds.

"Good?" asks beautiful man. We nod and thank him. Ian moves to pay for the taxi, but the driver refuses our money all three times. Both men stand with their hands over their hearts and bow.

As they turn to leave, beautiful man stops, asks himself a question and fumbles through his pockets. Asks something of the proprietor who shuffles away and returns with a pencil and paper. Beautiful man writes his name, Mustafa, and telephone number, and passes the paper to Ian.

"If you have problem," he says and shakes Ian's hand. He smiles shyly, bows to me and backs out the door. Ian and I set our bags down in our room and are about to settle down to a nap when there is strange thudding at the door. It is the proprietor. He drags himself into the room on his crutch. His pace is even slower than usual. He is balancing a tray of tea and biscuits.

When we emerge from our room a few hours later, there is a man seated beside the doorway. He stands up at the sight of us and offers Ian his hand.

"Hello, friends," he says. "I hope you are well. Mustafa tell hello. He is sorry with you he cannot be, but I am his brother, Hassan. Are you ready for meal?"

Ian looks to me, smiles and shrugs. "Sure."

Hassan flags down a taxi, opens the back door for us—"Please, you are welcome"—and we drive to a small restaurant by the sea, where Hassan orders swordfish kebabs, rice, yogurt, salad and colas, and asks us why we are here.

When we tell him we are on our honeymoon he nearly impales himself with a kebab skewer.

"I am sorry you did not come to our country twenty years before," says Hassan when the choking subsides.

"Twenty years before here was beautiful country, many people from Europe came for their honeymoon. Twenty years before you could go to disco, maybe to bar with music jazz, or a café in outside, or to beside sea for swimming." He's antsy now just thinking about it.

"Here was rich country, do believe me, we had all thing. But from time of revolution, from that time, here is not our country. It is. . . . how I describe for you. . . . it is sadness. Now we are poor. Our money is useless, and there is no place to spend. Before revolution here was like Europe, so much beautiful thing and fun and rich. Now, you can see, there is nothing. Our revolution took our life."

Hassan gets up from the table and pays for the meal. We walk towards the water—the sea is close but inaccessible—and sit on a stone wall that holds us from the memory of swimming.

"Before revolution here was beautiful sea, many beside sea and boat. It was place for honeymoon. Many people came from all place world for fun. When I was boy, seventeen years, I did meet girl from Emrika. Sandy. Her father did work here in Iran, he was geologist. I did meet Sandy beside sea—she was beautiful one—and after several week together, we become love. But she did life in Tehran, and I was here beside sea, so after our holiday we did write letter. We each other did not see again, only when we did send picture."

Hassan reaches into his wallet and peels a tattered photo from the leather. It shows a lanky, strawberry-blond girl in a bikini. She holds a can of Pepsi-Cola and poses like a model in an advertisement.

"Our revolution become next year, 1979," he sighs, taking a long sad look at the photo. "We did write letter after that, but after several month she did not write for me. I blame our government. I think it made afraid her. When our revolution became very severe with killing in street and hostage in Emrika embassy, it made afraid all Emrika. Even it made afraid many Iranian. Many people did leave country and try escape. Here was very fanatic revolution people, everyone fight for power in government. Emrika did think: Iran become crazy! But really Iranian was same people, only difference, we have some fanatic with power. Everyone else same." He takes one last look at Sandy's photo before replacing it in his wallet.

"After from that time of revolution I must in war, you know about our war with Iraq, when Hussein did invade into our country with help of Emrika weapon and money, and we must defend. Everyone must fight.

"You are kind people," Hassan says as we walk back to the main road. "I do think you are kind with our people if you for honeymoon come here."

We drive to the inn in silence. Hassan walks us back to our room and apologizes that we could not go to a disco or a bar or a beach. Asks what our plans are for the morning. Says he is sorry we will be leaving town so early. He wishes us the best for our journey, the rest of our honeymoon. And for long and happy lives together. We thank him, ask him to give our best to Mustafa, and wish him goodnight.

There is a timid knock on the door. It is either the middle of the night or very early in the morning.

"Mr. Ian?"

Ian gets out of bed, gets dressed and goes out into the hallway. I can hear the sound of voices but cannot make out a word. He reappears a few minutes later, stuffs something into his bag and lies back down.

"What was that about?" I whisper.

"It was Hassan and Mustafa. They brought us food for the bus trip tomorrow. And Hassan brought Sandy's address, says we could look her up when we get back."

"Where does she live?"

"Fort Worth, Texas. Poor guy. He asked me if I thought Iran was still a good place for a honeymoon. Then when I said yes, he said he would be very grateful if I could please mention that to Sandy."

WE SEEK THE TRUTH

BETWEEN DESTINATIONS. I cannot bear another minute of the day's heat. We climb off the bus in Gorgan to look for water. I have sweated so much that the back of my cloak is scarred with salt stains. Finding water is not just a priority, it is my sole purpose in life.

The moment Ian and I begin speaking English we are approached by two men, who wonder if they can help.

"Toilets," I sputter, urgently, perhaps rudely. The men smile and bow, pick up our bags and motion down a side street.

They walk ahead of us, peering back periodically to smile, ask if we are okay, ask where we are from—"Oh, Canada, very good"—if we like Iran, if I like my hejab. Ian smiles at this last question, and I pretend to trip and land my elbow into his back.

Outside a dilapidated brick building our bags are placed on the ground. Both men shake Ian's hand, then bow, deeply, with closed eyes, and stand with their hands over their hearts. We thank them, take our bags and go inside.

A mosque. Small, unremarkable, but home to reverent peace. And toilets. I leave Ian in the entrance with the bags, pee, perform ablutions, stick my mouth under the faucet, and am just readjusting my covering when I hear someone calling him.

"*En-ga-lay-see ba-la-deed?*" Ian's voice, asking if the person speaks English.

"A little," comes the reply. "You are Muslim?"

I lean my face forward, anticipating Ian's response, but hear nothing. Only the faint sounds of conversation. And the words: *Just a minute, I will get my wife.*

I leave the washroom and join Ian in the corridor. Next to him stands an old man in a long brown robe and a white turban. He does not smile, but stares into the air beside me, picks up our bags and shuffles through a narrow opening in the wall. The moment he is out of sight, we engage in a whispering match.

"What in the world did you tell him?"

"I told him I was Christian."

"Whaaaat? Why?"

"I don't know. I thought maybe he was going to invite me to pray with him."

"I don't really think it's a social activi—"

"—I just didn't feel like lying about being a Muslim to a mollah—"

"—You could have said you were *studying* to become a Musl—"

"—Look, I'm a little uncomfortable lying about religion in the middle of a fucking theocracy, so let's just—"

The old man returns without our bags. "Come," he says. Ian nods, and we walk in single file down the narrow stone corridor.

"Maybe we're being led to the arena: he looks a bit like a gladiator," I whisper. Ian does not respond. He only swivels around and gives me a glare that says, *I thought I just heard you cracking a joke. Please tell me I was mistaken.* I smile apologetically and walk the rest of the way with both hands over my mouth.

The corridor opens out onto a courtyard, a yard so replete with blossoms—orange petals, dangling just above our noses—that I stare, open-mouthed, for every inch of the space has been planned and manicured into perfect symmetry. A tree stands at either end of a shallow rectangular pool; the two trees are of identical height, breadth and shape. Identical. Along the sides of the yard fruit trees, berry bushes and flowering plants bloom with startling precision. There is something both calming and unsettling about the space, as with any place where nature has been disciplined.

Come, come, the old man motions from the doorway of a small stone building. We remove our shoes and follow him into a cool room of his house. No furniture, just a thick crimson carpet that nuzzles every corner of the room. He brings two long pillows and sets them on the floor at our feet. "Please sit," he says. And hobbles back outside.

Ian and I look to each other, shrug, and sit.

For about an hour.

Periodically we hear a rhythmic banging, actually more of a clanging, and I begin to wonder if this home backs onto a blacksmith's workshop or the part of the bazaar that houses the potmakers. The men that beat metal with little hammers until it holds food. I also begin to wonder what has become of our mollah. Has he left to report us—there was a Christian peeing in my mosque—or call friends to meet us or gather his family or take a nap? For some reason, it doesn't matter. What matters is that we are in a cool room surrounded by flowers, resting in the simple wonder of the day. For a moment, I take enormous pleasure in simply breathing.

Ian sits beside me. Frantic. I haven't been able to determine the source of his angst, just that there is some, and that relaxing is going to be difficult—impossible—until we have dealt with it. Between the banging and the clanging and the fact that we are confessed Christians, Ian is not delighting in his respiratory system as much as I; if anything his breathing is laboured. The flowers aren't doing it for him either. He has turned to his guidebook for solace, rereading the sections on "Religion and Social Customs" on the off-chance that he might have missed the sentences that dealt with mosque urination mores.

The old man appears in the doorway and motions us to follow him. We move towards the source of the clanging—Ian carries the Book, with his finger marking crucial sections—and come to a spartan kitchen, the sink piled high with pots. Beside this, a long wooden table is laden with food: saffron rice, vegetables and legumes, yogurt, flatbread.

"Please," says the old man, pulling out one of the chairs. "I bought too much food this morning. God sent you to help me to enjoy it."

We sit down at the table and devour the feast. We eat in silence, not out of awkwardness, but because it feels appropriate. When the meal is finished, we stack the dishes at one end of the table and begin conversation.

"You are English?" asks the old man.

"No, Canadian."

"Ah, vous parlez français alors. Ça c'est bien," he says spying the guidebook and raising his eyebrows in a manner that implies, may I?

"So you are tourists," he continues in impeccable French, flipping through the book. "I thought you were pilgrims, on your way to Mashhad. That's why I asked if you were Muslims. We Muslims are all pilgrims, we travel to Mecca at least once in our lives and to other holy shrines. So every pilgrim is our brother. But you are tourists. Well, it is another kind of pilgrimage. You can still travel to Mashhad to see the shrine of Imam Reza. I recommend it. Many beautiful buildings, even more beautiful than your Notre Dame."

He chuckles and smiles until his face is nothing but a series of wrinkles.

"Where did you learn to speak French?" Ian asks.

The old man doesn't answer. He is too engrossed in the table of contents. "Po-li-tic," he reads with a look of restrained surprise. He reads the entire section without changing his expression. He holds the book with his left hand and his forehead with his right. Both hands look as though they are wrapped in cellophane, such is the scarring. His fingers move like stiff plastic.

"This is a strange book," he says, handing it back across the table. "It tells you only what is not important." The old man gathers his hands into two fists and lays them in front of him. "You are pilgrims. You seek truth, is that right?"

Ian clears his throat, shifts in his seat and nods.

"You are on a pilgrimage, but it is a journey of the mind, not the soul. This is our difference. If you seek truth, then you must close this book. You must look into the eyes of the people. There you will hear the soul. If you hear the soul, then you will hear truth. Everything else is . . ." He searches the air for a word, squinting and looking up to the ceiling. "Everything else is a disguise."

"But don't you think historical facts are important?" Ian probes, turning to the chapter entitled "Recent History" and running his finger down the pages like a speed reader. "I mean, there's a lot here that you'd have to know to understand anything."

The old man smiles, not joyfully, and speaks to the centre of the table: "Iran is not a place, but a spirit. Iranian people live all over the world: Australia, Germany, Japan, France, Canada, America. Our spirit lives everywhere. But this ground—" he taps the floor with his foot "—this ground is our home, our heart. In this place you can feel us most deeply. In this place lives our language.

"Your book says that the Shah was a man, a leader of this country, king, but this is not true. The Shah was a wolf. He was not an Iranian, his feet never touched this ground, they stood on marble floors and private aeroplanes and platforms and foreign lands, but they did not touch here—" he taps the floor again "—he never gave the sweat of his feet to this dry earth. A man who lives above the ground will never touch its soul. And such a man he was.

"The Shah did not love his people; no; he hunted them. The Shah was a hunter. He tried to kill our soul. Your book does not say this."

Ian takes such an exaggerated breath that his nostrils flare.

The old man continues: "The Shah told our people: *We must be proud of our Persian history—We were a Great Civilization and will be again!* But he was not proud of our people, the history of their souls. No, he said our ways were uncivilized, that we must live and dress as the Europeans do. His thugs went into the streets and terrorized the people. They ripped off the women's Islamic clothing, beat them if they resisted, disgraced them, old women like my mother, and after that she did not leave the house, many women were the same, because they wanted to live with dignity, under God's eyes, and the Shah would not allow it.

"The Shah told our people: *We will have the world on its knees: we will have the third most powerful army in the world!* And the people watched. They watched him buy tanks and bombers and helicopters and guns. They watched him buy and buy and spend and spend. They watched the villages starve. They watched the war machines fill their land—my friends, please travel to our desert and witness the wasted fortune that rots there. They watched the world grow fat, and their mothers grow thin.

"The Shah told our people: *We will be as rich as Europeans—in one generation!* They saw the oil coming up from the ground, they saw the interest of the world, they saw the development, saw the easy life of the rich. The Shah told our people: *We will be a second America!* And he led the people to believe that this would make them happy. They cheered the foreign companies who came to help. They cheered and waited. They watched the Shah grow rich. They watched his friends grow rich. They watched them buy cars and build palaces, they watched them buy villas in Switzerland, fly to Italy for shopping trips, fly to Germany for meals, to America to buy second homes. They watched the oil go from their soul's land into everyone's hands but their own. And they felt the death of their spirit.

"The people watched, they waited, and finally, they spoke. They stood up and asked, *Why does the world become rich while we remain poor? This oil belongs to this land, and this land belongs to the people!* They stood up and said, *We do not need America to dictate our values, the way that we live! Why are their ways better than our own?* They stood up, my friends, and said, *The Shah is not our leader—he is one of them! Enough!* And you can imagine what followed: they were silenced. Killed. Tortured. Imprisoned. Exiled.

"No one was safe. Because the hunter must feel strong. If he is threatened, he panics and becomes so paranoid that he begins shooting every which way. He shoots at anything that moves, every rustle in the dark, every sound. He feels the fear of the hunted—and he does not like it.

"The people were afraid to speak, the Shah's thugs were everywhere listening. The people could not gather or discuss or question or read. The Shah's thugs were everywhere. And my friends, you do not know the fear that lives in the bones when you are among such monsters.

"Imagine that you are sitting in your home. You are an innocent person, you do not participate in politics, you are poor but happy. You are sitting at home with your wife, and there is a knock at the door. You answer to two men, strangers, who tell you you must come with them. Must. And so you go. You go to their offices, and you learn what you have done: Someone at your workplace heard you complain about your boss. You had asked for a day off to visit your mother, who is in hospital, and your boss refused because it was a very busy time at work, and you had taken too many holidays already. You came back to your desk and relayed the incident to a friend. And called your boss a tyrant. A tyrant! Why did you choose this word, sir? What did you mean by this expression? Were you announcing to your office that you lived in a tyranny? Were you trying to incite your office to think such a thing? Are you an enemy of the state? No? Well then why do you not belong to the Shah's party? Why are there no pictures of the Shah in your house?

"And all of the time they are asking these questions, they are pulling out your fingernails, one by one.

"The hunted learn to run. They run until they cannot run any more. They breathe heavily and cry easily. They look for shelter. They look for a place that is safe. They leave their work, they leave the streets, they leave the parks and the restaurants and the theatres and cafés— the Shah's thugs are everywhere—and they go to God. In the mosque they may gather, in the mosque they may sit in silence and meditation, in the mosque they may talk, touch souls, find peace. In the mosque lives their spirit.

"And in the mosque they hear the voice of prayer and calm and assurance and strength. I remember watching the faces of men who listened to tapes of Imam Khomeini, those secret recordings we smuggled from France, and their tears poured and poured, because their eyes, their eyes were hollow. They had been beaten, tortured, humiliated. But the Imam believed in them, he gave them hope and strength in themselves. Belief in themselves through Islam. The Imam returned our people their spirit. Oh, my friends, God is great."

Allah-u-akbar.

The old man closes his eyes.

"These hands you see," he whispers, turning his shiny gnarled fingers round and round in front of him. "These are the hands of the hunted. They put these hands into boiling oil because I fought the Shah with words. And I was fortunate. Many were chained to a metal table that grew hotter and hotter. The frying table. We smelled our friends, frying to death. Friends who had fought with their voices. Died when their voices stopped.

"You do not know the soul of this land until you know these voices."

We sit in silence. Staring at this man's hands, listening to the screams held beneath the skin. Cockroaches the size of my thumb find their way to our dirty dishes, but they skitter and eat in peace.

Ian inhales and prepares to speak. "I've heard everything that you've said, more than you think. And I'm certainly not trying to deny the horror you've described, but you talk about it as if it weren't still going on. I mean, there's a reason there are Iranians all over the world: they don't want to live here. If Khomeini returned their spirit, then why do they all want to go and live in America? We can't go anywhere without someone telling us they want to move to Canad—"

"—You have read much about our revolution. You know many facts and dates and figures and opinions. But you do not know its soul. I try to tell you about our revolution, but you must listen more quietly. Even when I am speaking, your mind, it is shouting at me. Please allow it to listen. God has sent you here for this purpose."

The old man strokes his beard and closes his eyes.

"I followed the Imam's voice because it was the voice of our soul. I followed the Imam to our religious city of Qom and listened to his teachings, and I followed him into exile. For many months I studied with the Imam in Iraq, and for many years I lived in France. And so I lived in your West. I studied there. I have touched your spirit.

"The life of your West is good, very easy, with many pleasures, much fun and laughter, much comfort. Every being looks for this path, what is easiest and most comfortable, even in nature you see it: animals will take the worn path instead of making their own—of course they will, it is understandable. But it is their downfall.

"The path to freedom requires discipline, silence, concentration, a strong will. It is not a comfortable life full of luxuries and distractions and bodily pleasures. It is difficult. The most valuable lessons are always difficult. So are the most valuable lives.

"The unenlightened man will always choose the worn path. He will choose play over study, noise over silence, company over solitude, a comfortable life over an ascetic one. He seeks fun and laughter, tries to satiate his appetite, fill his life with comforts, conveniences, toys, luxuries. Each one brings pleasure, but never satisfaction, never peace. Because he looks for happiness outside of himself. And he believes that he will be content when he is comfortable.

"But I have lived with these people, these comfortable people, with their houses and cars and televisions and foods from packages. I have seen the eyes of these people, and my friends, I did not feel happiness. Pleasure, yes, pleasure they can buy on every corner. But they are not happy. They eat and eat and eat and are not nourished.

They talk of a future time when they will be happy, when they have this, or when that is finished, or when they will be able to afford this, or when they will look different, or when they will have more time to enjoy, or when they are more comfortable. But there is no today. Today is always unsatisfied.

"Your West talks very much about freedom. Especially freedom for women, and they criticize us, they say we do not give our women freedom. But they talk about freedom as though it were an object. As though it were something you could own or buy or legislate. As though freedom were something outside of people. Freedom is not something that can be given, it can only be found inside people. And I believe our women in Iran hold greater freedom in their hearts than the women in your West. My wife used to live in America, and she has told me that she asked one hundred women: are you happy with yourselves? are you happy with yourself in every respect? are you satisfied with who you are and how you look and what you do in your life? And do you know, my wife told me they laughed at these questions, but their eyes were filled with shame. Because they knew they were supposed to say, *Yes, of course, because I live in freedom!* But they could not.

"In death is the vision of life. I have watched your people die. And they do not die in peace. They do not want to die because they feel they have not lived. They have not done enough to make them satisfied with their lives. They live in regret and hurried efforts to make their lives complete. They do not accept their death, because they did not accept their life. Even in death their souls are not free.

"You say that my people do not want to live on their land, but I say they want to live the easy path. They want to live in Europe and America because the life is easier, and if you have ever lived such a difficult life as I have seen in some parts of this world, you would understand. Iranians go to America because it is easy to be comfortable there. But just because they stay in America, it does not mean that their spirits are free. It means that it is easy to live there.

"In the Islamic Republic of Iran we do not live for money. Our path is not the clear path to wealth, comfort, sloth. Our path is difficult, full of hardship and sacrifice, but our path is to peace. Our path is to God.

"The Imam returned the spirit of our people. He returned to us the value of our soul. If people choose to ignore this, if they choose wealth over spiritual peace, then that speaks of their emptiness. It does not say anything about this country.

"If you wish to see this country, my friend, then you must close your eyes. You will not see it until you look with your heart."

Allah-u-akbar.

The muezzin calls the devoted to prayer.

Allah-u-akbar.

The old man stands up and puts the dishes into the sink. Moves towards the doorway. We rise from the table and follow him to the courtyard, to our shoes and bags, to the taste of flowers. "Let me give you some fruit for your journey," he says, plucking colours from various trees around the yard. "Please accept this humble food as a gift from our land."

Allah-u-akbar.

"God is great, my friends. He offers you peace. Only you may choose if you wish to accept it."

We walk across the courtyard together and file down the corridor to the mosque, now pulsing with prayer. The old man kisses Ian on both cheeks and holds his eyes with a gentle smile. He closes his eyes and bows, slowly, to me. Hand over his heart. Disappears into the tiled room where a sea of men fall to their knees and touch their heads to the earth.

ʰᵔᏏ

Later, alone. I walk the filthy streets unable to breathe. I am shielded from view, left to putrefy under a heavy black mask. I knead my palms and my arms, trying to feel myself, hold myself, bring myself to life.

Men squat by the side of the road and sell skins of freshly slaughtered sheep. They lie in bloodied mounds, limp woollen carcasses, their legs collapsed and splayed like puppets'. I walk past them, animals gutted of their bodies, and hold the stench of rotting flesh in my mouth.

CONFESSION

THE MOST STRIKING THING about Abbas is his teeth. Which is not to say that the rest of him is unremarkable, but simply that his teeth are extraordinary. If I had met him anywhere else, I would assume he'd spent a fortune in straightening, polishing, whitening, brightening, not to mention time in front of a mirror working on the presentation of his twenty-odd perfectly shaped ivory white stones. But we are in Iran, where, generally speaking, vanity is not a national pastime. Where the soul is of greater value than the body. Where plastic surgery is not an industry. Where a face is a face. Abbas's smile is his own, and is the most beautiful I've ever seen.

Sitting beside Abbas's twinkling face is his cousin, Mohammad, who simpers and chuckles in an aw-shucks sort of way. And blushes constantly. His posture and manner are both so self-effacing that I silently rename him Eeyore.

A few moments ago, Abbas rescued us from linguistic frustration—Ian had ordered a salad for dinner and was presented with a bowl of raw onions—and invited us to join him and his cousin at their table. They had a brief exchange with the waiter, who nodded and left the restaurant.

"Please pay attention to this matter: this man has no vegetables," Abbas explained, pronouncing every one of *vegetables'* four syllables. "But it is no problem," he continued. "He goes to his home to take some vegetables from his mother. We wait."

We waited, as instructed, and exchanged life stories in the process. Abbas grinned the entire time, not the kind of Plasticene smile that is offered out of politeness or boredom, but a full-faced enraptured smile, both when he spoke and when he listened.

A carpet dealer, Abbas is. His cousin, Mohammad, a dentist living in Germany these last five years. Too bad we don't speak German, Mohammad says. "Finally I speak in German and it is my voice. For many years I could speak only like a child, many mistakes and small vocabulary. So many times I became frustrated, but now is good. I can find myself in this language, and finally I have some German friends."

Abbas laughs at his cousin's declaration. It is a pure, genuine laugh. An extension of his teeth. His whole body generates warmth and delight. "Everyone who is knowing Mohammad is liking him, so it is, Mohammad. So good, so funny. He is a good one." Abbas throws an arm across his cousin's rounded shoulders and pats him on the back. "And please," he says, returning to Ian and me. "What is this purpose for your now travellings?"

Mohammad finds our honeymoon answer extremely amusing. So much so that I'm not sure he believes us. Abbas does, though; it shows in his expression. His full frontal broadcast of pleasure. "And so is our journey something similar," he says. "Mohammad comes back to Iran for finding a wife. We are visiting two possibilities suggested from our families, but maybe these are not successful, is it so, Mohammad?"

A blush descends the length of Mohammad's face, squirms down his neck and hides under his collar. He chuckles, awkwardly. Shrugs. Shifts, clears his throat. "One is very nice, also a dentist, but I must be careful. Many women look only for an opportunity of moving to Europe. They do not like me, instead, they like my passport."

Abbas laughs and laughs until all his teeth are showing. All of them. "Poor Mohammad! Oh my cousin!" He leans over and hugs him again. "We find, we find . . ."

"In Europe they think it is a bit barbaric, this way to look for a wife," Mohammad says to his hands, which have not stopped fidgeting since we sat down. "Maybe you think so much also."

"Do *you* think it's barbaric?" I ask.

Mohammad's eyes leap from the table to meet mine. "No," he looks down again. "No, sometimes I believe it is barbaric how do people meet each other in Europe, you know, so often through alcohol or some kind of superficial meeting, parties or someplace other. It is so easy to . . . how do you call it . . . *act* as some other person. I had one German girlfriend, for two years were we together and only have I seen some sides of her, very good and kind, but only the outside, fun and happy, I could not see who *was* she in earnest. It was always something for showing other people. Now when she heard that I came to Iran to find an Iranian wife, she said oh I was typical Iranian man, to find a wife with my family's helping and so forth, but do you know, after we separated each other, she made some *computer dating.*" He turns, at this point, and tries, in Farsi, to explain the concept to an absolutely stupefied Abbas, who stops smiling for the first time since making our acquaintance and sits with his mouth slightly open, listening. He asks a few quick questions, then resumes giggling.

"Always the life of Mohammad is so inter*e*sting!" he announces, pronouncing all four of *interesting*'s four syllables.

Our waiter strides back in the front door of the restaurant and holds up a plastic bag overflowing with greenery. "Your vegetables!" Abbas announces, clapping his hands together. "Now they prepare many interesting and delicious tastes for you, as I demanded."

ಬಬ

Abbas meets us at our hotel the next day at noon and is all wide smiles and apologies. Mohammad is unable to join us, having arranged a final meeting with one of the prospective brides and her family. He will join us this evening and would like to invite us to dinner at a fine restaurant. It will be his pleasure.

I have to describe Abbas again, because there is far more that is striking about him than just his teeth. His whole face sparkles. Eyes that come alive when they engage you. Or when you engage them. In a place with the texture of a hundred different shades of black, anyone offering a splash of colour to the air literally radiates. One of these effulgent beings is Abbas. Not only because he is wearing a turquoise-and-pink striped T-shirt, but because he seems to enjoy wearing it so much. And thinks nothing of wearing it today, on our visit to the Holy Shrine of Imam Reza, one of the holiest, and by extension, the most solemn places in all of Iran. Ian, on the other hand, is dressed entirely in black.

"Please, Ian, and what about your clothings?" Abbas says, tugging at Ian's shirt. "So much black and serious. Are you a Hezbollahi or some other religious organization?" Then he laughs, *exactly* this sound: "Ha ha ha."

Ian flips to the page in his guidebook that explains that men and women must dress *extremely conservatively* in order to enter the shrine complex. Abbas takes the book and scans the pages on the city of Mashhad, the Holy Shrine of Imam Reza, "Tips and Hints on Cultural Sensitivity," "Dangers and Annoyances." Looks up without changing his smile.

"Where it is written how to meet Abbas and Mohammad?" he says with an open-mouthed smile. Then again: "Ha ha ha."

We walk to the shrine complex along one of Mashhad's main streets: a roaring, bustling six-lane avenue jammed with traffic, business and life. At a small nut shop, Abbas buys us a tin of some of the most delicious I-don't-know-whats I've ever eaten. Made with butter, he explains. And pistachios. And sugar. And maybe some other things. Ian and I snap off bits of the brittle as we walk, until the tin rattles empty with the scratches of crumbs. By the time we reach the complex gates, we both have day-after-Halloween gut aches.

"Please pay attention to this matter: you must go this way," Abbas says, guiding me in the direction of the women's entrance. "And we this," he says to Ian. I join a group of women huddled outside the entrance, and I am just about to walk behind the curtains when a man holding a rainbow-coloured feather duster shouts to me and shoos me away with his duster. I turn, bewildered, to Abbas, who exchanges a few smiling phrases with the man, a few more, and a few more, eventually laying a hand over his heart and stepping away.

"I am sorry. It is my wrongness," Abbas explains through a gargantuan grin. "The book of Ian is correct: it is necessary wearing chaador for visiting Shrine of Imam Reza. Really your manteau is very fine. Only for visiting such holy places maybe it is necessary also chaador. Please excuse."

We return to the hotel and I uncrumple the balled-up chaador from the bottom of my bag. I have managed to avoid wearing it until now, not out of rebellion or mulish disobedience—though I have tendencies in both directions—but because in my plain black manteau and scarf I am already dressing on the conservative end of the spectrum. A calf-length spring coat and light-coloured scarf are almost as commonly seen as my get-up, depending on the city and the setting. Not that the sight of the chaador is uncommon, just that it is far from mandatory.

And there are no two ways about it: wearing one is a royal pain in the ass.

First of all, there is no such thing as "wearing" a chaador. There is only "managing to keep one on." And I don't say this as a frustrated novice, but as an observer of scores of women who have been dressing with it most of their lives.

The chaador is a living, wriggling entity, whose preferred habitat is the floor. Any woman trying to cover herself is not only fighting the true nature of the fabric, but also gravity, which has been in cahoots with the chaador since the beginning of time. The moment the chaador is on, wrapped in just the right way, covering all the right things, it begins its dogged descent, squirming along the sleek surface of the hair, hoping to make a clean leap to the neck, where it can secure a foothold for its plummet off the shoulders. An astonishing portion of the wearer's energy and concentration goes into minimizing the creature's progress, herding it back to its position around her face, leashing it to her fingers and fists, or clamping its skin between her teeth. It doesn't enjoy being corralled in this way. Thus the constant wrestling. The creature prefers damp, humid surroundings and feeds on sweat.

The literal translation of chaador is "tent," but from my own camping experience, this seems a poor translation. The sack-shaped coat and scarf I have on right now are the tent. The chaador thrown overtop feels more like the fly.

I join Abbas and Ian in the dusty alley outside our *mosafer-khané,* and they applaud my appearance with laughter and encouraging remarks. Abbas explains, in the best possible humour, that the chaador is just custom, nothing to take too seriously, nothing to worry about, nothing to be upset about. And that I look very nice. Now, are we interesting to hear his explainings of this Shrine of Imam Reza?

This is one of the holiest sites of Shi'a Islam, the branch of Islam whose followers believe that the Prophet Mohammed's rightful successor was his cousin and son-in-law, Ali. Those who adhered to this belief, that the

Muslim leadership should remain with the Prophet's family, became the followers of Ali, the Shi'ites. The majority of Mohammed's followers, however, believed in following tribal custom and choosing their leader by consensus. These became the Sunnis, the most populous branch of Islam to this day.

We stand now at the burial ground of Imam Reza, the eighth Imam according to the Shi'ites, and grandson of the Prophet Mohammed. Imam Reza was rumoured to be poisoned, and therefore martyred, in 817. He lies entombed in the very centre of the complex, but the Holy Shrine is off-limits to non-Muslims, so we will restrict our visit to the surrounding buildings, some of the most spectacular in all of Iran.

The shrine complex is owned by a large and exceedingly wealthy consortium. "Business," Abbas explains, "who is men of God." It plans to take over a large portion of the downtown core, envisioning large-scale expansion of the shrine, in all its glory. The consortium, which comprises over fifty businesses dealing in everything from biscuits to blood serum, also gives to many charities, and this place, this palace, is open to all people, all day and all night.

When we arrive back at the gates, I pass without problem and undergo a standard security frisking by an extremely bored woman with cow breath. A bomb killed twenty-seven people here last year. Rumour has it two women smuggled the device into the sacred area under their "tents."

I pass through security and step outside. Take two steps forward before being shoved to a halt by my first glimpse of the place.

The glare from the marble is blinding. Painful to the eyes. Opalescent stone, glass, mirrors, turquoise, gold, white, white, every possible shade of white. I stand in the base of a jewel, surrounded by sheer cuts of colour glittering under light.

We stroll through gatherings of arches and tiles until the voice of the muezzin unfurls and thickens the air, pulling people to the centre of this marvel.

Abbas smiles and gestures to the flow of people assembling for prayer. "Maybe it is interesting for you following also to mosque, for watching this devoting. It is not my way, but still I enjoy. I think people can have confidence in God, in any way it is good for them, something like private matter. I am Islamic, but only in quiet way, for same reasons I am speaking Farsi: it is my culture. Still, it is interesting for foreigns, it is so?"

The Great Mosque sits outstretched, one arc of its walls left open to a grand open-air courtyard. Persian carpets blanket the ground where hundreds upon hundreds upon hundreds of devotees stand, kneel, bow, submit. Breathe prayers to the sky.

A boy stands next to his father, stands as tall as his father's thigh, and learns the choreography of Islam. The boy tries to look stern and focused, but he is nervous, self-conscious, unsure of himself. He watches the other men out of the corner of his eye, sneaks peeks at the next move, then follows, hurriedly, a split-second late. His is a rushed, jerky dance of devotion, but it will improve. And the rhythm of this ritual will wash into his blood and live there as a lifeline. The line of his life. Something he would die for.

At the back edge of the carpets stands a collection of legs. Plastic tokens of an eight-year holy war. Artificial limbs of near-martyrs. Men who worship now with the help of able men. They stand, kneel, bow arm in arm.

I drift into the designated area for women: clusters of cut-out faces stuck to black drapes. I sit with a group of teenage girls who pretend to be consulting their prayer books but who whisper and giggle instead. They see me watching and wipe smiles from their faces, lower their faces to pages of script and begin moving their lips around prayers. A tiny girl in red tights and a miniskirt skips around heaps of cloaked women who sit fanning themselves, dizzy from heat and emotion; women such as she will become one day, this girl. This carefree child of Iran.

בּעֲ

Mohammad has invited us to the city's five-star hotel for dinner. Ian, who is a finicky eater at the best of times and has taken to schlepping around a box of Pablum that he dines on most mornings and evenings, is thrilled.

From a distance, the hotel is impressive, in that it is large, maybe fifteen stories, has a long circular driveway and a brightly lit entranceway. There is a crowd of very jolly, well-dressed people gathered around the main doors, so the place feels lively. "Probably this is a wedding gathering," Abbas explains, straining to examine the group as we wend our way down the driveway.

And see a sheep.

White.

Lying on its back, struggling against the three men who are holding it by the legs and the throat. And are about to slaughter it right here, metres from the hotel's marble entranceway.

"The wedding dinner," Abbas explains, putting his arm around Ian, who stands ag-g-g-gape. I don't hear what he says next. I've taken this moment to readjust my scarf so that it covers my head completely.

Inside the main doors is an atrium whose appearance is commensurate with the standards of a five-star hotel. Lots of mirrors and brass, chandeliers, plastic plants and bad art. The floor gleams and is dominated by an intricate mosaic with a polished gilded border. Beautifully inscribed in the coloured tiles are the English words, DOWN WITH USA. It is impossible to walk into the hotel without treading on it.

We are seated in the restaurant and given menus in Farsi and English. Elevator music jiggles out of one corner of the room. The wait staff stands outside the kitchen, bored out of their minds. There is no one else in the restaurant. With the exceptions of Imam Khomeini himself, his successor as Supreme Spiritual Leader, Ayatollah Ali Kha'menei, and President Hashemi Rafsanjani, whose portraits hang on every wall.

Mohammad seems nervous that we won't enjoy the meal, keeps saying, "I hope it is good . . ." as he scans the menu: salad, soup, shish kebab with rice, hamburger, pizza, spaghetti with meat sauce, spaghetti with tomato sauce, fish, lamb chops, beef chops, sheep chops.

"I'm going to have salad and spaghetti. Either that or the pizza," Ian announces excitedly.

Our waiter arrives to take our order. Apologizes that they are out of a few things: salad, soup, hamburger, pizza, spaghetti with meat sauce, spaghetti with tomato sauce, fish, beef chops. He recommends the sheep. Or the shish kebab, with rice.

If Ian sulked any harder I think his face would fold in half. Mohammad looks so distraught that he has actually begun to sweat. Abbas and Mohammad begin discussing the situation with the waiter, who shrugs and waves his hands in the air. *What am I supposed to do about it?* he gestures. *Go and get some vegetables from your mother!* Abbas and Mohammad seem to be saying. But it is hopeless.

We slump out of the restaurant, trudge back over DOWN WITH USA and out onto the bloodied pavement. Abbas runs to the road and flags down a cab. The waiter has recommended a place we could try, Mohammad explains between apologies, which he is now uttering at two-minute intervals.

An hour later we are sitting in a brightly lit, Muzak-laced, purple-plastic-tabled joint eating pizza and French fries. Ian is chewing huge mouthfuls of everything at once, and washing it all down with great, audible, cheek-squeezing slurps of cola. Mohammad and Abbas are munching away happily, relaxed now that they have finally pleased their guests.

Dinner discussion centres around today's announcement of a fixed rate of only 3,000 rials to the US dollar. Less than half what we managed to get when we arrived. The government has imposed the paltry rate to force a cap on frantic inflation and to try to get a handle on the economy. Anyone caught trading anything other than the fixed government rate will face execution for the crime of economic terrorism.

Even though we are the only customers in the restaurant, Mohammad is extremely uncomfortable talking about this in public. Abbas doesn't seem to pay any mind at all, though from what little I've come to know of him, he doesn't seem to fret about anything. He seems oblivious to the uglies of the world, not in a naive or blind way, more that he just doesn't allow those things to touch him. Abbas is a half-full kind of guy.

Mohammad, on the other hand, is more of a half-empty-and-oh-my-God-it's-probably-my-fault-I-must-have-spilled-it sort of person. But endearingly so. In the last twenty-four hours I've grown enormously fond of both of them.

We walk back to the *mosaferkhané* and continue the discussion of money, *sotto voce*, in our room. Abbas is all smiles and comfort. No problem, the new rate only means things will become a bit more expensive, that's all. Mohammad agrees, but worriedly. He thinks, mumbles to Abbas, stares up at the ceiling, is about to speak, then goes to the door, opens it, looks around the hallway, closes the door, sits back down on the bed. And offers to change our money for us at the old rate. He knows where to go to get the old—(he stops whispering, strains to the side, gets up, opens the door, checks the hallway again, closes the door, sits back down and lowers his voice even further)—the old black market rate. He could change $100 for us and it would probably last us the rest of our trip. If we are interested.

Once again, a man we've known for precisely one day is offering to break a law for us, commit an infraction punishable by death, so that Ian and I, two exceedingly privileged citizens by world standards, can make one hundred dollars stretch twice as far. So that we can buy carrot juice for four cents a glass instead of eight. Can find a room in a *mosaferkhané* for two dollars a night instead of four. Can take a two-hour flight for three dollars apiece instead of six.

Ian accepts. Takes a hundred dollars from his money belt and hands it to Mohammad, thanking him and shaking his hand. They confirm plans for tomorrow—we will have dinner at Abbas's parents' house—and shake hands.

Goodnights echo and I flop onto a bed while Ian walks our friends to the door. He returns and begins going over his schedule for tomorrow—the Holy Museum and Mosque of the Seventy-two Martyrs in the morning, Nader Museum in the afternoon, maybe an early lunch at the pizza place, Martyrs' Cemetery in the evening, well, or he could do that in the following morning before heading out to the bus terminal . . . flipping back and forth in his guidebook, orally ticking off the sites he's seen already, to be sure he hasn't missed anything.

I rise from the bed and grab my chaador. Walk to the door, turn the doorknob and my head.

"I'm going for a walk."

Ian nods, says, "Umhm . . ." and turns another page in his book.

Handle turns. Door opens. Door closes. Hallway falls tile by tile behind me until I am standing in dust. The street. The gentle air of evening. I curl up on myself and follow the path we walked this morning. Join the crowds on the street, the pilgrims. Join their midnight passage to prayer.

Dozens of boxy shops twinkle in the darkness, bare lightbulbs dangling over wares. I stop and buy a handful of pitted apricots, freshly sundried so that the juice still lives beneath the skin. My teeth break the sun seal and the soft flesh hugs my tongue.

I veer off into the bazaar onto hard-packed dust. Lift the shield of my mind and set it adrift, feel every part of myself as porous. I am conscious only of how my skin feels a part of this cloak. Of how my skin is a cloak.

The alleys are lined with prophets. Men filled with words and warnings and messages for us. Are we listening? they implore. Stamping their bare feet to the earth, they point gnarled, arthritic fingers at their audience: an audience of no one but us, the few people passing in the street.

A dark-haired man with the shoulders of a tiger raises his fist to the sky and pleads. He is sinew and fire and tattered clothes sewn again and again and again.

A young man, blond, eyes like hunks of wet jade. Striking. Hypnotic. Speaks softly. Glows. Stares at the air just above himself. Sings, chants. Gestures humility. This is his teaching.

A blind man stands in a long white robe and says nothing. His beard is scraggly and touches his chest. He leans on a staff. Barefoot, until an old man bows before him, places money in his hand and lays sandals at his feet. The blind man gestures gratefully, humbly. Holds the man's head to his chest, kisses him. Then looks up, stares at me. His milky blue eyes lambent with faith.

I blink and walk on. Fold into a crowd of chaadors, through security, and back into the shrine. Where a full moon hits the marble floor like a spotlight and sprinkles the air with light.

People stroll the night. Families. Zillions of kids, laughing, running round and around the open courtyards, dipping their hands into reflecting pools, having picnics. It might be two in the morning by now.

What time?

Two in the morning, those kids should be in—
No, no. *What* time? This is a state without time.
According to the Islamic calendar, the year is 1374.
The year is 1374.
I walk to the mosque, where bodies lie rolled up in carpets, against walls. The poorest of pilgrims, who use the worship mats as blankets and sleep under the breath of God. I join them, stretch out against the wool and wrap myself shut. Alone among strangers, I burrow a solitude in this quiet anonymity and let myself breathe.

I am bound in thin, taut ropes of colour, but feel weightless; cannot move, but am in every part of the sky.

ɷ

I have a confession to make. Ian isn't my husband. We aren't even lovers, just friends. We forged a marriage certificate just before leaving Montreal using photocopies of his brother and sister-in-law's document, and that is what we are using to get ourselves into hotels. Most proprietors don't ask and of those that do, two have scrutinized the paper very seriously while holding it upside down, so we needn't have worried so much about its appearance of authenticity. The thing we should have worried about, perhaps, is the effect that photocopying and whiting out names on a marriage certificate might have had. By the time Ian and I reached Iran, his brother's marriage had collapsed.

Before taking this trip together, Ian and I had been roommates for about a year. The first few months of our relationship were spent delighting in long, weekend breakfasts with pots and pots of strong tea, crusty bread and a stack of atlases. During the blustery days of winter, we would spend hours poring over maps, planning long, arduous treks through desolate corners of the earth or road trips across continents.

The only problem was my strong belief in travel as a solitary pursuit. And Ian's fear of travelling alone. He wanted to go to Bulgaria, though I've still no idea why. We settled on Iran because it was the only place I couldn't imagine going on my own. And for a whole stack of other reasons that had nothing to do with our relationship.

The year before we met, I had made my fifth trip to Yugoslavia. I went, in part, to visit friends trapped in the middle of war, but also because the media's portrait of the place—full of barbarians and void of humanity—made the world seem unlivable. I refused to believe that such a place of unalloyed evil truly existed, that that was the end of the story. I went because I believed there had to be more. And because I like to look for saints where there are said to be demons.

Iran became our destination for the same reason.

Ian and I make great companions, live together effortlessly, laugh almost constantly and only ever argue about my love of chaos, as he puts it, and his obsessive fastidiousness, as I put it. And we share a remarkable number of interests: long breakfasts, strong tea, Russian film, modern dance, music from Lappland and southern Spain, yoga, snowshoeing, brandy, and an irresistible attraction to rugged, self-assured men.

So Ian, my fussy, gay roommate and I are romping around Iran quite illegally. And not altogether happily, if only because our interests are not as parallel as we had grown to believe. He is primarily concerned with dead things (history, buildings, wars), and I primarily with living things. Sometimes I find myself wishing he would evaporate, which isn't to say that I don't still find him endearing. It's just that our differences have become painfully obvious here under this desert light, and the days of our squalid little Montreal apartment are a world away. The plan is, and always has been, to split up once we're out of Iran. Ian plans to move to Paris and become a mime. I'm planning to not have a plan and see where that takes me.

ᔭᔩ

Abbas picks us up at the hotel and drives us out of the downtown core to the quieter, more luxuriant suburbs. Mohammad will join us later, Abbas explains. He is attending to some urgent business.

Abbas's father, a slight, quiet man, is the first to greet us. His brother-in-law, another dentist, welcomes us with a friendly but serious expression. Abbas's mother is next, peeking shyly at us through the fabric that covers her. The cloth is pale green with tiny white flowers—I used to have sheets just like it—and she wears a thick smear of green eyeshadow to match. When the fabric slips from its place on her head, I can see that she dyes her hair reddish-blonde, just as Khomeini's wife apparently did until she was widowed.

Abbas's four sisters are decked out with the biggest hair, make-up and jewellery I've seen since I went to a wedding on Long Island, New York. Big curls with big bows, big rings with big rhinestones, big belts, big shoulders, big eyes and big teeth. Damnit. Big teeth. I shoot a fast panicked look at Abbas to scrutinize his smile. I decide it's congenital, this family's extraordinary endowment of tooth enamel, and become so focused on the teeth in the room that my vision goes wonky, and I begin to see every-one with two or three sets each.

I am also increasingly aware of how I look by compari-son: Dowdy. Small teeth (congenital), no make-up, the world's ugliest shirt, trousers that look like I've just come off an archaeological dig, a plain wedding band, and knotty ratty curls twisted into a braid.

They all stare, toothfully, and seem politely per-plexed.

I smile back and try to hide the holes in my socks by discreetly stuffing them into the cracks between my toes.

We sit down in the living room—sink down, actually, because the furniture is a ten-piece matching set of imita-tion Louis XIV chairs, all with puffy seats that deflate when you sit on them. It is the first time we have sat on furniture in an Iranian home.

The meal begins with a plate of cakes, passed around by one of Abbas's sisters, who insists I have not one piece, but four. I am handed a teeny plate and a teeny fork and enough cake for a birthday party. The next sister brings glasses of sweet lemon water, the next a plate of fruit, the next a tray of tea. Between bites—the more eaten, the more offered—there is a good deal of smiling but not a great deal more. Every time I look at Abbas's mother (I feel her eyes on me, like spidery fingers), she flicks her frown into a smile and says, *Hmmm.*

Dinner is slightly less staid, but I have a feeling that is because we are all too busy eating to be uptight. Rice and potatoes and kebabs and vegetables and bread and yogurt and the clinking of cutlery against ornate plates. Yellow with pink and blue flowers round the rim. Two bottles of cola completing each place setting.

After dinner, the men, the mother and I sink back into the living-room furniture while the dishes are cleared and dealt with by the sisters. The brother-in-law, a quiet man with thick glasses and the frown of an academic who takes himself seriously, leans forward in his seat and probes.

"And what is your reason for travel to Iran?"

He seems satisfied enough with my answer to sit back in his seat and rub his chin.

"You should come before revolution," he says, after some thought. "Economy now is very bad, very bad. In Shah time, dollar was seventy rial. Seventy! Just last week it was 5,800 rial and now with government regulation it is 3,000. Everything is so expensive for us, worst for young people, they can't marry or leave the parents' home. It is too expensive. Just rent deposit for small apartment in Tehran cost four or five years' salary. It is impossible."

"And in the Shah's time?"

He laughs and collects his thoughts. "It was perfect. In Shah time, everyone was happy, wealthy and healthy."

"Happy, wealthy and healthy?"

He nods firmly.

"Everyone?"

"Yes, everyone."

"Well, that sounds great—happy, wealthy and healthy—I mean, it even rhymes, but do you really think that's true? There must have been a *few* who weren't. What about SAVAK? I've heard horror stories about the Shah's secret service, what they were doing to peop—"

He *tsks* and throws his head back. "It is only propaganda from this government. They are killing even more people now."

A pause.

"But surely if everyone had been happy, there wouldn't have been a revolution."

"No," he says and rubs his hands together. "When people have everything, they always want more. They became greedy. Do you know what revolution men told? They told, '*Shah is keeping oil money for his friends—when we are power, we bring oil money to your door!*' He turns to Abbas and asks, "And did ever oil money come to your door?"

Abbas smiles wider and wider until his whole body is laughing. "No—ha ha ha—no—ha. No oil money come to door." Then he turns, perhaps in an attempt to change the subject, announcing: "I love so much my mother!"

His brother-in-law ignores him and carries on. "We did not know it would become like this. Iranian people did not expect any situation like this. They wanted only be like Europe, with democracy, that kind of thing."

"And so do you think there will be another revolution now?"

"No," he says, without even thinking about it. "People are hungry. They think about only getting bread to eat. In this condition, people don't think about revolution now. They know quality of life goes down after revolution, and now we can't afford it. Still we can't believe how far we came down after this last one." He shifts and crosses his legs under his chair. "No more. This is our state now. Everyone knows it."

As the evening winds down, Abbas's mother asks for a group photo. We all gather at one end of the room, Ian and I are asked to sit in elegant high-backed chairs, while the family stands around and behind us. The brother-in-law gets the camera ready, presses the timer and rushes around to the side of the group to squeeze into the photo. We all smile, hold still—and there is a problem. Something wrong with the timer. We exhale, relax, the problem is fixed and we return to our postures, smile, hold, hold—*hold*—must be another problem. Now three men huddle over the camera looking mystified.

Just as we get set up for the final attempt, smile, hold, hold—Mohammad walks in the door—*flash!*—so we have to do it all over again to include him.

"Here is your money," he whispers when he finds a private moment. "The highest rate I could get was 5,000. Still much better than government. I hope it is good for you." He moves to pass us a wad of bills from his coat, when Abbas spies the interaction and opens his mouth in a wide smile.

"Ha ha ha! I see you bring oil money to my door! Ha ha, look, you see? Here is revolution man, Mohammad! He is bring oil money to my door! Revolution is working! Ha ha ha!"

SEEX-MEEL-YUN-DO-LUR-MEN

O N A BUS. Where we have been for the last five hours and where we'll be for three more to come. It was desert when we started, and it is certainly desert for as far as the heat ripples will allow us to see. The only thing I am interested in doing is trying to figure out whether it is possible that I am urinating through my skin, as I haven't peed in three days. With remarkably little condescension, Ian assures me this is unlikely. I decide to try to take my mind off it, think about something else, so I concentrate instead on which moves faster: the sweat trickling down my arms into the palms of my hands or the sweat trickling down my legs into the soles of my shoes. Or the sweat trickling down my face and swan-diving from my chin onto my lap.

Ian, dear Ian, is not sweating at all. His nose is ever so slightly moist at the tip and, with the sleeves of his light cotton shirt rolled up, his arms are as dry as the wind. His skin runs a deep tan after all these weeks in the desert. He is talking and laughing with several people on the bus and looks so carefree and good-natured at the moment that I think I hate him.

Today, as every day, I am wearing black leather shoes, black socks, white cotton underwear with blue flowers and a tiny girly bow on the waistband, green cotton trousers, a white bra with some lacy bits that make my chest feel like a screened-in porch and metal clasps that sink into my skin like staples, a long-sleeved cotton shirt, a floor-length black polyester coat, and a black polyester scarf folded down over my forehead, back across my ears and clipped under my chin. It was 43 degrees Celsius when we got onto the bus. But it's a dry heat, as Ian pointed out this morning, so you see, you can barely feel it.

Four hours later. I am in the oasis town of Tabas, in a stuffy room with a fan that doesn't work, lying naked on a mattress that was a Belgian waffle in another life. I've let my skin out. I lie here letting air tickle the surface of my body. My pores stretch open and take deep gulps of air, breath after breath, as sweat bubbles to the surface. My skin sounds like a fish tank.

Ian is outside by the toilets, washing the salt stains from my trousers and manteau. I would do it myself, but there are no showers or washbasins at this establishment, only public toilets and a pump in the garden. And I can't go out without wearing the clothes I need to wash.

"We have dinner plans," Ian announces as he returns. "A man came up and started talking to me in the garden, really nice. He's a student, seems like a really nice guy, his English is excellent, and he's coming by in a couple of hours with a friend . . ."

I am too busy trying to iron out my skin with my hands to notice that Ian has brought back two buckets of water and is stripping down ready to wash.

We play with these buckets of water like kids at the beach: jumping in with both feet, sinking our butts in until our feet dangle over the side, splashing, slapping, gurgling, spitting, rubbing our skin with a rough wool cloth until we hear it sigh. The floor is covered with water. We fall into bed with drenched bodies.

And awaken to a knock at the door. It is the student and his friend, who tell us they'll wait for us in the garden. The floor is completely dry. The desert air licked it up while we were sleeping and now offers it to plants downwind.

It is early evening. The sky is scarlet, and the air smells of heat. Both men break into smiles when we appear in the garden. They are friendly, quiet, gentle. The younger one, Pirouz, is wearing black jeans, black leather boots and a black leather jacket. I find myself staring. Skin considerably darker than his friend's, eyes with enormous irises and almost no whites, smiles in that restrained way serious people do when they hear something witty, smokes. Friend, Mahmoud, looks as though he hasn't seen the sun in weeks, has one eye that wanders, smiles and laughs like a small child, does not smoke.

We get into their car, the biggest one I've seen in Iran, and begin driving to the edge of town. They speak softly to each other in the front seat and seem to agree on something. We drive along a long straight road that takes us out of the oasis and into the desert. We drive along this long straight road far beyond the last light.

Ian and I eye each other in the back seat, saying nothing. It occurs to me—quite suddenly—that we know nothing about these people, except their names, which don't really give us much to go on. I place one hand on the door handle and feel quite brilliant to have the foresight to prepare a plan of escape. I feel considerably less brilliant when I think through my plan and envision my black-bundled body tumbling onto the sand like a used tire. I remove my hand from the door and slap my cheek.

Neither man speaks. Pirouz rests his arm on the window and looks off to his right, while his friend drives. There is no radio. I watch the silence in the front seat for several minutes, then try to shriek at Ian with the pupils of my eyes, but he makes a strange sort of fish face and begins tapping rhythms on his thigh. I stare fixedly at this tapping until claws extend from my fingertips and pounce on his fingers. He looks puzzled and annoyed. Looks out his window.

Eventually, we pull over to the side of the road in what is, even by local standards, the middle of nowhere. The headlights reveal a small shack by the side of the road with crates stacked outside and a thatched palm roof extending over a few tables and chairs. The car is turned off, and the two men confer again. The driver seems to be explaining something to Pirouz, who nods and *umhm*s several times before leaning his elbow over the back of his seat to address us.

"Mahmoud would like me to tell you that he is very happy to bring you to this place. He is telling me that nineteen years ago, before the revolution, Steve Austen and his wife were going to visit this area, and my friend was going to be their driver. He wanted to bring them to this place, show them this place, but a few weeks before their visit we had the big earthquake, and they cancelled their trip. My friend was very disappointed."

I know Ian and I are both wondering the same thing (we are both wearing the same expression: bewildered relief), so I decide to put forward the question. "Uh, who's Steve Austen?"

"Steve Austen?? You don't know who is Steve Austen? You must know him, he's American. We received his television program here before the revolution and everybody watched it. Oh, it's incredible you don't know him."

Pirouz translates this surprising news to Mahmoud, who does a double-take and turns around in his seat.

"Seex-meel-yun-do-lur-men! Li-Mad-jers-Fa-ra-Fa-set!" He gestures anxiously at Pirouz and asks him to translate.

"Mahmoud wants me to explain that Steve Austen was his name on the program. His real name is Lee Majors and his wife is Farah Fawcett."

"*Oh,* The Six Million Dollar Man! Steve Austen! The Six Million Dollar Man! Yes, of course we've heard of that!"

Mahmoud claps his hands together and laughs. He is beaming, talking a mile a minute now, tugging at the student's shirt, making sure he is translating everything.

"OK OK, they were supposed to do some filming around here, and Mahmoud was chosen to be their driver because he owned the nicest car in the village. Every day he would drive them to where they were filming or anywhere they wanted to go. He decided that one evening he would bring them to this place, one of his favourite places, but then we had the big earthquake and they cancelled their trip. Mahmoud would like me to tell you that he was very disappointed at that time, but now it is nineteen years later, and he is very happy to meet you and bring you to this place. You are like Lee Majors and Farah Fawcett for him."

There is a rather deep silence.

"Well! That is certainly—*ahem*—it's, well it's very nice of him to say! Please tell Mahmoud we are glad to be able to make him so happy. We feel honoured to be his guests."

As he is listening to the translation, Mahmoud closes his eyes and places a hand on his heart. He gets out of the car, opens my door and takes a long deep bow as I step onto the road. Ian gets out on the other side and begins jogging in s-l-ow-ow-ow-ow-ow mo-tion towards the shack.

"Ah-ha!" shouts Mahmoud. "Seex-meel-yun-do-lur-men!" He is clapping and skipping after Ian. I am lagging behind, laughing so hard I can barely walk.

"I like your husband," Pirouz tells me. "But he is very silly."

We sit down at one of two tables set up for customers, and our friends nip into the shack to buy us drinks. We talk and sip orange soda until the sand around us turns black. For a long period we sit together in silence, the four of us, in private appreciation of this place. Somewhere in this darkness desert dogs sit on clifftops, blowing cries into emptiness. There is something about night-time in the desert. The sky feels so low somehow. And the air, it's as though it's being blown down off the stars. If I were alone here, I'd lean my head back and howl into the stratosphere.

"Mahmoud would like to take you now to meet his sister. And after that, we will go to the house of my mother for dinner. Mahmoud wanted to invite you to his house, but my mother just returned from the hajj, the holy pilgrimage to Mecca, so she must have the honour of feeding our foreign guests."

We drive back into town and park on a dusty street lined on both sides with high stone walls. Behind one of these walls is a large courtyard tumbling with gardens, fountains, ponds and a house. A young woman appears in the doorway, then walks so determinedly towards us, she rather looks as if she is snowshoeing. Her expression is radiant. She is shouting something to us that makes the men laugh.

She stops in front of me and kisses me on both cheeks. Then I watch her face elongate with surprise as Mahmoud tells her we are from Canada. She gasps and gawks, kisses me again.

"This is Mahmoud's sister, Siwa," begins Pirouz. "She tells me she was just sitting inside thinking how nice it would be to have some guests tonight, such a nice night, and then what happens, she looks out the window and who does she see: her brother, his friend and two strangers."

Boys of varying heights begin appearing in the courtyard. One by one they shake Ian's hand, nod to me and introduce themselves. Some bring chairs, one a table, another a bowl of fruit, another a tray of sweets, all at the prompting of their mother who stands beside me holding my hand. She talks constantly, with a voice like an English horn. Every sentence begins with enthusiasm and ends with the explosion of her face into smile. She doesn't giggle; she laughs, easily.

Her husband is a taciturn man with the face of someone who spends a good deal of time making gaga faces at
children. He is thin, gentle and moves like a dancer. His
smile is muted, it ripples all the way across his face and
rarely uses his teeth. After meeting us, he stands just off
to the side with his arms folded across his chest, watching
our conversation, grinning.

We all sit down when one of the boys arrives with tea.
Siwa asks Pirouz to listen carefully and translate everything. She asks so many questions, one right after the
other, that Pirouz must ask her to slow down, pause for a
minute, so that he can remember them all.

"She wants to know how did I meet you," he begins,
"so I told her that I was coming back from the park and
I saw a man in the garden of the traveller's inn. Then I noticed this man was washing some clothes, so I knew he
must be a foreign man, and I went to speak to him. Isn't it
right, sir? I explain to her that you are travelling across
our desert and breaking your journey here, in our oasis
village, but that you will continue your journey tomorrow, so we are very fortunate to meet you on this day. She
agrees that God has given us good fortune. She wants to
know also about your jobs, especially your wife's work,
about your family, why you are in Iran, what is your im-
pression of Iran, is this your first visit and when are you
coming back, because when you come back you are invited to stay here in her house."

Pirouz patiently translates, but each of our answers
prompts further questions from Siwa, and eventually he
surrenders, throwing his hands up in front of him. "I tell
her she is so curious, she forgets that you are her guests."

With this, Siwa pushes herself up from her chair and offers us some fruit, which we refuse twice before accepting. I take an apricot and sit back in my chair. She punches my arm, laughs, and dumps two plums, a banana, a cucumber and a handful of cherries on my plate.

Finally, it is our turn for questions. "Are all of these boys her children?" I ask. She cackles and says something into the sky.

"There used to be eight," Pirouz clarifies. "Three died in the earthquake, two girls and one boy. These are the five who remain."

Siwa calls to one of the smaller boys. He skips towards her and stands by the table, eyeing us nervously. She holds him around the waist. "This one has the same face of the dead son," she says through Pirouz. "Just the same. Every time I look at him, I must smile."

I trap the little boy's gaze for a moment and wink. He shrieks, puts both hands over his mouth and disappears behind the back of an elder brother, who reaches behind and pulls the boy onto his lap.

She is more serious now, tranquil, and asks something of her husband who nods, practically whispering a response. As she is formulating her next question, she motions to us. Pirouz runs his fingers across his forehead and looks into the distance, then turns to Ian.

"Now I must ask you something, sir, but please know that you are free to refuse if you choose. Maybe they will not be happy if you say no, but I will explain it to them in my own way, it is not a problem."

Ian looks quickly to me, resettles himself in his seat and stammers, "Y-y-y-yes, sure."

"Well, if it is fine, no problem with you, and please tell me if you object in any way and I will excuse you, but she has a request, sir. She would like to play ping-pong with your wife."

There is a rather deep silence.

"She would like to play to play, you mean the game with the—right now?—and the little white plastic, yes, like tennis only with a table—well, she didn't bring her own racket—"

"I'd love to play!"

"Well, she'd love to play."

"I'd love to play!" I repeat and clap my hands. The last time I played ping pong, I was about ten years old and hopeless, but the idea of playing now, under such beautifully ridiculous circumstances, thrills me.

My challenger seems even more excited than I. She leaps up from her chair, pinches my cheeks and runs up the stairs into the house with her chaador flowing behind her like a parachute.

"She must just change her clothings," Pirouz explains. "You can imagine it is impossible to play sports with such clothings." He crouches forward and pretends to adjust a heavy fabric over his head, securing it under his chin with one hand, miming a backhand with the other.

We start towards the back of the courtyard with all the boys in tow. "She is crazy for this game," Pirouz laughs. "Every day she is playing it for hours with the women of this village. She even started a club, a sports club for the women, and she is going there every day to coach ping pong, volleyball, I don't know what else they do."

Siwa skips out of the house in an outfit similar to mine (a manteau and headscarf), and holds my hand as we walk. Theirs is not a huge house, but its courtyard and gardens have such a luxurious use of space, I feel I am strolling the grounds of a palace.

At the back of the yard is a small concrete room. At one time, it might have been used to store tools, equipment, supplies. But no longer. Now it is filled by a full-size, top-quality, sky-blue, water-resistant ping-pong table. The nicest one I've ever seen, although I've not seen all that many. I am handed a green paddle. The men sit on either side of the table in silence, arms crossed, eyes trained on the ball. We flip a coin to determine the serve. My competitor crouches in a ready position.

The game moves at rapid-fire speed. There is leaping and diving, scrambling scampering, lunging and plunging, swiping and thrusting, charging and rushing and grunting. Wrists flick, paddles crack, balls are spiked, serves spin off the table and dance off the walls. The game is over very quickly. I have been utterly and unequivocally whomped. Crushed and shellacked. I limp to the sidelines and fall down into a seat next to Ian, who tries to reassemble my ego. "It must feel terrible to be chewed and spit out by someone twice your age who's given birth to eight children," he says out of the corner of his mouth.

Over the course of the next few hours, we watch as Siwa categorically massacres every member of her family. First her sons, youngest to oldest, then her husband, but not before she asks us to place bets. He chuckles away as she racks up points, shakes his head as balls go whizzing past him and smash into the wall. In between rounds, she calls to us, offering food. "Have some more cakes!" *Killer serve that leaves the opponent a crumpled mess.* "More tea— our guests need more tea!" *Thwack thwack thwack game*

point. "Someone peel my Canadian friend another cucumber!" *Punch dive volley volley volley SPIKE game over.*

With the final defeat of her husband, Siwa throws down
her bat and raises both fists in the air. The crowd goes wild.
She laughs until her cheeks blow up like balloons, then
asks us to please eat some more. She fills my plate again
with fruit and as she sits down beside me, I can feel Ian's
relief, so I say, "*Wait, wait, wait,* just one more game! My
husband was just telling me that he would like to play, too."

Siwa's face deflates into a strained expression. She looks
to Pirouz, who explains: "You are not a man of her blood.
Friends, please forgive her, but it is not our custom."

Ian is then invited to challenge any of the men in the
room. He chooses the eight year-old-boy standing in the
doorway.

"*Seex-meel-yun!*" Mahmoud calls from the sidelines,
and a game of slow-motion table tennis ensues. The games
go on for hours. We eat and discuss, perfect our serves,
eat again.

"Well," says Pirouz, "I hope you have enjoyed yourselves in this company—" Yes, yes, yes, we assure him "—
but we must go now. My mother will be waiting."

"Your mother?! Now?? But it's after midnight. I didn't
think—"

"Yes, I'm sorry," Pirouz interjects, "you are very hungry, but we will have dinner now. My mother is waiting."

Siwa and her family walk us back to the street and
make us promise to come and visit them again before we
leave. She kisses me on both cheeks and squeezes my
hands before letting me go. Tomorrow. Please come back
tomorrow. The whole family waves from the doorway as
we walk the dusty street to its end.

Around the corner behind a low mud wall is Pirouz's house, considerably more modest than his friends' and with an outhouse off to one side. His mother is sitting—sleeping—in the doorway when we arrive. She kisses me on the cheek and pulls her chaador tightly around her face as she nods to Ian. She looks exhausted. I feel wretched. But she has prepared our meal, as Pirouz reminds us, and she has been waiting.

"My mother asks me to tell you she is very honoured to invite you. She has just returned from Mecca, I told you, so it is a great honour to have you as guests in her home."

The house is dark. We pass one room where several children and an old man are stretched out on thick carpets, sleeping. At the end of the hall, Pirouz opens the door to a small room, and the three of us sit on the floor around a plastic mat.

"I am sorry that your mother has had to stay up so late," I say. "Please tell her we apologize."

"Oh, there's no need, no problem," Pirouz answers with a wave of his hand. "She doesn't mind. If she didn't have to cook now, she would only be sleeping. It is I who should apologize to you for giving you dinner so late. You must be very hungry. Forgive me."

He stands up and flips through a number of cassettes, selects one and shakes it in his hand saying, "Yeah, this one," and plunks it into the machine. "I got this in Japan," he explains, "but it's mostly American stuff. Probably you recognize it."

"Japan?"

"Yeah, I lived there for three years—that's where I got this," he says, pulling on his leather jacket and grinning.

"Lots of Iranian people go there to work, but I went as a student, for my first translation degree."

"You speak Japanese?"

"Of course," he laughs. "Fluently. When I'm not at the university, I work as a Japanese translator in Tehran. I work for businessmen or tourists, mostly businessmen."

He pauses for a moment and closes his eyes to listen to the music. The tape is a collection of seventies disco tunes sung by Asian pop singers with demonstrable pronunciation problems. We listen to "Deesko Infewno," "De Ye Dink Em Zexy," "Satewday Night Fevew." For what feels like repetitive eternity, we sit in silent contemplation of the long-play version of "We Aw Fambily." When the song ends, Pirouz revives himself and returns to Japan.

"Of course it was very interesting for me to live in that country, but after three years it was enough. Japanese people are so cold and unfriendly. People are like computers, you can't imagine it. All kinds of customs that were so strict: you must sit this way and eat this way and say this and don't say this. So many restrictions on living, everyone behaves like robots. After three years of living there I needed only the fingers of one hand to count my friends, and now it is four years later and I don't touch any of them. I wrote to them, sent them some gifts, but they didn't respond, only sometimes. I have a Japanese friend at the university in Tehran, and she doesn't want to return to her country. She loves it here.

"I don't know what you think about Western countries, but I don't think they are any better, really. Of course there are more things to buy, there is no question, but everything costs, even people. If I offer someone a gift, he wants to know why—maybe I am paying him back for something, or maybe I want him to do something for me later. I think people use emotions like money. You have been so kind, so I owe you something. You gave me this thing, so I must be good to you. People are not friends, they are businesses. Here we can depend on the good faith of people."

The door opens, and Pirouz's mother shuffles in with a large tray of food in her hands and her chaador wrapped across her body and held together with her teeth like a horse's bit. I lunge up to help her, but she only mumbles something to Pirouz. "Don't help her," he says. "You are her guests."

Three plates of saffron rice and chicken, three bowls of yogurt and a stack of flatbread are laid out on the mat. The old woman exchanges a few words with Pirouz and smiles. "My mother would like to thank you again for coming into her house. She apologizes that the meal is not so delicious, but she just returned from the holy pilgrimage and did not have much time to prepare."

Ian and I repeat every Farsi phrase of gratitude that we know, several times. She smiles again and adjusts her chaador, lifts herself back up on her feet and winks at me before leaving the room.

"My mother doesn't like the way I live. Oh, she thinks I have a Western attitude and such things. She gets so angry with me when I talk about my girlfriends in Tehran—I have two or three right now—and she is always giving me pressure to get married. So much pressure all the time, it was making me just crazy. Three months ago, she was bothering me so much about this that I kicked the door and said I didn't want to hear any more about it, and I left. It was a show, actually, because I wasn't really this angry, but just I wanted to make her stop bothering me about this. Now is the first time I see her since that time.

"It is a simple meal," he says, inviting us to begin. "As the Imam, our leader, ate. Do you know that he ate only rice and yogurt? Sometimes he ate some fruits and vegetables, not cooked, but most of the time he was eating only rice and yogurt. Six years ago he died." Pirouz stops eating and closes his eyes, takes a deep breath and continues.

"He was a good man, Imam Khomeini, a good and honest man. He never owned anything, you know, not even the rug where he sat. The house where he lived was a very small one, just next to the mosque. Yes, I can say he was a pure man, not like some of the mollahs we have now, corrupt ones. People say they have Switzerland bank accounts and live in big big houses in north Tehran. But the Imam lived as he told us to live."

Pirouz eats in tiny bites. A small spoonful of rice here, a taste of yogurt there. He has the delicate mannerisms that I have noticed of men in this country. The soft, almost effeminate, gestures: the sweep of a hand up to a mouth, rippling fingers across a chest, gentle laughter, the unimposing stance of someone in waiting.

"In the time of Shah—you know who was Shah?— well, it was a very different time than now. Completely different, actually. OK in some ways, there were good things, some very Western attitudes and styles, but it was not freedom at this time. It was dictatorship. Always you had to show you were loyal and supporting the Shah's regime. It was illegal to criticize it or any similar system. My brother was put in the prison only for editing a book about the French Revolution. He didn't even write it! He only edited the translation into Persian, but it was enough to show he was not loyal to the Shah's regime. We had to speak so secretly then, people spoke in sort of code. Everything was a symbol for something else. Black meant this, night meant that. After a while, our language lost its freedom. These symbols were like a prison for words. It stopped being language, it was just a tool. Now of course there are still some problems, but I think it's much better."

Ian folds his bottom lip under his teeth, then asks, "You talk about prisons for words in the Shah's time, but what about the fatwa against Salman Rushdie?"

After one more bit of yogurt, Pirouz puts down his spoon and pushes his dishes into the centre of the mat. He leans back on his hands and tilts his head so that he is looking at the wall above our heads. "I cannot defend him," he says carefully. "The fatwa from the Imam was a religious order, as you know, and I am not a scholar of Islam, I am not a holy man, so it is not for me to judge. I am not able to judge. It doesn't mean that I agree or disagree, it means I cannot argue."

He leans forward and runs the back of his hand across the stubble on his cheek. "I can choose to be silent on this matter. But I will tell this: if a man insults our Prophet, my religion, this earth of my society, then I don't forgive such a man. It is disrespect. I think if I spit in your face, you don't forgive me for this action. What do you think: do I speak truth?"

"Just leave your dishes," says Pirouz. "My mother has gone to bed, but she will clean them in the morning. Please," he says, when he sees me clearing and stacking our plates. "Please, it is not for you this work."

We walk back outside and down along the narrow street towards the House of Ping Pong. Mahmoud and Siwa's husband are stretched out on a thick carpet on the porch speaking in the low grumble of monks. They smile and pop up when they notice us in the doorway and ask us if we ate well, if we are feeling well, if we enjoyed ourselves, if we would like some tea, some cakes, if we are ready to return to our inn. *Yes, yes, yes, no no thank you, oh yes, I think we're both a bit tired.* Siwa's husband is wearing a wristwatch that I notice when he strokes his moustache with his fingers. It is three-thirty in the morning.

We drive, creep, crawl through deserted streets at a pace appropriate to the hour. Insects rattle the air and give it texture. The texture of an old wooden rocking chair with rounded arms and a back that creaks. At the end of one alley we turn onto the main village road, where street lights illuminate our way. At the base of one of these showers of light sits a young boy with his back flat and straight against the pole. His legs are stretched out in front of him and are crossed at the ankles. He is reading.

"It is the time for examinations," Pirouz explains. "Maybe this boy lives in a small house with many people. They are sleeping, so he comes to this light to study."

When we arrive at our room, we thank them again and arrange to meet the next morning. Our bus for the other side of the desert leaves at eleven, so they'll be here at nine, although they wanted to be here at seven, so that we'd have more time to talk, eat, visit the old part of the village, meet other members of their family, maybe even some neighbours, and the mayor.

"No no no, nine is fine, really. Don't worry about breakfast: we have some food for our journey . . . No no, we have an alarm clock, thank you . . . No no, I can't think of anything else we might need. Why, thank you, but honestly I can't think of any reason why we would need to call you between now and nine o'clock. OK, I guess it's good to have your telephone number . . . Yes, we had a wonderful time. Thank you again. We are very very grateful . . . No, we'd love to go for another little drive, it's just that we're a bit tired now. Even bionic people have to sleep."

We collapse into bed exhausted and pleasantly muddled.

We get out of bed exhausted and pleasantly muddled.

It's eight-thirty, but I would swear I haven't gone to sleep yet. Ian and I each take a handful of bread from a plastic bag we've been carrying around for days and sit on the edge of the bed, leaning shoulder to shoulder to hold each other up. Once we've managed to get our eyes to focus, I cloak body and hair, and·we stumble outside to brush our teeth.

Our friends are already waiting in the garden. They smile when they notice us and ask us how we slept. They hope we are well rested and in case we are hungry, they have brought some fresh bread—still hot from the coals—some soft white cheese, jam, butter and yogurt. Or would we prefer something else? They hold out their hands in offering, and we join them in the garden for breakfast.

After a brief stop at the mayor's house (he's not in, but we are invited in for tea by the man next door who notices us at the gate), we arrive at Siwa's door. She greets us with a mixture of elated words of welcome and scolding for being so late. Her children rise up from rugs on the ground and smile before rushing into the house to fetch food and tea. There is a group of very young children hiding behind some leafy plants by the fish pond. "Neighbour children," Pirouz says, throwing his chin in their direction. I creep over to them like a cat preparing to pounce, and they shred the air with screams and wild giggles before scattering across the courtyard and into the safety of the house. One by one they peek their faces out from behind curtains. One little girl waits until we are seated before tiptoeing onto the landing of the house, crouched behind a banana leaf that she holds in front of her face.

"She wants to know why don't you stay longer," Pirouz says for Siwa, who is seated beside me with her arm through mine. "She likes you very much, but she wants to know about you more. What is the name of your mother, for example, and is she working? And how did you meet your husband? Why don't you have children—this question is very important—and do you make some sport in your country? Her husband would like to know did you ever go to America, and is it a dangerous place? He says he thinks American government is bad, but American people are very kind, but he wants to know what do you think, and what are they thinking about Iranian people, are they thinking we are very kind?"

"Well. . . . uh, my mother's name is Susan and she is a music teacher."

Music! What kind of music? Does she play some kind of music? Can she play the piano? Siwa cheeps, as she leaps up from her chair and pulls her chuckling husband into the house. She returns with two metal legs and assembles them in front of me, her husband following with an electric keyboard the size of a killer whale. Extension cords begin appearing out of nowhere, and the apparatus is ready to go.

There is a rhythm section on the machine and Siwa sets this to Samba Groove I and pats the beat on my back. The instrument's tone button is broken and permanently stuck on Harpsichord. For the first few minutes, I doodle around with some jazz melodies, but the harpsichord keeps pulling me back to the eighteenth century, so I go with it. I play the first little bit of a Bach partita (with Samba Groove I) before plunking my face into the keyboard and convulsing with laughter.

More more more! Siwa is so full of admiration, according to Pirouz, that she has ordered two of her sons into the neighbourhood in search of a tape recorder. Several minutes later, a boy skips back with a machine held triumphantly over his head, and it is hooked up to the extension cord. With her husband! Ask her to play something with her husband, oh, please!

Ian and I embark on an ornamented version of "Chopsticks," replete with modulations, trills and glissandi that fly off both ends of the keyboard. The family stands around us with gaping mouths, like a choir in full chorus. The recorded version is played back four times before being kissed, pressed to Siwa's heart, and tucked into an inside pocket.

"I'm afraid it is time to go to your bus," Pirouz says with a hand over his heart.

"No no no no no!" Siwa protests and runs again into the house. This time she returns with a camera in one hand, and a chaador in the other. She hands the camera to her oldest son and pulls me to stand beside her; she adjusts the length of black fabric so that it drapes over her scarfed head and falls like a curtain over her cloaked body. The picture will show one eye, her nose, and part of one cheek.

The moment the photo is taken, she drops the chaador and leads me by the arm to the back of the house. To the ping-pong room. I am handed a paddle and told that she would like a picture of just the two of us together by the table. "She would like you to take off your scarf for the photo, if you please. You will take the picture, sir," Pirouz tells Ian. "We will wait for you outside."

Once the men have gone, Siwa peels the scarf from my head as though she were removing a bandage from burnt skin. She gasps at the sight of my flattened hair and plays with my curls, threading them through her fingers and stretching them out until they corkscrew back against my scalp. My hair sufficiently primped, we strike burlesque battle poses for the photo, then reclip my scarf under my chin and rejoin the men outside.

"We will take you to your bus now," Pirouz repeats. "You must say goodbye to the children, because they won't fit in the car." Each child offers us a handful of fruit as a parting gift. We get into the car with our pockets brimming with oranges, cucumbers, green plums, dates and cherries.

The bus station is this: the place where the road ends. Pirouz runs into a small building to buy our tickets, while Siwa's husband leaps onto the bus to ensure that we are awarded the best seats. There is a long discussion about the direction in which we will be travelling, which side will get shade, which windows will offer the best breeze, which seats have the most stuffing intact, and so on. Men and women scratch their heads, slide windows back and forth, test the springiness of seats, until they eventually agree on the third seat from the front on the right side. An older man collects his things from this seat, smiles at us and moves to the back of the bus.

Just before we say our goodbyes and climb on board, Ian asks Pirouz if there was anyone selling chocolate bars near the ticket booth. Pirouz translates this to Mahmoud and *BOOM!* the car's engine is started up—"*No no no! Please! Don't worry about it, really! I was just wondering! No, honestly!*" But he pleads to no avail. The two men peel out of the parking lot leaving ribbons of dust in their wake.

We wait with Siwa and her husband, who begin introducing us to some of the passengers. We wait and wait, until the driver explains that the bus is already an hour late, and we really must go. I give Siwa two kisses goodbye and nod to her husband; Ian shakes his hand and nods to Siwa. We take our seats, are immediately offered smiles and handfuls of sunflower seeds by the women in front of us, cherries and pistachios by the women behind.

The bus lumbers onto the road to the other side of the desert, and we bump along beside sun-scorched houses with domed roofs the colour of bread. Arcades of baked earth. Every home is shielded by high walls made of sand, dung, dead scorpions and the sweat of generations. Of this country we are able to see one eye, a nose, a part of one cheek.

Just as we settle ourselves in for the day's journey, the bus jerks and wrenches us from our seats. A car has cut across the road in front of us. It skids to a halt and tosses out a man carrying a plastic bag. Pirouz climbs onto the bus, sweating and huffing, tenders words of apology to the driver and hands us the bag.

"Please forgive our lateness. I am sorry, my friends, it is all we could find."

The bag contains four types of chocolate, two of each kind.

"Friends, please forgive us, but our country it is not perfect. We have not such things as you have, and perhaps it is difficult for you. But please try to enjoy, it will make us very happy if you enjoy. Keep your hearts in our people, my friends. We are strangers, but we try to be kind."

He kisses Ian on both cheeks, bows to me with closed eyes, and backs out of the bus with his hand over his heart. Mahmoud has pulled his car back to the side of the road. He leans his elbow out of the window and waves frantically as we pass. *"Goodbye, Li-Mad-jers-Fa-ra-Fa-set! Goodbye seex meelyun!"*

The bus inches into motion. The desert grows around us. My skin opens and leaks into my clothing. My eyes close.

When I open them several hours later, the sand for miles around is ribbed with windwaves.

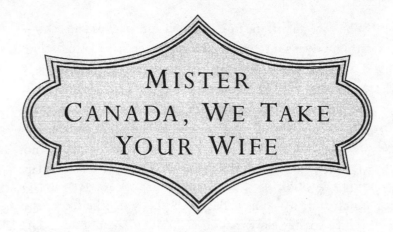

MISTER CANADA, WE TAKE YOUR WIFE

THE WOMAN BEHIND ME taps my shoulder and passes me a bag of cherries tied with string. From the string dangles a note:

In the name of God. Hello, My dear Friends. Well come to Iran. My name is Afsaneh Hosseiny. Iam very glad. Becues I see you, I am mathematic's student. I will be very glad If I know your nams and your's tel number. Sincerely yours Afsaneh Hosseiny. Tank you.

I turn around and thank the woman. She smiles and points to a woman behind her who points to a woman behind her who points across the aisle to a young woman who blushes and smiles, brings her chaador up to her face, shyly, and waves.

I write back. Tell her we are tourists, that we have enjoyed visiting her country and that we are on our way to Yazd. I give her our names and telephone numbers, and thank her for the cherries. Turn around and smile, wave, and pass the note back.

When we get off the bus, Afsaneh approaches and asks—timidly, eyes on the ground—if we need any help finding our way. This is her city, she explains, so perhaps she could help. I tell her we are looking for a *mosaferkhané* and she smiles. Takes my hand. Yes, she can help. Please come with me. We walk arm in arm to the main street. Ian trails behind.

Inside the taxi, she holds my hand, plays with my wedding ring, tells me I am beautiful, but I am getting too much sun. My skin is becoming brown, like hers. She points to her dark hands and hides them under her cloak. She asks me please to explain the term, "maiden name." My explanation confuses her. I go over it again and again.

"But for what . . ." she begins, adjusting her chaador for the *n*th time since we sat down. "For what purpose do woman change that they have same name like husband? They are two individual people, is it so?"

I ask her about her studies. Very difficult, she tells me. But she is working hard. What will she do after she has her mathematics degree? She pauses. Blushes. "Go to Canada," she says.

Afsaneh insists on paying for our taxi. Insists and insists and insists and insists. She points out a hotel across the road, then her university on the other side of the square. Nods to Ian, takes my hand and puts it to her heart. "Go with God," she says and kisses me. Adjusts the layers and layers of cloth around her body and gathers them up in one arm, heaves her books onto her hip and waddles away.

Ian and I are preparing to cross the street when she catches up to me. She laughs and pushes something into my hand, adjusts her covering again, then her books, and says goodbye.

It is a small jar. Some kind of cream. I open it up. It's make-up. Face whitener.

ဘ္ဘ

"Problem."

The word has been spoken so many times by so many different people that it is beginning to bounce off the walls; if I could, I'd lunge at it with a racket. I arrived about nine o'clock, and now it is nearly ten. I approached this postal clerk, this man here, and presented him my envelope. The saffron I wish to send to my mother. I had left it open to allow the package to be inspected, and my mother's address was written in English, with the word "Canada" repeated in Farsi just below. I explained to this man, in language that resembled heavily enunciated baby talk more closely than Farsi, I am afraid, that I wished to send this saffron to Canada.

"Ca-na-da!" he said, with a smile that lifted his eyebrows. "Canada very goood!"

I thanked him. He turned my parcel over on his hands and called the man working beside him, who dropped what he was doing and joined us. He bowed his head in greeting, then read: "Ca-na-da." Smiled. "Canada goood!"

Two women working at desks beside this man were called. "Canada?" they giggled. One of the women leaned over the counter and pinched my cheeks. The other one crawled under the counter, came up beside me and kissed my face four times. This woman called to several more employees on the other side of the office, whose faces lit up with smiles. Within minutes, we were all drinking tea.

Customers behind me in line either went home or joined our gathering. No one neglected to tell me that Canada was *goood* and most told me several times. All twenty-odd employees have come over to inquire after me and then after my husband, my mother, my father, my children—what? not even one? but why?—and to pay some attention to my parcel.

Almost an hour has passed and I still have no idea what the problem is, but there is enough of one to warrant the attention of everyone in the building, and at least one person has come in off the street to join the phalanx. My parcel consists of a plastic container of saffron, a one-page letter and an envelope. Each of these items has been weighed separately at least eight times by at least eight different people and all together by almost everyone in the room. The result is always the same: great discussion, scratching of heads, then a very patient and apologetic explanation to me.

"Problem."

My patience is fading. I had intended to visit the Jamé mosque in the cool hours of the morning, but I can feel the day descending, a heat that creeps through my clothing, weighs there and wrings my body of energy. My trousers are already damp with sweat. It trickles down my back, my chest, my stomach, my legs. My hair is soaked beneath my scarf. And it is not even noon.

My postal friends seem to sense my frustration and another round of tea arrives, this time with cakes. I try to retrieve my parcel, explaining that it is not worth the effort, really, my mother doesn't even use saffron, hardly cooks in fact, but they will not have me give up so easily. No no no no, they say and then discuss.

After several more interminable minutes, there is a swell of enthusiasm and a circus of hand gestures that would lead me to believe that we are finally close to a decision. My original envelope is discarded (to the loud approval of the office) and is replaced by one that is slightly thicker and twice the size. The saffron is opened and poured into a separate package—some protest here from one of my fellow customers, but after some discussion they continue—and the address is transcribed onto the new envelope, carefully, painstakingly, in what is apparently English, although I cannot make out a word of it, not one, even when it is six inches from my face. The young man who performed the job seems so deliciously proud of his work that I haven't the heart to question his effort and so leave it as is, resigning myself to losing everything to the experience.

Finally, packaging tapes of various widths and colours are considered before a thick grey one is used to seal the whole thing up tightly. The new parcel is weighed and some of the employees seem so pleased with the result, they have a spontaneous parade around the office. The men behind the counter pat each other on the back and the woman beside me claps her hands, laughs and gives my breasts a firm tweak.

I pull money out from beneath my cloak and shake my hand in a manner that asks, *how much?* but the clerk refuses my payment, raising his palms and closing his eyes. I thank him and offer the money again, but he continues to refuse it and motions in the direction of a man to my left, a fellow customer who has paid for me. Has paid to send a parcel to my mother. A parcel, I hasten to add, that is addressed so illegibly that it has precisely no chance of reaching its destination.

I stand there, gawping, trying to make sense of this. To refuse this man's offer would be the gravest of insults. But to allow him to pay, and a substantial sum at that, would be nothing short of absurd. I pause before responding. Waiting for I'm not quite sure what. My eyes skid across the faces that surround me, but every expression is stolid, unflinching. I stare into the hearts of strangers.

I have no choice. In the most elegant Farsi I can muster, I accept this generosity. I thank the man as gratefully as I can without going prostrate, offer everyone else my heartfelt appreciation, assure the room at large that Iran is good, very good indeed, and leave the building completely bewildered.

Outside, I stand with my face to the sun, searing the spirit of the morning into memory.

When I open my eyes, I am in the centre of a circle of people. They stare and are all talking at once. Are you sick? Please let me help you, my husband is a doctor. Are you tired? Come to my home, you may sleep there. Are you hungry? Do you want some tea? Where is your husband? Where are you from? What do you think of Iran, good or not good? Why do you stand here in front of the post office with your eyes closed?

I move around from voice to voice but have trouble answering. I assure everyone that I am well, not even hungry or thirsty, just a bit hot—several women giggle and tug my manteau—and people disperse, leaving me with smiles, best wishes and invitations to their homes.

One couple remains. The woman knows no more than ten words of English but says them in such rapid sequence that she sounds almost fluent.

"Hello how do you do my friend very good thank you God hello how do you do my friend very good thank you God."

She has been holding my hand these last few minutes and has not stopped smiling. Her husband bears a remarkable resemblance to a turtle, with droopy eyes, a head that seems to loll on the top of his neck, and a vaguely bemused expression. He doesn't appear to speak a word of English but seems very impressed by his wife's facility with the language. "Lida," she says, patting her chest. I tell her my name but she doesn't seem to like it, the way she crimps her face and says *uhh???* Finally, I assign myself the Iranian name Haideh, to which Lida makes some sort of proclamation to Allah and swats me on the arm.

Lida points to their car and offers to drive me to my hotel where I can rest. "It is hot now and will only get hotter," she explains in slow, enunciated Farsi. To be sure I have understood, she wipes my face with her palm and shows me my own sweat.

I decline, explaining that I can easily take a taxi, but she offers, again and again, so many times that I accept. Her face leaps into laughter. She hikes up her chaador and skips towards the car. I follow behind and make a move to open one of the back doors. No no no. We will sit together, all three of us, in the front. Despite the fact that the car has bucket seats.

While her husband climbs in behind the wheel, Lida squeezes to the very edge of the passenger seat and pulls me to join her. Between the two of us, there is so much black fabric that I feel we could upholster the whole car, but we sort through it all until nothing more of either of us drips out. In trying to give me as much room as possible, Lida has perched herself on the gear shift. We do the entire drive across town in first gear.

Halfway to my inn, I notice the mosque I had planned to visit before the post office ate my morning. As we pass, I turn my head to examine the tiled minarets, the spare elegance of its domes and arches; the grace of it all. Lida shrieks at her husband, beating her fist against the dashboard and pointing in the direction of the mosque. The car careens across one full lane of traffic—car horns spin the air into a hundred squeals—and onto a dusty side street. When I resume breathing, I notice Lida smiling so hard that her eyes are closed. She points to the object of my interest and pats my sweat-soaked arm.

We untangle ourselves from the car and visit the mosque, including the roof and winter prayer rooms, for which Turtle Man pays a small fee to an old man who wanders the grounds. The view from the roof pulls my eyes along the howling sweep of the desert and leaves them dangling at the edges of the earth. Inverse vertigo. I feel I will fall into the sky. I steady myself and attribute my state to the heat. It is at least forty degrees Celsius.

I take three deep breaths and climb down out of the sun.

Below ground, in the dark silence of the winter mosque, we sit on carpets and taste the air of shelter. We are here when the muezzin begins one of its five daily calls: the moaning that pleads for prayer. Peace. Respite from the agonies of a desperate world. Followers stream in from desert sands, cleanse their faces, hands, feet. They wash into the mosque like the tide, rising and falling to the gentle rhythm of worship. Lida takes my hand and leads me behind a curtain. Into purdah. Where pools of black cloth soak the ground. She joins the mass of chaadored women in the comfort of ritual and I sit to the side, watching her hide her shameful body from the eyes of God.

I watch until the moment ends, until the last call bleeds from the muezzin, until the silence has passed. Lida rises and smiles, comes to me, holds my hands to her cheeks. I hold the round brown echoes of prayer.

Back in the car—I have convinced them that the back seat, while being less exciting, is at least cooler—we resume the journey to my inn and are only blocks away when Lida notices the time. She reacts in such a way that I am sure I have made them late for something quite important, the way she taps her finger against her husband's watch and shakes her head, tsking and exclaiming. I move forward in my seat to apologize for delaying them, but Lida pushes the air in a way that says *Not to worry* and pats me on the head. I point out the inn, just up ahead on the right, and after they have both acknowledged the building by pointing, checking with me, and nodding, we drive right past it at full speed.

Several intersections later, I ask about my inn. Yes yes, they both saw it, but look at the time: it is almost one o'clock. I must be starving. We double back across town before parking outside a restaurant and retreating from the sun. Turtle Man orders a long list of food, which he recites with his eyes closed and one finger up in the air. Elegant glass pitchers of dark liquid are set before us, and I reach for a glass. It is at this moment that Turtle Man speaks to me for the first time:

"You want Pipi Zam Zam?"

I ask him to repeat himself.

He wets his mouth, closes his eyes and speaks again, this time more slowly. "You. Want. Pipi. Zam. Zam?"

It is sheer curiosity that makes me say yes.

"In Canada, Coca-Cola," Turtle Man explains as he fills my glass. "In Iran, Pipi Zam Zam."

We get through an entire pitcher of ice-cold Pipi Zam Zam before any of the food arrives. And it does, by the trayful. Three bowls of yogurt, three salads, three helpings of curried spinach, three plates of rice and twelve shish-kabobs the size of gladiator swords: chicken, cow, lamb, baby lamb. By the end of the meal—we have scarcely made a dent—I am ready for a nap. I relax into the back of my chair and flap the front of my scarf to try to point some fresh air in the direction of my skin. This prompts Turtle Man to speak for the second time all day:

"You like hejab?"

"Do I *like* wearing this?" I ask with what must be a strained expression.

"Yes. It is joyful?"

I shift in my seat, now a full-blown pool of perspiration. "Uh, I'm not sure about joyful, but it's certainly warmful."

He doesn't understand.

"Hot," I explain.

"Hot." The two of them repeat the word aloud, then launch into a long interchange. The next thing I know, the bill is paid, the dishes are cleared and I am being pulled back out to the car.

Turtle Man has stayed in the restaurant to make a telephone call, so Lida and I sit together in the back seat holding hands.

"Hot," she says and fans me by flipping the pages of the Koran in front of my face. I close my eyes and draw the breeze in through my nostrils, open my eyes and watch the script flutter under my chin. I ask Lida if she is hot, and she nods sheepishly and adjusts her chaador. She rolls down her window and lets in some fresh air. "From God," she says pointing to the breeze.

Turtle Man returns and looks into the rear-view mirror. "You like cold?" he asks.

I nod, unsure of exactly what it is I have agreed to, and we drive away. Away away away, as far as we could possibly go from my inn without flying. At the edge of the city we turn onto a dirt road that goes in one direction: straight. Directly across the desert. When my friends begin rolling up the windows, presumably in preparation for a journey into this sandbox, I feel justified in asking the obvious question. "Uh, please excuse me, but where are we going?"

"To cold," says Turtle Man, with a loopy inflection in his voice that seems to imply the words, *Where do you think?*

I settle back into my damp seat and try not to notice the palpable increase in temperature as we draw away from the city's few trees and fountains and deeper into the dunes that create the view on all sides.

Every few minutes, Turtle Man looks into the rear-view mirror and asks, "Hot?" in such a genuinely inquisitive tone that he seems unable to predict my response. The first few times I chuckled and said "Yes," but as he continues to pose the question I wonder if perhaps it would be better to say "no."

No. It only makes it worse. His face has a spasm, and we almost drive off the road. (Such as it is). He spins around in his seat and shakes his head at Lida, then twists further in order to face me and ask the question again.

"Hot, hot," I assure him. "Very very hot." He gives an audible sigh of relief and goes back to driving. A few minutes later, he looks at me again in the mirror.

"Hot?" he asks.

"Yes," I reply.

He smiles, nods, and his eyes go back to the road.

I sit here now, in dread of the next reprise of the question; it is rather like waiting for an electric shock I know will arrive. I try to enjoy the view—sand sand sand— then I clench my fists and hold my tongue between my teeth, smile flatly, and try not to curse. Lida sits beside me, watching my every expression. From time to time she smears her palm across my face, wipes the latest curtain of sweat on the seat, says, "Hot," and giggles.

It is an hour later, and we are still driving. The scenery has not changed; neither has the conversation. A few minutes ago we passed a man in flowing white robes, walking. We have been driving for over an hour with nothing, not even a cactus, in sight—and yet this man is walking. Presumably somewhere. My spirits lift.

The horizon teases me with shapes and forms. There is a fork in the road just up ahead. To the right are faint sketches of a mountain range, perhaps, or is that just my imagination? No it looks like colour, something of colour. Green, green! It must be an oasis of some kind! Oh God oh God oh God oh God oh Allah, whatever it is, please let there be Pipi Zam Zam.

Where the path splits, we take the right fork towards the colourful signs of life. I close my eyes and say "Hallelujah" aloud. And then. Then I do the unthinkable. I spy something, a cluster of something, domed structures, nestled deep in the horizon to my left and strain my eyes to get a better look. Point and ask Lida what that is, way off in the distance, then retract my hand in horror. Try to take it back. No no no no no. I'm not interested at all. No, honestly. But it is all too late. She is reporting everything to her husband.

I had forgotten that my looking at something ensures that we are going to cancel all previous plans and go there instead.

Before I have a chance to protest, Turtle Man is throwing his arm over the seat and backing up the car, backing up backing up, turning the wheels, moving forward forward forward onto the other road. Away—I think I need to repeat that—*away* from the verdant hills in the distance and in the direction of a handful of arches carved into sand in the far-off reaches of this desert.

If I were able to move from the seat, I would be beside myself, but as it is I am stuck in this costume as if packed into a sack. I sputter my objections, assure and reassure them that I have no interest in seeing whatever it is, that I was just looking, not even looking, just turning my head, stretching my neck; in fact, the whole time I had my head turned in this direction my eyes were closed. But I am babbling in English, to which they listen with great interest and no comprehension. I am so worked up about this detour that the only thing I can manage to say in Farsi is, "No thank you please no please no thank you I am very grateful but no please no. I am very hot."

It is a quarter to five, though it has taken me several minutes to determine this as my eyes seem to have lost their ability to focus, just as they no longer seem capable of depth perception or colour differentiation. Everything I see is somewhere between flat and grey. Even my hearing has done me the favour of failing, blocking out everything but the hum of the car motor and indiscriminate babble. I exist in a gauzy two-dimensional state.

Turtle Man has just parked the car, and I am fumbling with the handle. I crack the door open and reach for fresh air so desperately that I look like I'm swimming. The air feels anything but fresh; in fact, I believe it is actually hotter. I stand on sun-blasted ground and survey the place. Desolation. The horizon ripples a sort of ethereal liquid image and is flat in every direction. Hollow. It is not that my sight has failed me, I realize, it is that this place can hold neither distance nor time. I clench my cheeks under the sun and endure its torture. Resign myself to the fact that I am entirely at its mercy. Entirely. My clothes cling to me like airtight packaging. When I peel the scarf away from my neck, there is a hissing sound.

Lida takes my hand and guides me towards the only land formation in sight: a crag that looks like a stern forehead with a series of tiny sand dwellings that hug the base of the rock face like teeth. We walk slowly—my legs move like gelatin that hasn't quite set—and as we climb, faces begin to appear, peering from cavities in the setting. They wear white caps and scarves, do not smile, and chatter like cicadas. My friends seem unconcerned.

In a coarse archway at the entrance to the settlement sits a man. He is as old as this land and as beaten. Worn by decades of heat and hunger, he wears a white stitched hat and is barefoot. His feet are an elephant's: thick cracked soles and nails like tusks. He does not rise, but speaks to us from the ground, pinching the skin across his forehead as he talks.

Soon there are women and children poking heads and bodies around walls. They are wrapped in colour and trepidation. I trudge towards them and down an alley that pulls me further into stone. The air grows sweeter, gentle and cool. There are women on either side of me now, guiding me, holding my arms, but I am scarcely aware of them. I am fixated, instead, on the texture of the air. How heavy it is.

There are hands on the back of my head, pushing and guiding, peeling black cloth from my hair. I have come to the core of this civilization, a cool hollow lit by candles, and I hear a slapping sound, a harsh whipping of life against stone. The women lead me to the far corner of this cave, press my head gently until my lips are lodged in a cleft. I choke at first, from the shock of it, then swallow the water that trickles from this rock.

Blackness.

I awaken in a room built of sand and dung, filled with smoke. The ceiling is a open dome and beneath the aperture lies a smouldering fire, pungent with sandalwood. The old man from the archway stands above me, lost in incantation, while Lida holds my head in her lap. I try to move but cannot, try to speak but find that I do not have the strength. My eyes rise to the sky and I fall into blackness again.

This time it is a breeze that lifts me into consciousness.

I am outside, stretched on a carpet that smells of centuries. The sun is low, long and gentle, settling against the earth in pinks and mauves and a hundred shades of brown. I sit up from under a layer of sand and feel my head like a wound at the end of my neck. Lida arrives with bread and tea. I eat slowly and in small bites. Each one feels like a meal. Several women tend to me with cool wet cloths and pebbles of salt that sting when I place them on my tongue. When my head clears, I see Turtle Man by the car, filling the tank with a plastic bottle from the trunk. Lida raises her eyebrows and nods towards him. Ready? she implies and aids me to my feet. We hobble down the dusty foothills and wave to the community standing together by the arch. Turtle Man smiles and opens the door for me. "Hot?" he asks, and somehow I find the energy to smile.

I fall asleep again and expect to wake up at my inn. Instead, I wake up in total darkness by the side of the road. Lida is alternately tapping my hand and attending to the intrepid coils of hair that have escaped my scarf. She eases me from the back seat, and my body convulses in a chill. We are not in the desert any longer. The air is kind. And I can hear a river.

Lida takes my hand and guides me along the roadside. There are trees on all sides of us. I can feel their breath, and I trip over greenery, feel my manteau soaking up the day's earlier rain. We come to a mud wall, which we use to guide our steps away from the road, down a slight hill and deeper into the foliage. To a scene that makes my eyes bulge.

They stand around the pond like statues. Ten of them, at least, hands on their hips or on the shoulders of others. They look at me, stare, and offer nothing in their expressions. In the pond float melons and other large fruit, red-petalled flowers and glass lights, bobbing gently along the surface. Lida takes my hand and leads me to the pond, dips my fingers into the water and strokes droplets against my face.

"Cold," she says and kisses me.

The group is smiling now, children giggling and approaching me with offerings of food: nuts and fruit and candy and cakes. Turtle Man introduces his family one by one: father, mother, grandmother, older son, younger son, older daughter, younger daughter, brother, brother's wife, niece, nephew. After everyone has bowed or shaken my hand, Turtle Man explains to the group that we met in the post office, went to the mosque, then a restaurant, then to a Zoroastrian prayer site where I almost died (he imitates me fainting, and this sets the whole group laughing), and that is why we are late. Her husband—

Just hearing the word sets my stomach aflame. I cup my hand to my mouth and gasp. He must be sick with worry by now. We had arranged to meet back at the inn in the afternoon, but I'd become so disoriented. He will be beside himself. "I must go, please, my husband will be very worried—"

"No problem," Turtle Man says with proud assurance. Using a mixture of Farsi and mime, he conveys: eat— telephone—inn—husband.

"You called my inn from the restaurant?"

He nods.

"Did you talk to my husband?"

He nods.

"But he doesn't speak Farsi. He won't understand."

Turtle Man closes his eyes and smiles, demurely. "No Farsi—English." He clears his throat, points his index finger into the air and repeats his message: "Mr. Canada," he recites. "We take your wife. We make her cold."

It is true: suddenly I feel cold all over. Even closer to death than I did several hours ago. I remove my hand from Lida's and stand up. I explain in Farsi, English, mime and hysteria that we must go immediately, we absolutely must, that it has been a wonderful day, very cold, thank you, but my husband will be very angry, and I must return this minute.

Turtle Man says something to his father, who rubs his chin and nods. The two men leave without a word. A few minutes later, I hear a car starting.

"Your husband," Lida explains. "They bring your husband."

"They are going to drive all the way back to the city and bring Ian here?"

Lida nods and pats my hand.

"But how long will that take?"

She shrugs and consults her mother-in-law.

"Maybe four hours."

I try to imagine the scene that Ian will soon endure. Pacing (no doubt) around the inn, having tried all day (no doubt) to contact some sort of official somewhere to try to track me down. Then being approached by two men he has never met, one of whom says, "Mr. Canada. We have your wife. Come."

But I am beyond a tantrum. Haven't the energy for an argument. I scarcely have it in me to be upset. Instead, I find the situation so thoroughly absurd, that I begin to laugh. And once I begin, I cannot stop. I laugh until everyone around me has joined in, Lida the loudest of all, with great belly laughs of relief.

"You very happy are," Lida tells me. "You love very much your husband."

The sky cracks and sheds the day's pressure. The children shriek and gallop into the two-room house behind the pond. Another clap of thunder has them squealing like piglets. Lida and her sister-in-law retrieve the fruit from the pond and, by the time we reach the house, we are soaked through.

Turtle Man's mother meets us with dry clothes and draws me into the kitchen to change. I have been given a black T-shirt, a yellow blouse, green trousers, red socks, and a purple scarf. Plus a white bedsheet to cover myself. Mummified, I walk back into the main room and am met with approving smiles.

"No men," Lida says, removing the bedsheet. She lays it on a corner of the carpet and points to it to be sure I have seen where it is. "For men," she says and points again.

One by one, the younger children come and collapse on my lap, each time with offerings of food. They giggle and joke among themselves, sing what sound like nursery rhymes and shriek with every clap of thunder. The two older girls sit just to the side, studying, reading their lessons aloud, seemingly oblivious to the noise and excitement around them. I curl up on the carpet and zonk out.

When I wake up, I am a sea creature. The children are lying around me in starfish formation. They lie on their stomachs, propped up on their elbows, chins in hands, full of dimply smiles.

"My name is Mitra," says the oldest one of my starfish limbs. "I am fourteen years old. How old is you?"

She seems to like my response. She points to my wedding ring and asks, "How old?"

"How old was I when I got married?"

She nods.

"Twenty-six," I tell her. And all twelve eyes in the room swell to twice their normal size.

"*Twenty-six?*" she asks in English, then Farsi, then sign language. "Twenty-six? Twenty and six?"

I nod the room out of disbelief.

"I marry," Mitra says, sitting up. She takes a deeply creased photo from her pocket and offers it proudly. It shows her in a tinselly dress, her face painted so heavily it looks like it's covered in icing, and her hair in tight ringlets dancing to her shoulders. Beside her sits a man with a life three times the length of hers.

"You are married?"

She nods.

"Why don't you live with your husband?"

She pauses, bites her bottom lip, leans towards me and whispers: "I go when my blood start."

Mitra's cousin sits up and reaches for her schoolbook.

"My name is Farah. I am thirteen years. I learn your language. Want you read?"

She opens her schoolbook to a lesson called "A Day in London," curls up beside me and rests her head on my shoulder. Mitra sits behind Farah and begins playing with her cousin's hair. Another child stretches out and rests his head on my leg. The youngest child of the family, not yet two, installs himself on my lap and leans his face into my breast.

I read, "We are in London. It rains. It is very cold. Everyone is sad because the weather is dreadful. Churches are empty, but shops are full. Most people drive cars, but they are very expensive. Many people are without food. The Queen wears much jewellery."

When I look up from the page, every child but Mitra and Farah is asleep.

"You did travel to London?" asks Farah.

"Yes, I've been to London."

"And it has true?"

I glance over the story again. "Well, yes, I suppose everything is true, it's just not . . ."

"My father live in England," Farah continues. "Soon I live there."

"Your father is English?"

"No," she says. "Please wait."

Farah calls to her mother, who appears from the kitchen with a large envelope. She is smiling proudly. "England!" she chirps, patting her chest, then tapping the heads of her children: Farah and the boy asleep on my leg. The envelope contains several copies of approved immigration papers and a photo of a man who must, *must*, be Turtle Man's brother. He is beaming, holding an English passport like a trophy.

"We move after one month to England," Farah says timidly. "Please tell to me: I become happy?"

At this question, the two cousins give me their full attention. They lean into each other, entwine arms and legs, innocently, affectionately, and I look at them, their identical eyes and smiles, and try to imagine the divergence of their lives. Mitra marrying at fourteen while her cousin begins life in England. Mitra leaving school to have children while Farah studies, learns English, grows up in London, maybe goes on to university. I stare into the soft faces of these girls and try to imagine them meeting again, ten years from now. Farah will return for a visit. She will wear fashionable clothes and will wear a chaador with disdain. She will speak a refined English and will fit awkwardly into her mother tongue; it will no longer hold her. She will have developed a taste for philosophy over coffee, will have grown used to speaking her mind, will have had many friendships and a heartbreak that will have left her unsettled but independent, will have become successful, enviable.

She and Mitra will gasp when they see each other after all these years. They will hug and separate and hug and separate and kiss each other on the cheek again and again. Then they will sit across from each other staring, wondering how the other one got so old. Mitra will have four children; no, five; and will wear this, them, in her face. Her arms will be thick, strong, her hands calloused, and she will cry easily, not because she is sad, but because her emotions will not live behind her mind. Farah will be shocked to see her old friend and will think it pathetic, her life, all these children, this cooking and praying and serving; this waste. The visit will be pleasant but awkward, forced in a way neither of them expected. Farah will find an excuse to spend the rest of her holiday in Tehran and will return to England without seeing Mitra again. They will be cousins always but never friends, because each will have a wisdom the other cannot understand.

The girls stare at me, waiting for an answer.

"Yes," I say. "You will both be happy."

They turn their faces together and smile. Lean into each other and touch noses, then fall back against the carpet laughing.

"You are hungry," Lida says, ducking into the room with a bowl of dates and a glass of water. She kneels and takes the immigration papers from my hands. "No go London! London goood no!" Lida whacks her niece with the bundle. Farah giggles and tumbles away. Mitra picks up my scarf and swats her cousin, who howls in facetious pain. The children are all awake now, offering their own slaps and punches and squirming around like giddy jellyfish. Farah's mother has come in from the kitchen to investigate the source of the screaming, but is landed with a pillow in the face before she has a chance to tell us off.

Before long, every spare pillow, sheet, scarf, shoe and book is being hurled around the room. Some of the kids are laughing so hard that they are launching into coughing fits, others are screaming themselves hoarse. I am whooping and shrieking and being tickled mercilessly by Mitra and Farah. I am yelling "Stop! Stop! *Staaaawwwp!*"

—when Ian appears in the doorway.

I don't know why none of us manages to catch him. There is the shock of seeing him, of course, the confusion of being in the middle of a play brawl, and the guilt at hearing his words: "Oh my God, I thought you were dead." But why we all just watch as his whole body relaxes and falls into the middle of the carpet, I don't know. I can only say that we do, and all seem to feel rather badly about it.

Thankfully, he doesn't seem to notice. He wakes up with his head resting on a pillow, surrounded by food and well-wishers. We get through the initial "I thought you went to the post office" . . . "I did, but then I met these lovely people," and settle down to a delicious meal of eggplant, eggs, potatoes, spinach, saffron rice and Pipi Zam Zam. The moment the meal is over, Turtle Man stands up and the entire family thanks us for coming.

We reach town just before dawn. Turtle Man and his father wake the innkeeper, who gives Ian a big smile and a slap on the back—*There you go, I told you she would be OK*—and gets the full story from our hosts. We exchange the appropriate handshaking and bowing, trudge across the courtyard to our room and fall into bed fully clothed.

THE GREATEST TEA HOUSE IN IRAN

THE HALLWAY ECHOES the footsteps I drum down the stairs.

"Come on!" I yell to Ian and smear my nose against the window, straining to see. Nothing. I pull away and gather my manteau in my hands. *"Come on, I think they're coming!"* Adjust my scarf, folding a low visor over my eyes, stuffing stray curls out of view, holding bite-size pieces of the fabric in my mouth while I fumble through my pockets, fumble fumble fumble for—there it is—the clip that fastens the fabric under my chin. *"I hear them—What in the world are you doing up there?"* I sail down another flight of stairs to a broken window and inch one side of my face out through the crack. There is a gathering at the end of the street, but I would need to slice off part of my nose on the broken pane to get a better look. *"Would you haul your sweet ass down he—"* A couple come in off the street and begin climbing the stairs towards me. I weasel back out of the window and assemble myself.

"Salaam," we say to each other. The woman smirks shyly, lets her chaador fall open at the front. The man puts

his hand over his heart and bows his head. They are our neighbours from across the hall.

Ian ripples down the stairs, and we walk to the end of the street so quickly that clumps of black fabric keep getting caught between my legs. Traffic is stopped. A crowd has formed on either side of the avenue, but it is a thin one, in fact calling it a crowd is stretching it. Most people seem to stroll the sidewalks oblivious to what is going on in the street. We join the fray of interested observers and watch the procession drag, slowly, towards us.

The parade is led by a truck carrying speakers. Behind it walks a man with a microphone, who feeds the speakers to distortion with the wails of prayer. Behind him, row upon row of men lope and sway forward, answering his calls with a droning song. They are dressed entirely in black, most with freshly shorn heads. Each man carries a mass of chains that hangs from a wooden handle. Some carry two flails, one in each hand. At regular intervals in their song, the chains are slung over one shoulder, then the other. Back and forth. Over and over. The movements are choreographed and rehearsed: put your right foot forward, and your chains over the left shoulder. Right foot back, chains over the right shoulder. Right, *bash,* left, *bash,* two steps forward, repeat.

Some of their shirts are torn at the shoulder, some have a shiny spot where the chains crash each time. At the end of each group of men comes a handful of boys carrying junior-sized flails (considerably fewer strands of chains with smaller links). They are teeny boys with stringy arms and legs, some with big smiles, others with the stolid expression of frogs. They follow the steps of the adults in front of them, some giggle and chase their friends around, and others rest the chains on their backs like a bag of dirty laundry and sing prayers until their arms are rested.

Most of the flagellators appear to be a good distance from the enthusiastic though there is a handful of lively swatters up near the front. One man's shirt has been ripped open, exposing the bloodied mark of the flail, a wound that he aggravates again and again by thrashing the raw skin. He moves in fierce commitment to this act of suffering, deprivation, abnegation. He walks towards God. Such is his expression.

They say that the devoted do not feel pain from this exercise, it is those watching who feel pain.

The latter is certainly true.

This is Ashura, the commemoration of the martyrdom of Imam Hussein, third Imam of the Shi'ites and grandson of the Prophet. Hussein and his followers were killed in the battle of Karbala in AD 680, and the loss is mourned every year at this time by devout Shi'ites.

The most impressive flagellating, we are told by the man on our right, is found in Esfahan, where some men end up with blood streaming down their faces. "Here," he continues, "you get a lot of men just doing it for show."

We take one last look at the parade—no photos—and turn down a side street. Everything in Kerman is closed, not a morsel of food in sight. We walk and walk and walk until we reach the outskirts of the city. Ian is grumbling, I'm collecting pools of sweat in my shoes. We are growing hungrier, thirstier and more intolerant. The sound of the nearby parades (they are coming from all corners of Kerman towards the main mosque), is putting us both on edge.

Everything is closed save one small shop. The door is ajar, and a metal grate is open a few feet off the ground. There is a light on and the sound of a man's voice. We duck under the grate and poke our heads in. The owner looks surprised and tells us he is closed. Says a series of things I don't understand and is about to shut us out completely, when Ian pleads with him in English. Tells him we are very hungry, points to his stomach and growls.

At this, another, much younger man pops up from behind the shop counter. He looks like a hip, slicked-back American teenager and I gasp, despite myself, and stare.

We gawk at each other—the young man's eyes move between Ian and me as though he were watching a tennis match—and wait for the other to speak. Finally his eyes settle on Ian.

"You American?"

"Canadian."

He leans both arms on the counter. "Ho-ly-shit . . . ," he says, with equal emphasis on each syllable. He looks down and shakes his head, then throws it back as though he'd just stuck it in a barrel of cold water and was coming up for air. Laughing. A chirpy Woody Woodpecker sort of a laugh that gives away his age. Young. He vaults over the counter and lands his leather boots on the floor next to us. "How are ya. I'm Tip," he says to me with an outstretched hand. I accept, but shake his hand with great discomfort. It is the first time a man (aside from Ian) has touched me in weeks. It feels so odd, so forward, strangely disrespectful. I pull my hand away quickly, wipe it on my cloak—yes, honestly—and look away.

Ian laughs and shakes hands. "Nice to meet you. Well . . . ," he says and clears his throat. "I think you're the first Tip we've met here."

"I bet," Tip says, combing a hand through his stylish sopping-wet-look hair. "My real name's Abdullah, but in

America they could never say it right, they'd always say Ab*doo*la and shit like that, and then my girlfriend just called me Tip one time, as like a nickname, and I just started using it. What are you guys' names?"

Ian and I are too stunned to respond. Tip fills in the silence.

"I was totally nervous when you guys walked in here, I mean, you look like you're real Iranian with your black clothes and all. And then when you started speaking English I was totally freaked out. I've met foreigners at hotels in Tehran and stuff, but I mean, are you embassy people or what?"

"Tourists," I say like a robot. Moving from the flagellation parade to this conversation has made my mind twist into rotini.

"Tourists?" Tip laughs and shakes his head, translating our conversation to the shopkeeper and holding the most seductive pose I have seen in months: hip cocked out to one side, thumbs hanging out the belt loops of tight blue jeans. It is strange to watch him stand this way, so posed, so poised. So sculpted. So presented.

The shopkeeper mumbles to Tip and nods his head in our direction. Tip translates: "My friend wants to know why you'd come here, I mean, are you just on your way to India or what?"

"No, we're just travelling in Iran. We're on our honeymoon."

Tip spits a laugh onto the floor. "Man, you guys are fucking *nuts*." He chortles and translates for the shopkeeper, who scratches his forehead and asks for clarification. Twice. He looks at us, dumbfounded, then smiles and introduces himself.

"Karim," he says, shaking Ian's hand. "Karim," he repeats, closing his eyes and bowing to me.

The two men exchange a few words, then begin taking things from shelves around the shop and putting them into a bag.

"I invite you to eat at my house," Tip says, squinting at us from beneath bangs that continually fall into his eyes. "It's the beginning of Ashura today so everything's gonna be closed. It's like total shutdown city." We duck under the grate and follow him to the end of the street. "I've got my motorcycle, so we'll have to find a taxi for you guys and just like meet there. I gotta stop and get some fruit at my friend's house, so if you get there before me just like wait outside."

Tip flags down a taxi, explains the directions to the driver and negotiates a price, which he pays.

"Okay," he says, laying a hand on Ian's shoulder. "I'll meet ya at my place in like ten."

Tip's apartment is immaculate. Im-ma-cu-late. Nothing out of place. Everything—floors, tiles, tables—is not just clean, but sparkling. Nevertheless, there is a comfortable warmth about the place. It is a place that has been well looked after. Respected.

"Do you live here alone?" I ask. Because I am sexist.

"Yeah, I been here about six months. Here, have a seat," he says, pulling back one of the chairs at the dining table. Ian and I sit down and look at the walls. Posters of cars, sunsets, arrangements of plastic flowers and a Disney-type drawing of a warrior that dominates the main wall of the apartment. There is a neatly printed note in English beside the telephone:

15 minutes exercise every day
Water plants once a week
Clean up every other day
Cut down on useless expenses

"So how long did you live in the States?" Ian calls into the kitchen.

"About twelve years," he replies. "And three months."

"And how old are you now?"

"Twenty." Tip comes into the room to set out placemats and glasses, then returns with cutlery and plates, all of which he wipes with a tea towel before placing on the table. "I'll just be a few minutes," he says with a shy nod. I follow him into the kitchen and ask if there is anything I can do to help with lunch. He turns around and smiles. "Thanks," he says and holds my arm. "I think I got it all under control." It is a beautiful, genuine smile. His eyes are malachite crystals.

Tip busies himself in the kitchen for the next half hour, then lays the table with a spinach-yogurt salad, a dish of walnuts and white cheese, and a plate of tomatoes and peppers sliced and arranged in stripes just like my grandmother used to do. "I hope you like this drink," he says pouring peach-coloured liquid from a tall glass pitcher. "I made it with grated melon and rosewater. If you don't like it, just tell me, no big deal. Don't just like drink it." He giggles like a child.

"So why did you come back to Iran?" Ian takes a sip. "Oh, God, it's delicious . . ."

"Thanks." Tip smirks and takes a sip himself. "I came back 'cause my parents came back. Wasn't my choice really. We lived in like a *real* good part of LA. My high school had over five thousand students, and they had all kinds of tennis courts and Olympic-size pools." He laughs and shakes his head. "No *shit*." Refills our glasses.

"It was my dad that was wanting to come back here. My mom was okay with it, she had family here and stuff, but I didn't really get it, I mean I didn't know shit about Iran. Every single one of my friends was American. I thought it'd be pretty wild to visit here for a while 'cause I just finished high school and what the fuck, I mean I wasn't going to college." Tip spills a bit of yoghurt onto his placemat, so takes it into the kitchen, rinses it, dries it and lays it back down. Replaces his plate. Resumes eating.

"The first month was great, I mean a lotta dinners with relatives and stuff. We always stayed up in North Tehran, so you know it was still like, well, *kinda* like America, and I was okay with it, but by the second month I really wanted to go back. My dad didn't want me to go. He said it'd be *good for me* to stay and *learn* about this place, how people live, and then he said he wouldn't pay for my ticket. We had a major fight about it, he was yelling at me telling me America had poisoned me and saying I didn't value a goddamn thing, and that's what the revolution was about. I was totally pissed at him. He was always real strict with me, more than my friends' dads, but in America I guess I got away with a lot. Now I been here three years, and I ain't got away with shit."

He smirks.

"Did you get enough to eat? I can make tea or something. I got these great cookies I buy all the time. Once I ate a whole roll in one day." He smiles mischievously and begins clearing the dishes. I follow behind with a stack of serving plates. "Oh, that's great, thanks. Do you mind taking these out?" He hands me three short glasses. "This is what they drink tea out of here. I like it better than those big mugs they use in America. You know, here you just have a little bit, but it tastes real good. There, you have a whole big thing and it tastes like shit." He laughs, and his eyes squint into crystals again.

We sip our tea and munch on digestive cookies.

Tip stares at the table as he speaks. "When I decided I was gonna go back to America on my own, I went to the British embassy to ask about an American visa. I had my green card and everything, but I needed like this stamp and—*shit!*—they took my passport and they like punched this *hole* in it." His eyes widen as though he were watching it all over again. "I can't tell you how that felt, it was like . . ." He grabs the front of his shirt. "It was like someone just like . . . you know . . . just like being totally trapped here, you know?" He takes another cookie and sits back in his chair.

"Then for two years I had to do military service so I could leave the country, you know here every guy's gotta do two years, so I did my serv—"

The telephone rings. Tip answers, says a few quick words. Replaces the receiver. Continues.

". . . Yeah, so I did my service, and then I could leave except I needed money, for the ticket and shit, so I worked as a translator for a while, got like three bucks a day, that's pretty good money here, but shit, for three bucks a day I was gonna be here forever, so I got this job as like a driller. It's this uranium mine, and it's mostly refugees that work there, Afghanis mostly, so I worked there doing drilling for a while, but I got the hell outta there when they started extracting the uranium 'cause there was no safety standards, no protection. It's like totally radioactive shit, and those guys are just pulling it out in their own clothes, some guys with no shoes. Only the real desperate guys stayed for the extracting. Anyone who knew shit got the fuck outta there." He slurps his tea. "D'you guys play cards or anything?"

We clear the table and Tip gets a deck of cards from his closet. Ian goes to the toilet. While he is gone, someone buzzes the door to the street. "Oh," Tip says and goes back to the closet. Rustles around with some paper or plastic and comes out with a rolled-up newspaper. "I'll be back in a sec." I hear him run down the stairs, let someone in off the street and talk to him for a few seconds on the landing. The main door opens again, the man goes outside, Tip strides back up the stairs and comes into the apartment carrying a hamburger wrapped in waxed paper.

Or no, it's a wad of money.

He counts it quickly and expertly, snapping each one of the bills as he peels it from the stack. He walks back over to the closet and buries the money somewhere in its depths. Closes the closet. Sits down. Begins shuffling. Ian returns from the toilet.

"So, you quit the uranium mine," Ian begins.

"Yeah," Tip replies and deals us seven cards each.

"So, what do you do now?" Ian collects the cards and sorts them in his hand. "What are we playing?"

"Let's play rummy." Tip gathers his own cards. "I do like odd jobs and stuff."

"And you can save enough to buy your ticket?" Ian asks. The telephone rings again. Tip gets up and answers.

"*Salaam,* Daddy!"

It is a short but lively conversation, fast-paced and full of laughter. He hangs up.

"That was my dad. We get along real good now. I haven't told him I'm saving to go back to America. He'd be totally disappointed, so I just tell him how I'm doing and stuff. Who's going first?"

We play a few hands. The telephone rings again. Tip answers. Speaks briefly. Sits down again. We play until someone buzzes the outside door. "'Scuse me." Tip gets up and goes to the closet, rustles paper and plastic, and leaves the apartment with a rolled-up newspaper.

"Do you know what's in that?" I whisper.

"In what?" Ian looks up from his cards.

"In the newspaper he just left with."

"No, what?"

"I don't know, but watch what he gets for it."

We hear the outside door close and Tip bound up the stairs. He comes back with another fistful of bills, but this time counts them behind the closet door. All we hear is the snapping. He buries the money deep in the closet and sits down again.

"Is it my go?" he says nonchalantly.

Ian and I smile at him and he grins, smugly.

"What? Did I already go?"

"I'm not sure."

"Oh," he says, sifting through the discard pile a bit. "I don't remember what I put down last . . ."

"What do you sell?"

"What's that?" Tip flips up his face with a look of inno-cent confusion.

"What are you selling?"

Tip smiles and sorts his cards.

"Come on," I laugh. "Do you really expect us to believe you're selling newspapers out of your closet?"

Tip shifts his eyes between the two of us. Smiles. "Opium," he says and then asks, with a child's excitement: "Wanna see?"

Ian and I look at each other and shrug. We all get up and go to the closet. Tip rummages through a heap of clothing, unwraps several layers of plastic, and pulls out a stick of opium the size of a pepperoni.

"This gets you about three years in the slammer," he says calmly.

"Only three?" Ian asks, staring at the opium as though it were alive.

Tip convulses and laughs. "Three's enough, believe me." He wraps it up and hides it again and closes the closet door. We sit down at the table and pick up our cards.

"Okay," Tip says. "So whose go was it?

We play cards for the rest of the afternoon. Until Tip suggests a walk. "Lemme just grab a different shirt." He opens the door to the next room and pulls out a neatly folded shirt from a cupboard. "Oh, by the way . . . This is my room." He leaves the door open and we step inside, take a look around. It is as orderly as the rest of the apartment, holds more photos of cars on its walls, plus another of the cartoon-like warrior posters.

"Who is that guy?" Ian asks. "There's another picture of him in the living room."

Tip buttons a long-sleeved shirt over his T-shirt. "That's Hossein. He was one of the Imams, one of the big leaders. He's the reason everyone's out there beating the shit out of themselves. I just bought the poster 'cause of the Komiteh—they're sort of, I dunno what you'd call them, they're like the revolution cops or something. They make sure everyone's following Islamic law and that. They've only been on my ass once, a couple of months ago, I went across the street in boxer shorts. I was just like wearing them around here inside, and then I needed something from the store, and I totally forgot I was wearing shorts. I just went out. I didn't even notice till these two guys came up and started asking all kinds of questions, and then they wanted to see my apartment, but they just looked around a bit and didn't find anything. They were like asking me questions about the revolution and the Koran and stuff, but I was real lucky. My dad talked to me a lot about that kinda stuff, so I knew what to say so they left me alone. But the next day I went out and bought this." He flicks his finger against the poster and laughs. "Looks good."

The only thing on the shelf above his bed is a box of condoms, placed in the centre of the shelf and set on an angle, as one might set a framed photo. Ian flicks his finger against the box. "And these?"

Tip laughs, a cool-dude kind of chuckle, and sticks his thumbs through his belt loops. "It's empty." He guides us out of the room and shuts the door. "I used 'em all."

"Is that, uh, I mean . . ." Ian searches for the best way to ask. "I guess I'm surprised you find that many opportunities considering . . . I mean I think you're *attractive*, it's just . . ."

Tip turns and looks at Ian with a strange, puzzled, smile.

Ian sputters as we leave the apartment, then twists himself around and around on the staircase trying to explain himself. Tip opens the heavy outside door and puts an arm around Ian, leading him onto the sidewalk. "You mean, how the hell does a guy get laid in a place like this?" Ian sighs, relaxes. "Well, *yes*."

As we walk into the old section of town, Tip eases into a steady monologue that is probably half cathartic and half didactic. He looks at the ground as he talks, scuffing through the dusty streets, walking like a cowboy. "There's lots of like liberal families left in this place, you know, and it doesn't matter what the government says or what the mollahs say, people are just *people*. You know, you probably see all these girls walking around all covered up and think they don't ever wanna have sex or anything, but there's a lot of stuff going on, I mean, you can tell by the way a girl looks at you what she's like, and so there's a lot of like looking and kind of secret stuff you can do to get someone, but man it's hard for some girls. It's like a totally major risk for them to do anything. Some of them say it's like living in jail, everybody watching you and wearing the chaador and stuff. I mean it's shitty for us too, but the girls have it the worst."

Tip leads us through a series of narrow alleys into a part of the town that feels abandoned to history. "I come here a lot," he says, looking around at the emptiness and smiling. We turn into a courtyard made of adobe arches and space. "You know what I love?" he says, leaning against one of the mud walls. "People lived here like thousands of years ago, but you can just like . . ." he scratches the grainy wall and shows us the dust on his fingertips ". . . and it comes right off in your hand. Sometimes I dunno why it doesn't all just fall down. It's like time just kinda leaves this place alone." He puts his hands in his pockets and straightens his arms. Smiles, then squints into the distance. "C'mere. I'll show you this great door."

Hunched at the end of an alley like a hoary old hermit sits the door. Thick and worn. Bolts like fists. A brass latch that shines with the oils of its owners' hands. It is an ancient creation. Created with wisdom and respect. And it sits here now, refusing to die.

"I'm gonna build a house in America with a door like this." He runs his fingers along the wood and cups the door's mammoth lock in his palm. "You just wonder, like where's the key now? Sometimes I look at the old keys they sell at the bazaar, I've bought a couple, but I never found the one for this place. It'd be wild to find it and go inside." He lets go of the lock and knocks his fist against the wood. "Probably I'd go in and be totally disappointed. There'd just be like this room with nothing in it, and in my head I got the place filled with all kinds of neat shit."

We leave the ruins behind us and walk back towards the modern-day bazaar. Between rolls of carpets and open sacks of spices we turn and take tiled steps down below ground. Immediately it is cool. The air is moist and smells of cardamom.

"This is the greatest tea house in Iran," Tip says, leading us into a room that makes my eyes take deep breaths. Vaulted white brick ceilings speckled with colour and various shades of light. Patterned mosaics on the walls. Deep, thick slabs of stone at our feet. We walk to the centre of the room, where a platform is suspended over a small round pool. On the platform is an octagonal table with low benches. We sit. Look up into the highest point of the ceiling, and look down into peach-coloured curls. Goldfish, swimming beneath us.

"Lemme just go and see what they've got to eat," Tip says, taking a long-stride hop back onto the floor. I watch him walk, greet the men working at the samovar, shake hands, nod and gesture. They know each other, it seems, the way they fall into easy conversation and gentle smiles. I watch Tip lay a hand over his heart and bow humbly, gratefully, sheepishly; the way I've watched so many other Iranians do. I wonder if he knows how many of these gestures have crawled into him, how many of these mannerisms now live in his body and come to life, naturally, when he speaks.

I love watching men talk to each other here. Love the way they stand in themselves so comfortably, without guard. How will he stand when he returns to America, I wonder. Will he keep the light grace he has right now—in this simple, beautiful moment—or will he adapt himself to his surroundings and learn to stand like a bulldog again?

He turns in our direction and nods. Smiles. Turns back to his friends and touches his heart again.

"They're bringing us a whole bunch of stuff. I hope you like it. And this is on me—no arguing." He sits down beside Ian and looks at the two of us, one after the other. "So what's the deal with you guys? Are you really on your honeymoon or are you just shittin' me?"

We smile and divulge our secret.

The next day we meet Tip at his apartment for lunch. Given time to prepare, he assures us, he is actually a pretty good cook. And he is right. Saffron rice with roasted vegetables, pan-fried potatoes and chicken so soft and sweet, I have trouble chewing it without groaning. Tip cuts two opium deals while we are eating and one more over tea. A good day, he whispers, dunking another cookie into his tea.

Once the table is cleared and the dishes washed and put away, we agree on a few hands of blackjack before embarking on the day's outing. In place of poker chips, we use Tip's favourite cookies. Each player has the option of eating his/her money at any point in the game, but there will be no loans from the bank. The package of digestives is empty.

We play for the better part of an hour, until the chips begin to deteriorate and the table is covered in crumbs. "Okay," Tip laughs, running a wet cloth across the table and catching the crumbs in his palm. "Enough illegal shit. Let's go out. There's this really great shrine just outside of town I wanna show you."

He closes the door to his room and changes into cotton trousers and a long-sleeved shirt. I put on my manteau and scarf, plus the chaador Tip suggested I bring today. Ian rolls down his sleeves.

"We can take a taxi part of the way, then ask around in the village and see if someone can take us the rest of the way." Tip locks the door to his apartment and bounces down the stairs like a kid.

The taxi takes us to a small, dusty village about half an hour out of town. Tip pays the fare, after offering once, twice, three times, then asks us to wait by the side of the road while he looks for some transport. We watch him go from shop to shop, leaving each time with shy nods and thank-yous, hand over his heart. At one point, he disappears down a side street and is gone for quite a long time. I am beginning to wonder what is going on. Ian is reading his guidebook.

Tip reappears at the top of the street with a small boy walking beside him. No. Not a boy. A very, very small man. Small, as in comes-up-to-Tip's-waist small. Tip introduces him as our driver, and the man bows, graciously and amiably, and gives us his name: Mehdi.

Mehdi smiles constantly and has a helium voice that makes everything he says sound like an exclamation of joy. Every time he speaks, I automatically raise my eyebrows and smile.

We pile into the cab of his truck and sit with the seat as far back as it can go, so that Mehdi has room to stand behind the wheel and drive standing up. The truck is the perfect size and shape for him, as he is just high enough to peer over the wheel when he moves his foot forward and touches the gas pedal. About halfway down the street, a man waves down the truck. Mehdi hops back onto his right foot and kicks his left foot into place on the brakes. Opens the door and lets in his friend. The man greets us and settles back into the driver's seat behind Mehdi, who stands between his friend's legs and continues driving. The two men talk and laugh, every once in a while Mehdi takes his hand off the wheel and pats his friend's knee. At the edge of the village, the man pulls his right leg back over the seat and gets out the driver's side.

The shrine itself is unremarkable, though it is packed with people who think otherwise. Throngs of mourners pulse in and out of the building; the wails of pain can be heard from the street. "They're not really crying about the guy who's buried here, I can't even remember whose tomb it is anyway. It's all about Karbala," Tip explains. "That was where Hossein—the guy whose picture I have up in my apartment—that's where he got massacred with all his supporters. It's like the biggest story for Shi'ites." He stares at the crowds and shakes his head. "It's amazing, you know. This massacre happened like two thousand years ago. Imam Hossein—he was Ali's son, the Prophet Mohammed's grandson—he's up there in Karbala with all his buddies, the Shi'ites, and *wham!* they just get totally slaughtered by a great big army of Sunnis, only you never say 'slaughtered,' you gotta say 'martyred.' That's some-one who dies for God. Shi'ites love that stuff. It's like if something bad happens to you, let's say your son dies, and *Jesus*, in a country like this almost everyone's lost a son or a brother, and so you're sad, but then you just think, well, he must've been a martyr, he's up there with God now havin' a great ole time, and suddenly it's okay, still sad, but you know, it's like you can accept it."

We go inside, I through the women's entrance, Tip and Ian through the men's, and arrange to meet back at the truck in half an hour.

I am the only one in the mosaic-tiled room not weeping. No, that's not true. There are handfuls of young girls dot-ted around the room who just look sad but overwhelmed, though they could probably burst into tears if they were asked. The body-smush crowd is trudging towards a large gilded cage. As we draw closer, I notice the ornate coffin behind the bars. The women around me are beside them-selves with grief. Wailing and moaning and wiping the pain from their eyes. Some have messages gripped in their fists. They push these through the bars, as close to the cof-fin as possible. Please take this message to God, I imagine the women saying.

On the other side of the cage are the men. I stare through the bars at their faces. Closed eyes, whispering lips, expressions of submission and grace. One man grips the cage with both hands and rests his forehead between two bars. He closes his eyes and begins to whisper his prayer, then he squints, flinches, and his face erupts with tears.

I pull my chaador tightly around my face and squeeze away from the crowd into a cool corner of the room. I sit. Feel my eyes as a periscope that peers out of this costume, allowing me to see, stare, observe—unnoticed.

A widow settles herself at the edge of the room next to a mollah—they are the only men allowed on this side of the shrine—who sits cross-legged with a Koran in his lap. He turns to her and begins speaking, softly, gently, without facial expression or gesture. The woman weeps and weeps, shaking her head and pulling her white veil further and further across her face. Curling it around her fingers and gripping it in her teeth.

The exchange lasts no more than a few minutes and ends when the widow passes a handful of crumpled bills to the turbaned man. He closes his eyes and bows his head, tucks the money under his *aba*. The widow pushes herself to her feet and waddles away. A young woman with a downturned lip folds herself onto the same place on the floor and another counselling session begins.

Outside, the boys are anxious to go; actually, Ian is the impatient one, Tip doesn't seem to know what anxiety is. Mehdi has offered rides back to the city to a large group of men. They just barely sardine themselves onto the bed of the truck, but wave their hands insisting that they can fit a few more. Mehdi jogs back to the shrine site and offers transport to a family of eight. They decline, once, twice, then graciously accept. How they manage to find room for their bodies I'll never know, but they do, with the exception of a small child, who rides up front with us. The toddler sits on my lap and smiles, then settles into me as though he'd known me all his life.

On the way back to the city, we pass a one-legged man on a bicycle. It is a strange sight. One I've never seen before. Ian follows the cyclist with his eyes and turns to me. "Did you see that? I'm not sure if that's beautiful or sad."

Mehdi turns to Tip and asks him what Ian has said. Tip tells him, then translates Mehdi's response: "It is both. You feel sad, and the man feels beautiful."

A few miles down the road, there is a lone man walking. Mehdi slows down the truck and asks Tip to see if the man needs a ride. How we are going to jam him in I have no idea, until I see Mehdi open his door and squeeze forward against the steering wheel. The man nods and thanks us, then hops in and sits behind Mehdi in the driver's seat as he is instructed. As Mehdi pulls the truck back onto the road, he asks Tip to translate again:

"Maybe a man with such small legs is something sad for some people, but I must thank God for this beautiful gift. I will always be able to help one more person than the man with big legs." He smiles a full-face wrinkly smile and pats the hitch-hiker on the shin.

As we wind back into the city, the road widens and hardens. It is now a four-lane highway split by a grassy median. Three cows graze there, and a goat. The little boy on my lap shifts in his sleep and begins snoring into my neck. Quiet snores that sound more like purring. Seconds later, Mehdi slows down in the middle of a straightaway. A tiny boy on his tricycle is trying to make his way across four lanes of traffic. Cars slow on both sides. The tricycle crosses. Traffic picks up.

Mehdi lets us out in the city centre and refuses, once, twice, three times to accept payment from anyone. "It's one of those things about people here," Tip explains. "Being like a good, real generous person is like more important than anything, *definitely* more important than making money." He turns around and looks back at Mehdi, who stands beside his truck laughing with some of his passengers. "I kinda like that."

Tip walks us the rest of the way back to our inn. The flagellation marches continue to wind through the main arteries of the city towards the central mosque. Men in black with chains.

The streets sag with mourning. Sheets of black velvet drape buildings and doorways. Here there is no traffic. The only sounds are the melancholy droning of prayer and the shrieks and laughter of children playing on the sidewalks and watching the parade.

Persian carpets have been laid across the road outside mosques along the route. The men stop, rest their flailing arms, and pray in unison, bowing their scarred bodies to the ground. They are led in prayer by a young boy with the voice and sensitivity of a trained singer. A plangent tone that shimmers like a peacock. It is a hypnotic scene, this mass of black bodies falling like feathers into blocks of crimson set into the dust while a boy's voice fills the air with light.

"Is this sad or beautiful?" Ian asks.

Tip shrugs and stuffs his hands in his pockets. "Maybe it's both."

He drops us at our inn and apologizes, again and again, for not taking us out for dinner. He has to catch the overnight bus to Tehran in less than an hour. He promised his father.

"I'll give you both my addresses: my one here and my cousin's in California," Tip says with the end of the pen in his mouth. "Hopefully I'll be there soon. My cousin owns like this video store and stuff, and he told me I can work there when I get back, you know, it's not great money but it's pretty easy, lotsa free time. Maybe you guys can like come and visit. I'm gonna buy a car and just go out to the beach all the time, start surfing again. We can just go out and like totally party." He passes the addresses and winks.

"So when you finally make it back to America, do you think you're going to miss this place?"

Tip laughs and puts his pen back in his pocket. Looks right in my eyes and gives me a deep, broad smile. "No fuckin' way."

He shakes Ian's hand and slaps him on the arm. Turns to me and smiles. Bows. Hand over his heart. He walks backwards a few steps, turns and waves. "Hey! Don't forget to write me!"

ॶॵ

On our way to the bus station, we stop to buy yogurt and juice. The shopkeeper is busy serving a young woman, so we poke around looking at stacks of canned beans and eggplant caviar. At one point, the shopkeeper overhears us speaking English and stops in mid-sentence to listen. I catch his eye and he returns to his customer, exchanging a few whispered words with her before returning to business. I hear her whisper the word *hand* in English, and I look over again. This time they both smile, the woman pays for her goods, and the shopkeeper disappears into a back room. He returns a few seconds later and walks over to Ian.

"Hand!" he demands. "Hand! Hand!"

Ian wrinkles his forehead and brings his hand up slowly in front of him. The shopkeeper takes hold of Ian's fingertips and pulls them towards him, palm up. Then he brings a closed fist from behind his back, places it in Ian's palm, opens his fist, finger by finger, and walks away. Ian is left standing with a handful of fresh pistachios.

ၢ

It is early. The air is cool and smells of rested flowers. Palm trees outside our room are scrubbed by pale light. There is the sound of plants yawning, of insects chattering their teeth against leaves, of heat settling onto yesterday's footprints. It is a day in which the earth will dance.

I join the air outside. It is pink and colours my cheeks, teases my nose with the smell of bread and pulls my teeth into view. I smile at a roasting sun and begin walking. My body is an anonymous cloak, a vehicle of no consequence. It acts out of purpose, moves to transport me, allows me to walk in my mind. I live here weightlessly in my eyes. My days are spent lounging beside these reflecting pools, watching the world sparkle inside my head.

I walk in a labyrinth of dust, through the empty bazaars and alleys of Bam, which wander and twist like roots in search of water and fresh wet soil. Water purls in canals along the path. I am wrapped in this sound: the cries of laughter from pebbles and damp earth.

Black clouds blow out of doorways. They hold the hands of children, who scatter and giggle and skip, riding imaginary toy horses along the path. These clouds are women, like me, black figures who stalk the morning. Our eyes touch and hold each other. *Salaam*. I feel their breath as they pass, quietly, through space, and they turn, recognizing me as a stranger, and wave with their teeth.

There are men, too, at certain turns in the maze. But I am left untouched, by sight and by mind. They walk beyond me in their wanderings. They stare at walls, flying dust, their own thoughts. I am invisible today, such is the feeling. Some would call it a freedom.

I walk until the earth perspires into my feet. Until I am conscious of my body again. Until my thoughts are dragged down into my chest.

How hungry I am, suddenly.

There are dried fruits lying in heaps next to a child with an outstretched hand. I gather enough dates to fill my pockets and offer my money three times before it is accepted, graciously, by the boy who is selling them. The dates are tropical cockroaches in size, shape and texture, but they melt in my mouth like warm chocolate and I eat them by the handful, spitting skeletons into my hand as I walk.

To the edge of town, to the ruins of a medieval castle built from the earth for miles around. It dwarfs me upon arrival. Towers over me so that I must lay my head on my spine to see its height. It stands boldly, in elegant death. Its walls are forbidding, topped by saw-toothed edges. As thick as time.

I am alone here. Which means that my imagination can run wild.

My hands run along sun-cracked walls, grainy and thirsty for the oils of living skin. My tongue glides along the curves of doorways, arches that crunch against my lips and let me taste sand steeped in centuries. My eyes sink into the colour of these ruins and become terra cotta beads, smooth and hard against my eyelids when I blink.

There is a fox. It holds itself motionless with its ears cupped to the wind, then lowers its head, moves cautiously through crumbling walls and disappears, retreating from the smell of life in the area.

I move further along the whispers of this past. Stepping into the broken homes of the dead, across fortifications and ramparts, climbing into aqueducts hollow with the echoes of water.

The sky sighs and it begins to rain. I turn up my face, open my mouth and fill my body with water. The ground thickens. Colours deepen as raindrops cling to my lashes and break against my eyes. I pull my cloak up over my knees and climb down the castle wall. My foot slips on a toehold and I am yanked off balance. Locked into a costume that binds my body shut, I have no choice but to tumble and roll, tearing bits of the decrepit wall with me as I skid and slide—thud—to the ground. Then sit on the floor of this empty world and feel the rain pound against my veiled head and soak through to my hair.

It is pouring now. I crawl to an arched refuge and huddle, hold my knees in my hands, hold my spirits up, sing campfires songs and lullabies, listen to a muezzin wail in the distance. I sit, waiting for the rain to beat down the castle and wash me away to sea.

So Much
Ridiculous

THE VISA EXTENSION OFFICE in Shiraz must also be the office of a number of other things. If it isn't I cannot explain why it is so full: the only tourist I've seen in the last two months is Ian. We sit down and prepare to spend the entire day here. Being gracious.

The man in charge sits behind a desk and does a lot of talking. He is surrounded on all sides by people, but does not seem to mind. Does not order them away, does not ask them to stop leaning all over him. He listens to as many of them as possible and looks exceedingly patient.

I watch him for as long as it takes to understand the protocol (the more you lean, the faster you are dealt with), and walk up to the desk with our visa extension forms and photos. He smiles, nods, and asks someone to fetch two chairs, so that Ian and I can sit down in front of him.

We sit until the only people left around the desk are two women, one on either side of the man, both leaning so far over the paper on the desk that he can no longer see it. Finally he breaks, throws his hands down on his desk and asks the women to wait outside. He huffs and holds his head in his hands. Stares at the paper on his desk. Then at us.

This man has the power to kick us out of the country tomorrow. And I'm not ready to leave yet. I smile.

He huffs again. "What country from?"

"Canada."

He looks down at his papers. "Please," he motions us to lean over his desk. "Can you understand?" He shows us a telegram: ULT/SOUND NEG. SMALL LESION. NOT NEC. ABNORM. POSS DIAG: KIDNEY STONE.

Ian and I read the telegram, first silently, then aloud. Then lift our heads and look around the room.

"Is this the visa extension office?"

The man nods. "Please, what it mean?" he asks, pointing to the word "NEG."

"Negative. This ultrasound test was negative."

The man nods and points to LESION. Ian explains. Then the word KIDNEY. "Uh . . . this," Ian says, pointing to his side. "There are two . . ."

The man looks confused. I take a piece of paper and draw the shape of a kidney. The man purses his lips. Calls back the two women and explains everything to them.

They smile and nod, smile and nod. Lean way over the desk and pinch my cheeks. So hard it hurts. Smile and laugh, pinch my cheeks again and talk to Ian as though he were a saviour.

The visa extension takes no time at all. There is no interrogation, nothing of the grilling I was expecting. Only this question as we make our way out the door: "You like hejab?"

I smile and say nothing. It is the easiest response.

We attempt to flag down a taxi, but all are either full or not going in our direction. Eventually one does stop and prepare to take us, but when asked he quotes a price much higher than the one we paid to come out here, so we begin haggling. Haggling haggling haggling, until we attract several men off the sidewalk who enlist in furthering our cause. The last man that comes to our rescue leans into the cab, says something definitive and slams the door, then smiles to us, bows his head and points to his car.

He will take us, he explains. But first we have to go and pick up his mother.

His mother is an ebullient woman with the determination of someone who *gets things done*. She is babbling at breakneck speed long before she reaches the car, waving her hands around and above her head as she speaks. Once she settles herself into the front seat and receives our introductions, she fixes her gaze on me and tells me I should marry her son.

I point to Ian.

What does he do? she asks as though Ian were invisible.

He's a writer, I tell her.

She looks at Ian, makes a loud *pffft!* sound and waves him away like a bad odour. Then she makes the suggestion again: Marry my son, she whispers. He's a doctor. And he plays the piano. She laughs, heaves her upper body over the front seat and pinches my cheek.

Ian explains our plans to the doctor: that we are on our way to the tomb of the great poet Hafez, so if he could drop us off within walking distance, that would be great.

The doctor translates this for his mother. She *tsks* and hoists her arm back over the seat to explain that whatever our plans might have been, they've now changed. We're all going to her house. Hafez has been dead for six hundred years, so there's no rush to see his tomb. She, on the other hand, is seventy-two and might be dead tomorrow.

The first seven hours of our visit are spent watching videos: the wedding of her youngest daughter, the wedding of her oldest son, a pirated copy of the film *Ghost* (starring Demi Moore and Patrick Swayze) that is obviously the product of excessive copying: it is all static-snow with the occasional shadow that would suggest a figure on the screen, and no sound. The last video is a concert by the doctor. While we are watching this one, the doctor's mother sits beside me, nudging and pointing to the screen, even though I am already watching. Her son sways dramatically behind the keyboard and pounds out an extremely opulent version of "Some Enchanted Evening." His mother turns to me, raises her eyebrows, points to my wedding ring and nods persuasively.

"Do you watch film *Not Without My Daughter?*" the doctor asks quietly, sheepishly.

"No, but I've heard of it."

"You know it?"

"Yes."

"Please answer me: what is purpose of this film?"

"The purpose?"

"Yes. Is it for America some kind propaganda?"

"Well, it wasn't actually a government film—"

"—but it is very exaggerated. Not true Iranian life."

"Most American films are very exaggerated. That's just the way they are."

"But American people believe bad thing about Iran."

"Maybe they do, but I don't think *Not Without My Daughter* is entirely responsible for that. It has more to do with what people read about terrorism and fundam—"

"But that is something from government, not from people. I think government America do many kind of terrorism, for example America South: Chile. America Central: Nicaragua, El Salvador, many war and group terrorist. Vietnam also same. They kill many innocent, only because those government is not same like America. But this is something from government, not people. In Iran we know this difference. We say, sometime government America no good, but people America good. This most important. Also we see film from America, maybe about men bad with gun and drug and crime and government with lying and corrupt, but we say, this is film, something from imagination, maybe some true, but small."

His mother is yelling over her son's voice, demanding to know what he is saying. He tells her we are discussing *Not Without My Daughter,* a film about an American woman who marries an Iranian man. On a visit back to his country, the man's personality transforms into that of a violent fundamentalist beast. He beats her, holds her hostage in their home, and she is forced to flee the country illegally with her daughter.

When the doctor's mother learns that this is what we have been discussing, she bawls out her son and covers my ears with her hands.

Dinner's ready. The doctor's four sisters have been working on it since we arrived.

"Do you like some wine?" the doctor asks us.

"Uh, wine?"

"Yes," he says, pulling a plain green bottle out from behind a bookshelf. "I have only red."

"Uh . . . sure."

He pours three glasses.

"How illegal is this?" Ian asks, staring at his glass as though it were about to explode.

The doctor shrugs and looks blasé. "Not much. Maybe fifty lashing."

The three of us raise our glasses in cheers. Ian puts his glass down immediately, without taking a sip. I inhale the liquid so hurriedly that the *gulp!* is audible from across the room.

"You like meatloaf?" the doctor asks.

"Oh, yes. Meatloaf sounds great," I say, surprised that such a down-home American meal would be served in an Iranian home.

The doctor goes to his tape machine and puts on a much-pirated copy of a Meatloaf album from the seventies.

"And how many lashings for playing American music?" Ian squeaks.

The doctor smiles and takes another sip of wine. "Just a few."

It is almost midnight by the time dinner is over. The doctor's mother invites me to come back again tomorrow, but I explain—because Ian and I are both in need of solitude—that we have a very busy day tomorrow and after that we will be leaving Shiraz.

Leaving? she asks.

I nod. Thank her for a lovely day and meal.

Leaving? she asks again.

Yes.

She doubles over laughing. *"Not leave!"* she shouts. *"Not without my doctor!"* She laughs and laughs and laughs. So much that she has to sit down. Her son is so embarrassed his cheeks are glowing. His mother sighs, wipes her eyes and kisses me. She nods to Ian and says something to the doctor.

"My mother tell, don't be offended, sir. She is my mother. All mother are same."

ಎ

Alone in a mosque. Tiles of turquoise and the yellow of yolks. The beiges of sunburnt sand. Patterns of script swirl and circle each other, twisting and swooping, spinning into vines and flowers and teardrops that fall from the tip of the dome and get larger as they reach the walls. The temple is sobbing.

I stand in the centre, stare up into the dome, hold my arms out to the side and spin spin spin spin the colours smudging together until it feels as though I've dived into water, the shapes blurring and my eyes crossing I go flailing about the empty room trying to stay upright, shrieks and heaves, slapping these chilled hard walls crackling back at me in echoes until my butt bounces against the stone floor and the place is filled with laughter.

The sound God probably longs to hear.

ಎ

It is the sixth anniversary of the largest funeral in the world. The day when ten million vessels of sadness soothed the parched streets with their tears. Beating their fists to their own heads, stamping out the pain through their feet. Because it is too much for the body to bear, the pain of loss. The mourner wails out of necessity. Wails for the man whose words formed the life of a nation, whose teachings pierced time and resurrected faith, virtue and pride. The man whose eyes gored impiety, whose peremptory gaze set the Americans running like dogs. Khomeini's face was seen on the moon that lit the sky on the night of his return from exile. Such a man they lost six years ago.

It is said.

The television in the main room of our inn carries images of weeping masses of men and women groping the air for strength to bear this grief. They paw at ghosts.

The innkeeper enters the room, watches for a few minutes, then shrugs at us with his shoulders and lips. "They try to look sad," he says, beckoning us to follow him. On the wall hang portraits of Imam Khomeini, Supreme Leader Kha'menei, and President Rafsanjani. They are hung in the same manner as in every other inn, shop, office, restaurant in the country: in descending order. Imam Khomeini's portrait sits at the greatest height. One or two centimetres below that to the left hangs his successor Kha'menei, with Rafsanjani's beardless face taking third place on the podium. The innkeeper takes a seat behind his desk, runs a finger along the path of his nose and raises an eyebrow at Ian. As he pays for another night, Ian slips him a deck of cards we have carried from Istanbul.

(The previous evening, as we retired for the night, the same man had called us to his desk and initiated something of a charades game by shredding up bits of paper and sitting regally like a king on a throne. The more puzzled we looked, the more frantic he became, until eventually, after he had counted to ten so many times I thought he'd gone completely potty, we finally got it. Although chess was recently decriminalized, cards remain illegal and are, therefore, widely coveted. We have learned to shuffle quietly in sheltered locations.)

The innkeeper shakes Ian's hand and grins until his eyes twinkle, takes the playing cards and slips them into his pocket. His eyes flicker to the television—shots of bawling men shaking fists into the sky—and he makes a *shhh* gesture, smiling at us like an impish child. Ian and I put our hands over our mouths, hunch our shoulders and tiptoe onto the street.

I am wrapped tightly this morning; my nose emerges from black fabric like a chipmunk from a hole. It twitches, sensing delicacy in the air, a fragile balance. I am on edge today. Wary of setting people's tinder sensibilities on fire on this day of mourning. Ian wears a black shirt and trousers (his sanctity suit) for the same reason.

Shops are closed, the streets hollow, traffic is light but customarily life-threatening. Our bodies hesitate, bend, twist, leap and lope between cars until we plant ourselves firmly on the other side of the street and resume walking. We move towards the city centre in search of food and mourners of Imam Khomeini.

There is a pulse surrounding the main mosque as it prepares for a day of prayer. Thick Persian carpets are being rolled out across the courtyard to cushion the knees of the mourners, men gather around fountains to cleanse themselves of the impurities of an imperfect world. We skirt the crowds, sure that even in our gait we give ourselves away as infidels here for the spectacle, but our clothing affords us anonymity, and we are noticed by no one. Still, it is not our place. Our presence here feels irreverent. And is. We retreat through the twisting alleys of the bazaar, into softer light. And then we hear them.

At first it is the sound of childhood. The sound of late pancake mornings, rough wool skirts, knots being drawn out with a fitch and twisted into braids, the deep black grain of polished wood, and books with pastry-flake pages. That sound. It is as faint as a breath and yet it is all we can hear. It rolls above the traffic and turns the air into waves. We are drawn to it as to a scent.

We walk in tranced silence for several minutes, getting closer and closer, until we come to a high stone wall. "It is coming from behind here," I say and stand back on the road, running my eyes over the bits of jagged glass that run atop the wall.

"Yes, I can see bells! It seems inconceivable, particularly today, but just ahead there it looks as though there might be an opening of some kind, a gate, it will be locked, surely but hey, look the doors are open. Let's get a bit closer, just peek our heads in and *oh*—"

We are caught in the doorway by the seraphic gaze of a man, bearded, dressed in white, a length of plum fabric hanging from his shoulders like a scarf, and a skunk-striped collar around his neck. He stands in front of a domed building with his arms open at his sides.

Welcome.

As we draw towards him into the courtyard, the man's expression changes: suspicion and uncertainty fold his forehead into pleats. But he holds his stance and gestures to the open door beside him.

Welcome.

We exchange words of greeting, nods and standard responses, and follow him into the dim peace of a church.

This is a curious place. It has the reverberant shape of
a mosque, with dry arches and a dome like a monk's bald
head, but the formal arrangement of furniture Christian-
ity demands of its servants. The apse is made with sand-
coloured bricks. Arabesque ornaments twirl around it
in graceful simplicity, with turquoise-tiled crosses spun
into the design. Stained-glass windows offer sunlight in
lozenges of blue, red and green. It has a restrained elegance about it that makes me take deep breaths and
smile. The air has the smell of summer shade.

We take seats in the tenth and last pew and hold our
hands in our laps, uncomfortably. There are several rows
of people seated in front of us. I count the backs of twenty-
three heads, nine scarfed, fourteen hairy. Six children
who would stand at a height lower than my bellybutton
play in the aisle, one wearing a T-shirt with the word Buf-
foon written across the chest. The bells send out a final
call and we listen to the silence that follows. The minister
takes his place in front of the altar and conducts the Christian house into prayer.

The minister seems very capable, in that he speaks
for a long time without losing the attention of his audience, and with an impressive dynamic range. For the first
little while it is enough to enjoy the service as a vocal
concert, but words without meaning quickly grow dull,
and after half an hour I feel my enthusiasm yawning. And
then there is the singing, which is some of the lamest and
lost I have ever heard. The melody dies several times in
mid-phrase, only to be resurrected by a woman with
pursed lips who sings out of tune at top volume. In fact,
the entire ceremony is so cerebral, so lacking in passion
and zeal, that it is impossible to exult in anything but my

own supreme boredom. I begin to envy the children who have squeezed away from their parents and now flutter in and out of the church like pigeons. Ian passes me a note that reads "Allah Schmallah—I'll meet you back at the hotel, OK tenthead?" and weasels out of the building before I can decide if I want to join him.

Before too long, the service is over and the scant congregation filters by, giving me inquisitive glances as they pass. I notice the minister eyeing me too as he exchanges a few words with a woman in a pink coat. She nods, then approaches me, smiling.

"Excuse me, please, but are you a foreign lady? Canada? Oh, Dios mio! You are almost from my home! I am from Mexico! Welcome welcome! Our father was interesting to know who are you people—where is your husband?— in black dress, so serious, he was thinking maybe you are some Muslim fanatics!"

Whooping laughter shakes her body and pushes tears to the rims of her eyes. She is larger than life: a loud friendly voice that is immediately engaging, semaphoric gestures, wide billiard eyes and a smile that shows both rows of teeth. In addition to her pink manteau, something of a statement itself, she wears a lurid pink headscarf with a colourful fringe thrown lightly over her head. Her blonde hair leaks out from all sides.

"A*iiii!* So funny, fundamentalists from Canada! But why are you wearing such blackness? I know: you are scared from this country, I know! My family also was scared, too much television, stupid books, and not knowing our real situation, then they came for visiting, and I showed them it is not how they thought, so much kind and good, and now they understand much better, soon you will be the same, yes! Oh! I have an idea! I think that maybe you are becoming tired from your travels and want to rest for some time in our city, so you see, you can stay here because in our church we need an organist! You can learn! I am here nineteen years, yes, I see you are surprised, and here there are such good people, my husband, for example, the most kind from all men, we met in America, my father was working there, but he did not expect his daughter to meet some Iranian man, heee heee heee, and now I am here nineteen years, two beautiful children— but what is your name? My name is Esperanza and you are my friend, but everyone of our church will want to meet you now, please come with me, and I will introduce you to our wonderful people, we are a small group, but this is the best kind, I think so yes, this is Khosro and Jahan— I am telling them that you are our new organist—and Hossein and Farhang and Kamran and this is our father, I call him *el guapo* [the hunk], heee heee heee, and he is from Armenia, he is only here for few years, a very good man we all like him very much, during the revolution we had also our minister from Armenia, but one night his throat was cut by some cuckoos, poor man, and his wife, very nice lady, she was from America, and she went home after that, I can understand that, and this is Siwa and Lida, and *oh*—you must meet my friend Emma, she is from England so you can talk for days in your language!"

I am yanked back towards the entrance of the church, my head still bobbing from the string of recent introductions, to a staid figure in a pale blue coat and a scarf tied tightly under her chin. I am introduced as a Christian friend from Canada—the woman's wrinkles recede into a tired smile—and told to exchange life stories while

Esperanza returns to the minister to reassure him that I am a harmless tourist.

"A tourist?! Good Lord." Emma winces, then simpers. "Oh dear, pardon me, you can tell I'm not a regular. I only came back to the church three years ago. It's Pentecost today, you know, I thought I should at least make the effort—a tourist? How's that, then?"

I explain.

"I should have you talk to my daughter," she says, staring at the air between us. "She dies of boredom every night. She's sixteen, poor thing, there's nothing for her here— they'll bring around cakes in a minute. It's Pentecost today, you know . . ."

I turn and look in the direction of food, leaving Emma's daughter somewhere between here and boredom. A man arrives with a tray of cakes and insists I take four. Insists. Another man appears with glasses of orange soda, which he points to and says "*CA-NA-DA,*" before tumbling into laughter.

"It's the orange drink," explains Emma. "It's called Canada here, though come to think of it, I've no idea why. This man has asked me if it is a national food in your country, but I've told him it is not, and he wonders if Canada is famous for its orange soda. And if you have any children. He's just trying to be friendly, you know. They're all just trying to be friendly."

Their questions answered, the men bow deeply before resuming their rounds with cake and Canada.

"I beg your pardon? Oh, I've been here, what, twenty-two years now. I've seen it all." Emma chuckles and rolls her eyes, holding herself with her arms around her ribs. She has a chiselled mouth and pale eyes, her expressions are measured and rationed. "It's much better now than it has been," she muses, looking around at the trees in the courtyard where we stand. "We're able to do almost as much now as before the revolution. Everyone talks about missing the good old days, but the only thing they really miss is the television, stupid American talk shows, European serials. People no longer have the freedom to be perfectly stupid, that's all. And I remember the way men used to leer at me. I only had to wear trousers and a smart blouse to get the men going. Even if the hejab were to go eventually, I might take off the scarf, but I'm keeping this," she says firmly, tugging at her manteau.

Esperanza returns with more cakes.

"And I see my friend Emma keeps you all for herself! *El guapo* welcomes you, heee heee heee, but he thought you and your husband were devoteds of Imam Khomeini coming to our church to make some trouble, did you know about today, the anniversary of his wonderful death? *Aiii,* I am so wicked! But I tell you some truth about me: I am not in Señor Khomeini's fan club, oh no! I don't know what am I going to do if I go to heaven and see him there, oh I will be so angry!! Heee heee heee . . ."

"You've no need to worry about that," Emma cuts in. "God keeps him where he belongs." The two snigger with their hands over their mouths, delighting in the pleasure of outlawed desecration, then tuck their lips into their mouths as if caught doing something indecent.

"I remember when I had to make my token conversion to Islam before I married." Emma laughs. "I didn't speak Farsi at the time, so I went with my sister-in-law and the two of us sat behind a little curtain while the mollah said all sorts of things I didn't understand. I think we were supposed to be praying, but we just spent the whole time giggling. He didn't seem to mind, though, he simply jotted down the name of another convert and away we went."

"I baptized both of my children when I was visiting my family in Mexico," whispers Esperanza with a grin as wide as her face. "Sometimes they come with me here, but I don't push them, no, but every Sunday I say with a very happy voice, Hello, my wonderful children, does anybody want to come to the church with their lonely mother? And sometimes, do you know? They come! And then it is beautiful, or sometimes, like today, they prefer to stay at home, so I am not so lucky. You must meet them! First I drive Emma to her home, and you can meet her daughter Maryam, then you may come to my Mexican home for dinner, oh yes! But first come to see the rest of our ground!"

We stroll around the small but pleasant grounds, view the minister's quarters, a lovely rose garden, and what used to be the Christian hospital (now the Muslim hospital).

"We had so many bombs from Iraqis! I still remember, do you remember, Emma? We had some here and here." She points to corners of the property. "And soooo close to our beautiful church, but our colour windows, they did not break, not one! It was a miracle—" she kisses her hand and shakes it at the sky "—certain it was God's miracle! How can small windows stay like this, so perfect, when we have bombs just here? My son says it is only big glass, thick like camel's teeth, but I know it was a miracle."

After saying goodbye to each and every member of the congregation, we leave the church grounds. A car door is opened for me. I sit in this car and retreat from the conversation and draw imaginary outlines of my new friends with the blackest part of my eye. I colour them with the cadence of their voices and laughter, draw their stories as the sinew of their lives. They gesture the texture of themselves, Emma with the movements of a fine, thin brush, and Esperanza with bristles splaying out in all directions.

The car turns onto a narrow street filled with boys in the middle of a game. At the sight of our car, one boy scoops the ball and the rest line the street like toy soldiers, nodding and smiling as we pass. For a moment, I feel very regal. We park on the street and pass through a high gate—as essential a household fixture as the lawn is back home—to Emma's flat. The scarves come off the moment we are inside. Emma hangs her manteau in a closet. I throw mine over the back of a chair. "I cannot take my manteau off," Esperanza squeals. "It is so hot in these months, I wear nothing under! Heee heee heee . . ."

Emma leads us into the living room, then vanishes to fetch some food. We sit down on corduroy furniture and look at bare walls, listen to the murmurs of a man's patient voice in the next room.

"It's Maryam's tutor," Emma explains as she joins us with a tray of watermelon. "She's just finishing a two-hour session in maths. It's one of four different sessions per week, poor thing. All she does is study. There's nothing else for her."

Emma's forehead has become the repository for guilt; anxiety crouches between deep creases on her face and neck; she has no spare skin on her body. She places the plate of fruit in front of me, and I dive into it with both hands. Watermelon juice pours into my palms, forms rivulets along the length of my arm and drips from my elbow. Emma takes a seat at the end of a sofa and continues.

"She has her regular classes, and then she must take Arabic, Koran, religion and civil service on top of everything else. I'm sure this is what tires her. She has a tutor for Arabic and Koran, and one more for chemistry. It's too much, but all the children have them. I just wish she could study something she enjoyed. Do you know, she can't even find English classics in her school library."

Esperanza clears her throat and sits with a very straight back. "You are making such a bad story, Emma! Oh my friend, do not believe it is so bad for our children. Maybe Maryam's school does not have a good library, so she should come to my children's school. There are other schools. And so much studying? It is true, they are all good students, learning many things, but so bad? I don't think so. They can do sports, for examp—"

"She tried to do sports! She went to one of the girls' gymnasiums—there are *two* in this city and over fifty for boys—and was sent home for wearing a T-shirt and short trousers! There are great high walls surrounding the place, not a man in sight, but she was told she was indecently dressed! Oh she was furious when she came home, said she hated it here and wanted to—"

"It is just the age! My children say sometimes similar things, they hear it from their friends, I think, silly ideas. All teenagers are unhappy for some time, but we can be happy to have good children with good manners and good schools. With their education, they can go anywhere if they want, but they will come back—"

"I admit Maryam runs circles around her cousins in England. She finds the girls her age so childish and silly.

And when they compare what they are learning in school, it's ridic— Pardon? Well, of course I've *thought* about going back, but it's not a possibility. My husband is a doctor, you see, and he wouldn't be able to get a good job there. His future is much better here."

Emma hunches with her arms held straight, elbows locked, and her fists on her knees. It is a peculiar, awkward, position. I watch her. The way her eyes never settle as she is speaking.

"It's too much here, I admit, but England isn't the same place I left twenty years ago either. There's . . . oh look, there's almost too much freedom now; there don't seem to be any values left at all. When I listen to the problems my sisters are having with their daughters—" her eyes reel to the ceiling "—Lord, I am so *thankful* I live here. Two of my nieces suffer from anorexia, one is pregnant at sixteen, their best friends are having abortions and drug problems and they *all* have grown up obsessed with the idea that they must be seductive-looking in order to be women. Why why why? Why must they dress and act that way? For every Tom, Dick and Harry on the street? And then they talk of my poor poor Maryam, so oppressed in this country, oh I could murder them! They simply do not see how atrocious their own lives are! Of course they have freedom, but at what cost? They are being so manipulated—I can scarcely bear to look at them. And yet they find it so tragic that my daughter grows up in Iran . . ."

Emma is no longer awkward. She sits with her head resting in one palm, the other hand gripped around her thigh, and her legs crossed. Her eyes are fixed on a spot on the carpet. She blinks heavily, as do people who are weary of arguing.

"The same in Mexico! So many problems for the youngs! Smoking and drugs and teenagers, they don't respect! We hear such big problems in America: their schools are full with guns and students don't respect! Here our youngs listen, and our schools are very good places—"

"Well, yes, although I don't like being told that I must wear a chaador when I come to the school to talk to one of Maryam's teachers. It's something fairly recent, I used to be fine in just a manteau—"

"I don't know what silly things you are saying, Emma! I go to my children's school just like this . . ." Esperanza smooths her manteau against her lap with thick fingers. "And I am very welcome there, I think maybe you try to look only at bad things—"

A sliding door opens to the next room. A tidy man with a sheaf of books under his arms smiles and nods—no eye contact—and proceeds to the front door, followed by a young girl who scans the room and follows her guest. Emma rises from her seat and joins them in the doorway, chatting briefly with the tutor, thanking him and wishing him a pleasant evening.

Esperanza leans towards me while Emma is out of the room. "You will see maybe they are thinking some negative things," she whispers. "They do not trust enough in God."

Emma returns with Maryam, who wears a pleasant face, without smiling. She is slight, like her mother, but has a fuller skin and shoulders that hold strength and resolve. Her Iranian blood must live close to the bone, as it is invisible along the surface; her complexion is carved of alabaster. Approaching, she offers me a radiant smile in greeting, and I rise to shake her hand.

"Please sit down," she says, giving my hand a firm jerk. She walks with a confident elegance and sits on the floor on the other side of the room. I can't take my eyes off her dignity.

"My mother tells me you are a traveller," she says in a thick, plummy voice. "Could I ask you how you chose to travel in this country?"

I explain.

"You haven't had any difficulties, problems with the authorities?"

Esperanza flashes me a knowing glance, then returns her eyes to her lap.

"Even I do, occasionally, and I understand the customs. Just this past summer," she says with her wide eyes trained on mine, "we were up north on the Caspian Sea coast— have you travelled there yet? Yes, it's lovely, isn't it? Well, my father's parents have a summer house there, by the sea, and we usually go up there during school holidays. It was the first day of the summer holiday, I was riding my bicycle around the sea and my manteau kept getting caught in the pedals." She stands up to demonstrate.

"So I tied it up, here, just above my knees. Well, it wasn't ten minutes later, and I was stopped by two men—do you know about the Komiteh? It is a fanatic group. Yes, these men were from this group, and they told me I must get off immediately, that I couldn't ride a bicycle because I was a woman. I stopped and asked them why I couldn't ride; in the Koran women rode *horses*." She laughs and looks to her mother, whose mouth is relaxed around a smile.

"Well, they were a bit surprised by this, and one man said something like that was a time of war, I don't remember exactly, they just muttered some things, but then they told me to forget that because the *real* problem was that my hejab was improper. I was wearing a scarf and a manteau, which is perfectly acceptable, just tied, you remember, above my knees." She demonstrates again.

"So I quoted the Koran again, because you see it doesn't say exactly what must be covered, only that a woman must be dressed modestly, which I was. But they were getting angry and I knew that it didn't really matter what the Koran said, it only mattered what these men decided, and in the end they brought me home and talked to my father, telling him he needed to be more careful of me, and my father agreed and thanked the men for rescuing me, but when they were gone he just laughed and told me he was proud. But I can't ride my bicycle! It just sits there, getting old, like me."

She laughs, a short staccato chuckle, but anger grounds her voice quickly and pulls it into silence. Emma's eyes lunge to touch a spot on the carpet. Esperanza clears her throat, dusts tear ducts with a baby finger. Maryam leans forward and clutches a slice of watermelon, laughs as juice rains from her fist onto the table. She leaves the room to the kitchen, returns with a tea towel, wipes the mess, returns the tea towel, returns to the room, seats herself. She seems unacquainted with the awkward postures and gestures expected of someone in the depths of puberty. It is rare to watch someone so firmly planted in their earth. My mouth holds the word, *sagacious,* when I look at her, and I wince at memories of myself at this age, when skin and hair were of life-stopping importance.

"So you see, all of my Koran studies are worth the effort," Maryam smiles. "They keep me out of prison, at least."

"Is that true?"

"So much ridiculous!" Esperanza spouts, then erupts. "This is one small story and was she in some danger? No! It is much exaggeration! There are different customs here, yes, and so no bicycles for the girls, my daughter also she does not like, but she has two shoes, she can walk instead! And me, I did not have a bicycle in Mexico, so it is no problem for me, more important is that we are happy! God gives us so much wonderful, we must not always think about bicycles and hejab—"

"Except when we are arrested for—"

"Not arrested! They are so silly these girls at this age! They did not arrest! Only to warn and tell to your parents. It is only stories of arrested, OK, maybe some times after their revolution they took some women without proper hejab, but only to some office where they had to promise not to do it again, finish!"

I tell Esperanza about a book I had read before I left Canada. The interviews it contained with women who had received lashings for indecency: wearing nail polish or lipstick, having hair showing around the edges of a scarf. But she is laughing so hard she is barely listening.

"I don't believe a word! Hahahaha—who wrote this book? I think some people will say anything to make some money! Hahahaha—"

"It could have happened!" Maryam insists. "Those things *did* happen ten years ago, I remember people talking about it. That sort of thing doesn't happen any more, but it could have happened during the revolution."

"What happens now?"

"For nail polish or lipstick? Oh, nothing happens with that now, it's much less strict, some girls even wear blue jeans under their manteaux. Once, when I was in Tehran with my grandmother, we saw a girl wearing open shoes, like sandals, and she was wearing nailpolish on her toes!" Maryam's face sputters in disbelief. "I think it is more free in Tehran. If a girl did that here, they would take her and put her hands in a box with—" she fumbles with the English word and turns to her mother, who prompts, "— with cockroaches."

"Oh, so silly girl! They say those things only to frighten you! They are only stories, and you see, American women, they listen and write these stories in their books! Haha-haha—I feel sorry for people they need to say bad things about other people to make their money. Do you know Betty Mahmoody?"

They all groan and slap their foreheads in unison, as though the movement had been choreographed.

"Have you read this dirty book, *Not Without My Daughter*? Oh, she is a stupid woman—pardon to God for these words, but it is true. And there is also a movie! My family gave it to me, the video, and I became so angry, oh! She is a very rich woman now, I am sure, you see? She makes millions of dollars to tell all America how bad is this country. But it is not truth—"

"I read it," Emma says in such a way that each word takes a swipe at the air. "I don't think she's lying, but she strikes me as a profoundly stupid woman, she even admits that she was naive, totally uninformed, made no attempt to understand local customs. She couldn't even get her facts straight when it came to writing the book, which she didn't write, by the way, it was a ghostwriter, the same fellow who wrote that awful book about Turkey, oh you know. . . . *Midnight Express*—another great anti-Muslim book from what I gather. And there were so many factual errors, her writer obviously had never even been here! In the very first chapter you can see what sort of person she is. She didn't even give these people a chance, and they are so kind, you've seen them, it's extraordinary how kind they are. One of the first things her husband's family did was slaughter a sheep in front of her, for a feast to celebrate her arrival, they do it here as a show of great respect, it was done to welcome her, not a way to try to scare and disgust her, but poor Betty just could not begin to understand, oh honestly! If she had had *any* cultural sensitivity . . ."

"Only to talk about this Betty, it makes all the blood go to my cheeks." Esperanza is still holding her forehead. "It is a sad story, yes, of course, but there are many many happy stories, did she tell? No!" Hands on her chest now. "Did she tell about me and my wonderful husband—you will meet him, we will go to my home now," she says, pushing herself upright. "No! It is not for a book, such stories. It is only a bad story they will make a movie. You do not become rich from good stories."

"That's certainly true," adds Emma, who joins Esperanza on her feet. "No one is interested in hearing about my kind, gentle husband, or any of his kind, gentle brothers and friends. No one is making films about me, or the tens of foreign wives I know, who live here because we *want* to, and there are far more of us than there are Bettys."

We walk together towards the entrance. As I wrap myself up for the outside, Maryam laughs at my severe black cloak.

"You look like a very good Muslim! You must be very sad about Imam Khomeini" (long smile) "and tomorrow there is another holiday, but I'm not sure if it is a happy or a sad holiday. Just look at the television in the morning and see if the people are crying or laughing."

Emma laughs along with her daughter.

"There are so many of these holidays, it's hard to keep them straight. And some of them are rotating holidays, like Ramadan, so one of these years, a day of mourning is going to coincide with some joyous occasion like Khomeini's birthday. My husband jokes about how they will celebrate then." She moans and slaps her chest, then snaps her fingers in the air with a cheerful grin. Slap (moan), snap (smile), slap, snap, slap, snap.

"You see how much fun it is to live here?" Maryam rolls her eyes and looks at the wall. "Best of luck in your travels," she says after kissing me on both cheeks.

And I wish her luck, too, although I'm not sure why.

Esperanza's car. As we are driving, I try to imagine this place as home. Which is impossible, I know. But I do it anyway.

As I am imagining, I hear wisps of Esperanza's monologue. How beautiful is the weather here, she is so fortunate to live in a country with such nice weather, not like me whose body lives like ice cream, in and out of a cold place. How friendly and generous are the Iranian people. How tasty are some Iranian dishes, like chicken with sauce of pomegranate juice and walnuts . . .

And so on.

I watch her. Her indelible smile. Her determination. Her commitment. I let her mood swim over my own, pulling me back back back to memories of Mexico. Memories of that indefatigable Mexican spirit, the ability of even the most destitute to celebrate prosperous lives, to find pleasure in another's smile, in the magic of children, in the simple miracle of existence. To see life as a gift to be enjoyed. In whatever form it is given.

We arrive at the gates that veil her home.

"Here we are in Mexico, heee heee heee," she says, after unlatching the gate and pulling the car onto court-yard stones. Gate closed. Scarves off. We walk up steps to her house, and she pauses before opening the front door.

"My children are also silly teenagers," she whispers. "Sometimes they say some negative things also, but it is just the age. My daughter, fourteen, my son, seventeen. When they are older they will become wise. But in this time, they—"

Interrupted by a girl opening the front door into our conversation. She is smiling with both rows of teeth, very small teeth, teeth that make her look younger than her fourteen years. Long deep brown hair, skin the colour of cinnamon.

"*Buenas tardes!* It is my daughter! Shaadi, I present my new friend from Canada." (Tiny teeth open to let out a breath of disbelief.)

The explanation moves into the house and into Span-ish. Where we met, what I am doing here, that my hus-band waits for me at our hotel. Shaadi continues to smile. She looks at my face as though she were touching it. Her mother excuses herself and runs off to change into other clothes. I remove my manteau and sit on a sofa by the window. Shaadi sits beside me. And takes my hand.

"You are a traveller?" I nod. She smiles. Squeezes my hand. "Please, can I ask you a small question?" I nod. She smiles. Squeezes my hand. "Why do you come to this lost country?"

"And I see you become friends with my daughter! My daughter also has travelled, to Mexico and Turkey, so you can speak about many things! But first we will speak about our dinner—heee heee heee—because there is not so much to eat in my house, but is no problem, we will make some potatoes, some salad—oh yes, I have a good idea: when my husband and my son return, I will ask them to get us some hamburgers, it is a good idea? We have one restaurant near to here, where we can take the hamburgers and bring them to our home—so many good things we have in this country!"

Esperanza's eyes widen and attach themselves to the window.

"Already they come!"

The gate opens and two men walk through, one with such a severe limp that his entire torso buckles with each step. The limp of a disease rather than an injury. Esperanza runs to the front door and calls something to the men, who laugh.

"I tell them to come to help me make the dinner, heee heee heee. . ."

The lame man arrives first and bows to me with a hand over his heart.

"This is my husband, Hassan, you can speak with him perfect English, he lived for four years in America, and this is my son, Majid," she says of the tall stocky boy behind. He mumbles something to his mother, which she translates:

"He asks you please to call him Mario, this is his Mexican name, because he thinks after the high school he wants to go to Mexico for studying, heee heee heee, but right now he goes to restaurant to buy some hamburgers."

The men bow again and return outside. We watch them from the doorway, her husband hobbling like a broken puppet.

"And so you see, it is impossible for me to return to Mexico," Esperanza says on her way to the kitchen. "My husband is not so strong to move to another country and begin his work, so I must be happy to be here. And it is not difficult with such a kind husband, friendly friends, beautiful weather, some delicious food, but secretly—" she hunches her shoulders and lowers her voice "—our Mexican food is much much better, heee heee heee . . ."

"Of course it is," says Shaadi, who is peeling potatoes. "Many things are better in Mexico. Most things." She is laughing now. "Everything is better in Mexico! *Viva Mexico!*" She calls to the ceiling and shakes the potato peeler in the air. We are all laughing now.

"*Bueno,* my beautiful Mexicana, you will make some fried potatoes and a salad? And I will sit with our guest, good?"

We leave Shaadi and return to the living room.

"It is natural to love Mexico," says Esperanza as we settle ourselves on the sofa. "Of course I also love Mexico, it is my home, and sometimes it is difficult to live here, I can tell you, especially in the time of war, when I could sit right here on this chair and watch the bombs drop on the city, *aiiii!* Oh, I wanted to leave! Sometimes I could see even the missiles going right over—" she makes an arc with her finger over her head "—and I prayed so much! You saw how kind was the Lord with our church, my children don't believe it was a miracle with our colour glass, my son says it is only thick glass, but I know it was a miracle, and so I prayed for another miracle to save my house, but I didn't know how many miracles can the Lord do! And so in that time, it was difficult to live, but I think war is difficult in any country. I know you want to ask me about hejab and such things, and so I must tell about my good husband, so gentle, he knew it was difficult for me always to wear this hejab, but one day I became angry with always covering and I yelled like a Mexicana, *aaiiiii*, and I said, I want to leave this country! And I threw my clothes at my poor husband and I said, you wear this costume for one day, *one* day, and tell me this isn't hell, heee heee heee."

She covers her mouth with the palm of her hand, but continues to laugh. "And my husband was very understanding, and so he tries also to wear some hot clothes, to make me feel not so alone, and now it is summer and you see he wears a small jacket, heee heee heee. But it was not very nice, what I said about the hell, and I apologized to him, and to God, and now I am very happy here. Both help me to be happy."

The men return with a bag full of hamburgers, which Esperanza lays on plates, alongside Shaadi's salad and fried potatoes. Her husband says grace, and we embark on a meal that is the closest thing to McDonald's that Iran can offer. It is an evocative experience. I spend most of the meal watching this family enjoy itself, the way brother and sister laugh and live in each other, share jokes, words, the language of this country. I stare into the thoughts and shadows of these Mexican-Iranian children, trying to understand how their blood must feel. I climb into Esperanza's faith and imagine the world from there. And at the end of dinner, I listen to her husband tell me, so proudly, how much he loves her.

After dinner, I say, "It is late. My husband is surely worried. I must get back to the inn. No, really, I must."

There are goodbyes, but no good-lucks this time. It's not about luck, I realize.

The streets are empty now, as Esperanza drives me back. The smell of saffron rice makes pillows of the air, comforting ones I want to rest my head on. The sky is dark, but for the milky light of the moon. And Esperanza's teeth, enamelled stars, that twinkle from light years away. As we near the city centre, she asks again if I wouldn't consider the job as organist for their church.

Heee heee heee.

I point out the inn and she pulls up to the door. She takes my hand and tells me that someday I will know God and be happy.

I thank her for dinner. We exchange farewells and kisses and I wave from the street. I climb the stairs to the inn and am deafened by the wails and prayers coming from the television, which now sits on the innkeeper's desk and faces the street. The volume is up so loud the sound comes out shredded and crumpled. Just behind is the innkeeper's room. The door is ajar. I peek into the small crack of light and see him, with Ian, in the middle of a game of cards, the television masking the sound of shuffling to any mourners who might happen to walk by.

I abet the crime by not interfering, sit down in front of the television, stuff corners of scarf into my ears. And watch the sadness. Devotion and sadness. Watch it until it trickles the length of my spine. Until it cries within me. Cries so far inside of me that I no longer feel my skin.

I feel weightless, buoyed by a spirit of sorrow and bliss, by the voices and wails of faith. I float inside my mind, into a language without words, into a dim peace, where I rest.

When I awaken—Ian's hand on my arm—I feel I have touched this place.

ೞ

My request to call Canada is overheard by the three women behind me. They stroke my face, peek under the back of my scarf to see my hair. Smile and laugh and tug on my cheeks.

We sit down together and wait for an international line. For two and a half hours.

"Canada!" the clerk calls from the counter. "*Cabine chehar!*"

I rush to telephone cabin four, pick up the receiver and wait for the connection. I can hear the hollow line, how my breath sighs into a void. I feel my heart beat through my throat, listen to the quickness of it, how anxious I am to touch home.

She'll be outside, it will be evening—no, around noon. August, so fresh corn on the cob that will leave baby teeth marks in the butter. Thick slabs of tomatoes from the garden, sleeveless dresses and hair that's still damp from the pond. She'll be eating outside. Corn, tomatoes and a huge green salad with dressing that gives you garlic breath for days. Outside on the back porch, where she can see the hill, the sunflowers, the blue jays bossing the chickadees around. Surrounded by dogs: Sox, Alex, Sebastian, Mugs, who will be seated around her like parliament members—she is, after all, the speaker of the house—and the cats, Figleaf and Foliage, perched on the trellis like tightrope walkers or lying next to the dogs, ready to pounce on the first tail that dares to move. Having dinner. If there's a breeze, the poplars will shimmer like stalks of crepe paper—*ssshhhhhhhh*—telling the earth to be quiet. The air will smell of . . . I'm not sure. I close my eyes and try to imagine it. Can't. I smell this telephone, the last thirty people that shouted into it, the smell of dirt and sweat and cramped quarters made of metal and rubber and glass.

"Canada?" The voice of the operator.

"Yes, yes. *Baleh*."

"One moment."

I close my eyes. Wait for the first ring. She will put her plate down. One half-eaten cob lying on one of Gramma's crimson plates. The second ring. Open the screen door, hop over the fan. Third ring. Trip over Figleaf, who has followed her inside, and pick up. Fourth ring.

"Sorry I can't take your call. Please leave your name and number and I'll get back to you as soon as I can."

I hold the receiver with two hands. Press my head against the glass. Wait for the goddamn beep.

"Hi, it's me. Everything's fine. I just called to . . ." My voice cracks. "I was just thinking . . ." I chew my cheek and take a deep breath. "Maybe I'll try again later, it's just that it's sort of an ordeal to call—"

I'm cut off. Either that or someone has driven a nail into my stomach. I replace the receiver, slowly, awkwardly. Ache. Lean against the door until it pops open. Step into the open air of the post office. Walk to the counter. Wait for the cost of the call to be tallied. Try to breathe.

"Canada," says the clerk. "Canada very good."

I perform a thin smile. Thank him.

"I go to Canada," he says, smirking.

I nod. Pay for the call. Am about to leave the building when one of the cheek-pinchers takes my arm and asks me to wait. The other two have gone to get their husbands and will be right back. Will I wait, please?

I sit with her in silence. Wondering where my mother is, trying to imagine where she could be, why she didn't answer. I begin to wonder if something has happened, maybe she's fallen, slipped on the hill and broken her leg, unable to crawl back to the house, stuck out there for hours maybe days in the rain, and oh God, I should call someone to go and look in—

Nudged out of my neurotic stupor by the other two cheek-pinchers, standing in front of me with their husbands and questions about immigrating to Canada. They ask detailed questions about the immigration process, want my opinion about illegal entry. Should they rip up their passports on the airplane or not? How much money will they need for a good life? Is it better to apply as engineers or businessmen?

I cannot help them, know none of the answers. I know only what other immigrants have told me. That no matter how much money and how beautiful the life and the city and the weather it never quite feels like home, and why one piece of ground smells different from another no one knows, but it does and no matter how familiar it gets it will always be ground, never grounding. You get there—the other place—only to discover that home is deep in the innards and can only truly be removed by surgery, complicated emotional surgery, and nine times out of ten there

are unforeseen complications and there is haemorrhaging
and scarring and a dull ache like a cramp that flares up on
cold damp days or hot days, beautiful summer days when
everything is pleasant enough except when the wind blows.
And even the trees speak a different language.

I smile into the earnest faces of these men. Give them
the name of someone I know at the Canadian embassy
in Damascus who will be able to answer their questions.
Wish them luck. And happiness. I leave the building, the
sun slaps my black back, and I walk to my hotel listening
for leaves.

AN ANGEL
AT THE AIRPORT

T HE PERSIAN GULF. A heat that makes me grit
my teeth and squint, wilt, as I am drawn into it, as
my body is wrung out into my clothing. Diarrhoea
of the pores. Forty-eight degrees. Humidity so high that if
I pulled a sock out of my bag, it'd be soaking wet within
minutes. The socks on my feet were soaking wet hours ago.

We search for a bed for the night. Trudge. Ache. Feel
like I'm walking around on my knees, but look down
to see my legs outstretched. The bag in my hand feels like
a boulder. No room in the first inn. Or the second or
the third or the fourth. Fifth one stinks so badly of piss
and sulphur that the smell actually hurts. Leaning my
face through a hole in the wall to ask about a room. Yep,
they've got one, but no water. We'd have to use the public
showers at the end of the street.

Collapse.

The legs of a newborn foal. Bent and crumpled underneath me. Cannot stand. Cannot balance my weight over
my limbs. Flopped out on the floor like an unpitched tent.
Ian crouches with water, offers to hobble me downstairs,

away from the smell, back to the street. I stand, steady myself, and see a deer caught in headlights: a man with his mouth open in shock. Then slowly, slowly, smiling. Until all of his teeth are showing. "You are English speaking," he says in a breathy voice. We nod. He leaps from his seat and crouches beside us. "I am Amir. I have a Norwegian girl-friend." He pulls a photo from his shirt pocket. A pass-port photo of a fair-skinned woman wrapped in a sari. "This hotel is a little bit terrible, please let me help you to another arrangement."

Amir carries our bags. Ian and I limp down the stairs behind him. "You do already too much walking for this weether. Sir, you do not understand that heat of the woman in this clothing. It is very dangerous. Too much sweeting. You must drink very much to replace the sweet. Also it is not good to walk at this time, the hottest moment. Please wait in this shade while I search for your arrangement."

Amir returns with two possibilities. One very nice hotel with air conditioning and shower in the room. This is thirty dollars. Another is not so nice with "cool fan" and showers in the main hall, but much cheaper, 8,000 rials. Under three dollars.

Amir settles us in to the cheaper arrangement and says he'll come back to get us when the weather is cooler. "Sleep," he tells us. "It is the best thing for your bodies." We take his advice, but only after washing, one at a time, in the shower room down the hall. I begin perspiring again the moment I turn off the water. My clothes sit in a damp heap in one corner of the tiled room and the thought of putting them all on again for the walk down the hallway is so depressing, I decide to do the unthinkable. I leave on my plastic shower sandals, slip my soaking wet body into my manteau, button it down to my knees, tie my scarf around hair so wet it is dripping, pleasurably, down my back. Open the door and prepare to walk down the hallway like this. Bare from the ankle down.

I am a third of the way down the hall when two men walk out of the stairwell. I notice them noticing, my bare toes, my ankles, the bottom half of my shins; reacting as though they'd just received an electrical shock; looking away; walking to their room; taking one more peek as they close their door. I stop in my tracks feeling naked and shameful.

Amir wakes us with soft knocking. "Hello?" he whispers. "Do you sleep? The weether is much nicer now, good for walking."

Ian rolls out of bed and groans. "Just a minute."

I sit up to discover that my skull has cracked above my temples. Fissures that I can feel with my fingers. I would swear it. My eye sockets have been carved out with a pickaxe, and whoever did that also ripped my lips off.

"Have we eaten yet today?" Ian asks, massaging his neck.

"Watermelon."

"That was yesterday."

"Oh. Then no."

It is evening. The temperature of the air has dropped from forty-eight degrees to just under forty. The boardwalk along the water is full of people out for an evening stroll or going to do business in the bazaar. Amir takes us to a squalid restaurant that sells seafood fresh from the docks. He orders a strange assortment of squiggly things and sprinkles ample amounts of salt over each one. "Eat this, then we will go to my place to drink a lot of sugar. After that you will feel better."

We do as he says. His face is so full of concern we can't bear to disappoint him. When the last hunk of squidgy flesh is gone, Amir settles the bill. No no no no. He *insists*. We thank him and continue our walk along the boardwalk.

"This place," he points to a hut with a thatched palm roof at the edge of the shore. "This is my place I started with my friend. Just a small coffee house, but a nice one." He greets the men sitting outside next to the samovar with handshakes and introductions, then leads us to a bench overlooking the Gulf. "Would you like some tea?" Amir asks. We nod. "Good," he says. "It is our only product."

We drink glass after glass of sweet black tea spiced with cardamom, cinnamon, orange peel and ginger. With each glass I feel less ragged. I feel myself coming slowly back to life.

"I bring this recipe from India. For ten years I lived there, four years with my girlfriend." He draws the photo from his shirt pocket and shows it to us again. "We were together four years in India. I was buying and selling: silks, handicrafts, passports. Good life. After four years my girlfriend got accepted for school in England, and I came back to Iran. My mommy had a bad heart, I wanted to see her, but it meant also military service. Two years I did it, but I was like an animal in the cage, just going crazy wanting to get out. Whole time I was trying to plan how to get out. It was like a prison time."

Amir notices our empty glasses and hails his friend for refills.

"After military service I came here to Bandar-é Abbas. In my family village there is no work, so my friend from military asked me to come here, and we started this coffee shop for my Indian spice tea, but after one month a businessman asked me to work with him, smuggling from Dubai some electronics and kitchen machines for a big profit. First it was okay, then after twenty days our government made the dollar fall. Before, I could buy 8,000 or 9,000 rials with one dollar. Now, only 3,000. I lost everything. Two thousand dollars. It's all my saving." He takes a deep breath and finishes his tea.

"My girlfriend waits for me in India until I get my passport, after military service it takes about one year. Also she waits until I make some money, I need it for the trip and for starting some business for us. I called her after I lost all of my dollars. I told her not to wait for me, but she is crazy for being with me. She says she wants to come here, become Muslim. You see she sends me her photo looking like Muslim with something over her hair. She wants to be with me very much, but I know she cannot be happy here. I know it's not the good life." He stares at the photo and files it back in his pocket.

An urchin appears, a small tattered boy with dirt for skin. He lingers at an empty table, his head lolling from side to side, trying his hardest not to look at us directly. He is barefoot. His hair matted flat against his head. Amir calls to him and the boy approaches, timidly, keeping his eyes on the ground and a hand over one side of his face. Amir takes a handful of bills from his pocket and stretches them out to the boy. The boy takes the money and turns away. He has the ceramic face of someone who has cried all of his tears out.

"He is from Pakistan," Amir explains. "His father died and his mother remarried. That husband didn't want the children of another man, so she must get rid of them. It's very common in those countries. This boy doesn't know how he came to Iran or how long he is here. Now he sleeps on the street, so I try to help him. Sometimes people try to steal his blanket, sometimes the police pick him up, so I try to help. I give him money for food, or I give him some foods to sell, but he never asks. Only stands like this you saw, hoping I will help him. I know someone with a factory in Pakistan, maybe he can be happy there, in his home country."

We watch the boy make his way towards the bazaar, shrinking from anyone who approaches him, as though he were preparing to be hit.

"If I help him go back to Pakistan," Amir says, forcing a smile, "I'm sure God will give me a good life." He hails his friend and orders another round of tea. Squints, and looks out to the sea.

᠅

We hitch a ride to the airport on the back of a pick-up truck. It is crowded with women wearing bright red pointy masks that make them look like cardinals. (The birds, not the men.) They wear scarves as well, these bird women, brightly coloured like the rest of their clothing: relatively revealing swaths of fabric and tight, beaded leggings. And they wear sandals. I spend the entire ride staring at their toes.

We drop them off at the docks, where the toughest-looking men I have *ever* seen ferry passengers and smugglers across the Gulf in long wooden motorboats. These waters are so infested with sharks, they say, that you barely get a chance to notice you've fallen overboard. I spot our boatman from yesterday's trip to Hormoz, one of the Gulf islands: his scarred, squinting face, the long, dark scarf around his forehead. He governs these waters and knows it. A man of pirate proportions.

As we drive into the outskirts of Bandar-é Abbas, the wind picks up and hurls dust across the road in gusts. By the time we reach the airport, I have my scarf pulled right down over my face and feel sand crunching against my teeth. Ian is coughing and holding his eyes, trying to give the truck driver some money. The driver rolls down the window and a swirl of dust blows into his face. He refuses Ian's money once—*cough cough*—refuses again—*cough brush the sand out of eyes*—and accepts when Ian offers a third time. Cranks up his window and drives away.

Ian and I wrestle our way against the wind. The palm trees in the parking lot bend and recoil like Slinkies. Garbage tumbles around us and pastes itself against cars and walls. Minutes after we enter the terminal, the building loses power, and the windows become opaque. There is the sound of a hundred tiny fists against glass. Windows being pelted by blowing sand.

All planes are grounded. All ground transportation is blind and immobile. It's eleven o'clock in the morning, but somehow we all know we'll be sleeping here.

There is a kiosk selling newspapers, pamphlets by Islamic scholars, and posters of Imam Khomeini, Supreme Spiritual Leader Kha'menei, President Rafsanjani, Imam Hossein and assorted soccer stars. I buy a guide to proper prayer for children, illustrated with pictures of a pious preschool girl in a white sheet. There is only a handful of benches in the building and all are occupied. There is no restaurant or waiting room. But there are prayer rooms, segregated ones, and I know there will be carpets to rest on.

The women's mosque is a room with red woollen floors, as I had hoped. Women line the edges of the room, their backs against the walls, their children rolling around the centre of the carpet like circus animals. Many of the women have pulled their scarves down, eased out of their cloaks, some are breast feeding. It is unthinkably hot and stuffy. The sand storm has clogged any ventilation there might have been. The place feels and smells like a locker room.

I stretch out and unwrap myself. Use my scarf to wipe the sweat from my face, my neck, my chest, then use it to rehydrate myself, by putting it into my mouth and sucking on it. It is so hot that any measure of concentration is impossible. I sit, like all of the other women, and watch the children. Doze off. Try not to be hungry.

Every once in a while, someone ventures out to assess the situation. They always return with the same expression: raised eyebrows and a look of exhausted resignation. Sometimes a plea to Allah, but mostly not. The storm rages for hours. Then the cleanup begins, the rearranging of sand: shovelling it away from the building, off the runway, sweeping it off the planes and out of all of the cracks and openings. Periodically, Ian stands outside the door of the women's mosque and calls the latest developments through the curtain. Along with the news that he feels like he might be developing athlete's foot.

By eleven o'clock that evening, more people have arrived in the hopes of catching evening flights, but nothing is moving yet. The building swells and swelters with more bodies. I return to the women's mosque and try to stretch out, but my legs keep getting run over by children and more and more women keep arriving. I sit and take up as little room as possible. Ian announces through the curtains that there is talk of flights resuming fairly soon, and that he is hungry and in a terrible mood.

"You'd think they'd find a way to get some food out here," he grunts.

"Why would you think that?"

He huffs and stomps away.

There is a woman standing by the doorway. She walked in a few minutes ago and looked around the room, wondering, I suppose, if she could stand to sit down in here, and realizing that there was nowhere else in the airport to sit. Now she stares at me. The English-speaker. And starts a conversation with her eyes. *Can you believe this mess? What can we do? It's too hot for words. Can I sit next to you?* I shift and make room for her. She sits down and loosens her covering, fans herself with a flap of her scarf, smiles and introduces herself.

Fereshté asks all of the standard questions—*where from? what do you do here? what? why?*—and watches the other women in the room closely to see if anyone is listening in on our conversation.

"And how is your hejab?" she asks.

"Very hot."

Fereshté throws her head back and laughs. "Yes, of course it is hot. But is it difficult for you?"

I ask if it is difficult for her.

"Of course, but I must adjust. At my work—I am a laboratory technician—I have a white coat and a lighter scarf, but here the weather is very hot, and I must wear a thick coat, like you." She sighs and fans herself. "Even these young girls, Islam says they must start at nine years old. And for men—" she shrugs and looks at the ceiling "—they are free. Just with shirt. Very comfortable. Sometimes . . ." She leans towards me and whispers. "Sometimes I think God is a man."

Fereshté watches me, my reaction, before she laughs. Glances over her shoulder and smiles around the room. Suggests we go for a walk outside. The sun has set, and there could be a small wind.

I'd love to, but is she sure we have time? Couldn't flights resume at any moment?

"Oh no," she laughs. "There is nothing to worry. I heard the officials say that the first flight will be at three-thirty this morning." We button up and prepare to leave. "And probably they will give the first aeroplane to the families of martyrs."

We walk out of the airport and into the desert. At the edge of the parking lot I spy Ian flaked out on his back along with a dozen other men. He doesn't see us; we blend into the night. We walk and walk and walk. Away from the lights and the noise to a small spot of sand, where we sit. Lie. Watch the stars.

"I am embarrassed for you to see my country like this," she whispers. "There is so much bad to see, maybe you are thinking it is just a crazy place, full of bad people. And it is true there is a lot of bad . . . Of course you know about our revolution . . . well, I was supporting that revolution, but I didn't know this would be the result. Maybe only a few people guessed it. In time of Shah, our country was so artificial, very rich and beautiful, but inside it was like rotting fruit, just collapsing, without strongness or taste. We lived only for something outside. After revolution, everything is different. Many things are much worse, oh much worse, but some things, some important things are okay, more true. It is a difficult life, but some things are more honest. People are more clear, less artificial.

"It is so strange now to think about it, time of Shah, because in this time the life was so different. Religion was something almost like a protest, even wearing the chaador was something like revolutionary, it seems ridiculous now, but you must understand that we never imagined this. This result . . ." She curls up her hands in front of one eye, making a telescope with her fists, and stares at the sky. "I never imagined I would live this way, in such a place. This is not God's world, here, where I live. I am still looking for that."

She reaches over and brushes the back of her hand against my cheek. "Soft, young skin," she says and smiles. Brings her hand back to her own face and tucks it under her head as a pillow. "You live in a soft, young country. It decides your face."

We lie on our sides in the dark and watch each other's eyes. The stories they hold. She shifts her head and draws out her hand again. Returns it to my cheek, then dances the tips of her fingers along my forehead, my nose, my lips; leans closer and traces the curves of my ear, tugs at my scarf and twists her fingers into my hair. I close my eyes and smell her scent, her sweat; how much it smells like the desert. She leans away and smiles. Rolls onto her back and returns to the stars.

"Do you know what is interesting?" She is whispering, even though there is no one around. "God did not mean this." She lies with an arm thrown over her face, so her speech is muffled. "He does not mean this way, the way it is here. This black shame, so much fear and anger and killing. After revolution, the Imam changed law so girls can be executed at age of nine; for boys the age for execution is sixteen. And worse——" she lifts her arm and lets the points of her fingers rest on her eyes "——do you know about *mut'a* marriage?" I ask if she means the "temporary" marriages, those state-sanctioned arrangements that can last as little as twenty-four hours; that are known as "legal prostitution."

"Yes," she sighs and throws her arm back over her face. Speaks softly, slowly, dully. "They used the *mut'a* before executions. In early days of revolution, many thousands of girls were arrested for being supporters of opposition groups or for violating Islamic code and sent to die. Those people, those fanatics, believe that a girl who is virgin goes automatically to heaven, and they did not want these prisoner girls to go to heaven, so they arranged *mut'a* marriages with some prison guards, and these men—temporary 'husbands'—raped these girls before they were executed. And these men . . ." She turns, and says with a jaw so clenched it looks wooden, ". . . talk of *God*. God."

She speaks this last word as an echo, a hollow sound that falls into emptiness and dies.

We watch the stars.

And she sings to me. Softly. Songs from her childhood. Sombre, lilting melodies that sound like the gentle ripples the tide leaves on sand.

When her grainy voice breathes into silence, she turns and asks, Where am I looking, what do I see? I point to the deep, still light of a planet. Jupiter. With binoculars, I tell her, you can see its moons. She squints and focuses, trying to imagine. "How do they look?" she asks. And I try to remember when I saw them for the first time, way back when. Lying on the dock with my toes dipping into the lake, naked as a jaybird after a swim on a sultry night in July, and holding the plastic lenses up to my eyes. Hoping to get closer to the sky, I suppose. And there it was. That matrix of brilliant white light. I don't know if they were moons, actually, the things I saw. They were either moons or angels. Beams of angled light suspended in orbit around the glow.

"And please," she asks. "Please explain me about angels."

As I speak, she holds my hand. Closes her eyes. Smiles a faint, light smile and rocks herself, gently, in the sand.

The Colour
of Old Blood

EIGHT BRIDGES arch over this river.
Eight graceful stretches touch the land on either side.

Eight bridges as old as the idea that stone will allow us
to walk on water.

Observe this miracle: I am walking on water.

I sit in a tiny octagonal room, a teahouse under a bridge. I
am a troll drinking tea in a room with eight sides. And
something about this exercise delights me.

The room is thick with carpets and dark warm air. I rest
against tasselled pillows that smell of smoke and spices
and a people I will never understand.

I watch the others in the room, the men, the way they
lounge so freely. Beautifully. I look at the shape of their
chests, follow the outline of their legs through their
trousers. Sink my eyes into their dense, dark hair. Enjoy
the spectacle of beauty.

And look away, to the river.

I sit like a bloated sponge. Thick with sweat and the exhaustion of living in hiding. I must protect these men from themselves. Must shield them from temptation. They are unable to control their desires; as I am. So I must tent myself. Because they are not strong.

As I am.

ॐ

"Oh! oh! oh, I am without breath! Oh, let me some seconds for breathing kind friend! So quickly am I running to welcome you that air is leaving me! My breath is too much heavy! Can you hear it little bit squeaking? Oh, yes! Listen, my friend, when am I breathing: *pant pant wheeeeze pant pant*. Some small squeakings, I think you hear them. Haha! And oh my! There is also some sweating on me! Oh, dear! I am wanting to give you my hand, and then I notice there is some water! Please I am asking for your forgiveness! Only am I wanting to wish you hello! Welcome, my friend!"

I was on my way to a tea house, to lounge on thick woven cushions and suck on sugar cubes, when I noticed them: crosses spread into hot metal gates. Doors to Christ. I stretched to get a closer look.

The gates were surrounded on both sides by stone walls that were too high to climb. And locked. A deep iron lock that sank into the centre of the earth. I rang the bell and was greeted by a fuzzy intercom voice.

"I am a tourist," I told the box in stilted Farsi. "Is this a church?" The intercom went silent. I adjusted my scarf for the hundred-and-third time that morning and was tucking a sweat-soaked curl out of sight when I heard the *shuffle skid shuffle shuffle* of someone walking with slippers several sizes too large.

A key was put into the hollow door and clanged like pebbles rolling down a slide. A latch released, and the gate swung open to the reticent face of a boy.

"Hello, I am a tourist from Canada," I repeated in Farsi. "Is there a church here?" The boy looked puzzled, moved away and took baby steps backwards all the way across the courtyard and up ten steps into a house, leaving one slipper in the middle of the yard and the other on step number four.

A few minutes later, a man appeared in the doorway and gave me a giant wave that used his whole arm and wafted above his head like a flag. "Hello, friend! Please only to wait for some minutes! I must find some clothes for my feets!" He ducked back into the house and waved again, this time with a shoe in each hand. He fumbled awkwardly with the laces, rushed down the steps combing his hair into place with his fingers, got halfway down, threw his hands up in the air and bolted back up the steps, two at a time. "My keys—haha—I am coming so quickly I did forget having my keys!"

He is, without a doubt, the most animated and ebullient person I have ever met, not in a way that makes me want to retreat to the nearest dark corner; the opposite: in a way that draws me out of myself and into his world of enthusiasm. This is a man wholly enthralled by the art of living.

"Oh, my breath it is becoming slower now, aaahh. I am just returning from giving service in other church, much bigger one, did you see it on other side of city?" (No pause.) "You must see it sometime! Very nice, and do you know, we are doing whole service, even if we are only ten, and they are laughing at us, those secret polices, I know they are laughing, but we are continuing. Maybe they are thinking we are so crazy doing whole service for today only eight peoples, but we are doing! Haha! It is not forbidden, this service, but of course they do not like it. They are hoping maybe we will just stop, but we do not sit. No! I am like dog with big mouth. I continue saying, even when they do not like what am I saying!

"Please to join me visiting our church, a small one, okay, but oh such beautiful. First just to open door . . . there is some . . . sticking with my key . . . aha, here . . . please I will put my feets after your steppings."

It is a small church with a modest altar, an alcove lined with low benches and ceilings full of prayer. We walk in silence to the end of the aisle.

"Very beautiful stained glass," I whisper.

"You see how much beautiful! It is something very special. Come come! You see this one in corner? It crashed by Iraqi bombs—oh, they did put their bombs everywhere—and what did I do? Cry for the broken? No! I did collect all small pieces of colour glass and I did find some craft maker, you know, old one, so careful work he does, and he did make again this window so beautiful! Look, look my friend, look how beautiful! Maybe you say, oh, I can see some difference from other windows, OK! Also I can see some small differences, but it is not so important, I think. Important is how we are feeling and peoples when they are coming here they are looking at this work of my craft maker, and do you know how they are feeling, my friend?" (No pause.) "Of course they are feeling very good! Good they are feeling!"

As I stare up at the coloured light, my scarf slips from my head. I catch it before it falls and reclip it under my chin.

"Please you can remove your big black hat—haha, this is how do I call this costume—because I know these Muslims are telling to you always to cover, oh yes, we must not see hair of womans! Why? Haha! Do you know their explainings? They are telling something so silly about strong vibratings coming from hairs of womans and making the mans to go crazy. Imagine such sillies! Oh my friend, here you are on Christian ground, so do yourself as your home."

On the way out of the church, I yank down my scarf and use it to wipe the sweat from my neck. Outside, I feel unexpectedly raw. Vulnerable. After months in this country, months of living under the sheltered anonymity of this cloak, it is suddenly a strain to feel comfortable without it. My scalp tingles against the sunlight. As though my hair were on fire.

The children in the courtyard stop playing as we approach. A tall, lanky boy with red hair smiles and blushes all the way down his neck. A young girl looks me up and down, rushes over to her older brother and whispers something in his ear. The little boy who opened the gate holds a red ball in front of his chest. His arms don't quite reach around it. He looks at the ground and gradually brings his eyes up up up to my level, then bounces his gaze off to the side and drops the ball.

My friend struts towards the house but stops in mid-stride. "Oh, my workshop!" His hands fly to his head and he motions in the other direction, spins around and strides ahead of me. "I am wanting to show to you it—

yes, it is good idea, many interesting things I am keeping
there, some things, for example, tools and, well, such
things as tools and—here you are seeing with eyes from
your own head."

It is a meticulously organized shed, each hammer with
its own home, not a nail out of place. There is one wall
covered by several hundred keys. The way the light plays
on them from behind, they look like iridescent shingles
or scales. The wall looks like the side of an enormous
fish. "And to see my pipes," he says, throwing his arm out
to the side, pointing to the most extensive collection of
pipes I have ever seen. Chrome-plate pieces jutting out at
all angles. A giant metal hairball.

"I have one assistant, blind boy, so good, so good
worker he is. I am giving him tools, showing him some job,
he does it so nice, yes, so nice he does it. Not half an hour,
okay, maybe two hours, but he is good, no stealing from
me, no! Do not even come such thought in your head! He
is good, and I am happy for him." He locks the shed with a
heavy padlock and turns around to face his property.

"Oh, to look at so little, my friend, sometimes it is sad
thing for me. So much we did have before, so much
things confiscated: Christian hospital we did have, two
schools for blind, one orphanage. After revolution, little
thing after little thing, they did take it. For our schools
they told it is against Islamic law to have girls with boys,
but I told to them they are blind childrens! They cannot
see others! No, they did not know how to answer this,
only they did stand there looking at me with no teeths in
their mouths!" He laughs and shakes his head. I shed my
manteau completely and hang it over my arm. My shirt
grows crisp against the sun.

"First was our Christian hospital over there. They crashed it for no reason, and then they did begin to build this one, their own hospital, over here." He tosses his thumb in the direction of a shell of metal girders, a building in its earliest form. "They did start this building ten years before, so big and wonderful it will be, such things they told, but you see we have small stream here, they did not notice, it goes right under their so wonderful hospital." He squats beside the rivulet and scratches the damp ground with his middle finger. It is the sort of earth that makes good mud pies. "And so of course it is not good place for building, in fact it is impossible, so they cannot build. You know one smart mollah, clever one—yes, true, some of them are clever, they know truth—he told this problem is because of stolen land, and good Muslim cannot build on stolen land. So they leave it just like this, and now we must look at such ugly thing each time we want to come out and play with our childrens. Oh, so many things I can tell to you. Your eyes will become big like eggs when do you hear them!"

He continues speaking at such a pace that he cuts himself off in mid-word or mid-sentence as one story tumbles into the next. Details leak from both corners of his mouth. His eyes dance between memory and the present.

"They tell to you about tolerance? Haha! When they come here and talk such things, I bring them my list, list of everything they did confiscate and it puts, well, small holes in their chests, and then it is finished, their talkings. Oh, but it is getting better, this tolerance, even I must speak this truth. We are doing our service every Friday, on Sunday the peoples they are working, and church school for childrens also on Friday, you call it Sunday school—haha, Friday Sunday school—my wife is doing it, you will meet her in few minutes. And so tolerance is better, yes, I think so, but economy, oh my friend, our money it is like dead leaves on wet ground. Only nothing it can buy. My parents did come to this country to escape their countries—maybe I have Russian or Greek accent in my English?—and now look at us: we are same same."

At the top of the stairs, he pauses before opening the door to his house. "I invite you to our home where I live with my family. I do not ask to you if you are good person. Already I see it: your heart it is sitting in your eyes."

A tall blonde woman appears in the hallway. Her face is warm and worn, the way a face looks when it has had to work for its happiness. She approaches us and laughs with her husband as he explains, with animated gestures, what we have been doing. Her smile is restrained by her own face. Her chin is heavily scarred and holds taut the skin on one side of her jaw. It means that it is probably easier not to smile, that it is not a natural position. It means that her smile is precious.

"You can speak to my wife in English. She is good at this language. Even when she says her name she is practising this language: Karen is my wife's name. Haha! Please to let me to introduce my friend—oh, my goodness, in all my talkings I do not know your name! Oh, it is not polite from me. Please forgive! But my wife is used to me."

"Pleased to meet ya," she says, laughing. "Where're ya from?"

Karen, I learn over the course of the next few minutes, is from the one-horse town of Marion, Arkansas, and has been living in Iran for the last twenty-six years. From the age of eighteen, she felt called to do missionary work here, but was cautioned against doing this as a single woman. She chose, instead, to come to study nursing (at that time universities held classes in English) and to do her missionary work on the side. Although she had been brought up Baptist, she joined the Anglican Bible study group at the university because it was the only one around.

"Me too, I did join only because of no alternative! My parents were of course Orthodox, but me, I did not care. We are not such people to say, oh you are that and I am this, my way is better than your way, no! We are all Christians. We are all reading same book, OK some differences, but I think this is not so important. Main thing that we are enjoying, and we are sharing together some wine—aha! Yes! Oh, how clever am I to think this! Yes, my friend, we will drink wine together!"

He catapults out of his chair and out of the room. Karen watches the doorway and laughs, looks down and smiles. "We met at Bible study," she says, "and got married after college."

"So much naughty!" he calls from the next room. "Everybodies in Bible study we were getting together, you know, like couple, and at end of year we were all together in pairs, and poor minister he did not know what did he do. He was trying to be angry, to say, this is not purpose of Bible study group, such romantics, but really he was very happy for us."

Three wine glasses are placed on the table.

"Before we are sharing wine, first I must tell to you about woman who did teach me to make it. Listen, my friend: it was just after revolution, in difficult years, and

I was in prison—yes, it is another story I will tell to you later—and so my wife was here alone with some other foreign womans and childrens, and they were having many problems with revolution peoples, always bothering, trying to confiscate things, stealing from us. Once they attack to my wife, maybe you see some markings on her chin, and one doctor friend, he did fix her like this, so beautiful." Karen puts her hand on her husband's arm and smiles as far as her skin allows her. He takes her hand, kisses it, and washes it against his cheek.

"Every name you can imagine they did call us: dirty Christians, English spyings and such things. After revolution, we were everything! And so in this time, they put me to prison and here my wife and some other foreign womans were alone fighting these problems, and old Jewish woman from neighbourhood, maybe eighty years old, she did come to help. She was friend from some years, not close one, but she did come to sleep here with them and defend. They did not have heat, I did build these pipes later," he says, pointing to a heating system running along the corner of one wall. "You remember my pipes from workshop? Such beautiful things I am building with them," he laughs and rubs his fingernails against his shirt sleeve, then throws his head back in laughter.

"At that time there was no heating and this old Jewish woman she did bring some gas ovens and did sleep all in this room together, womans and childrens. Revolution peoples were giving so much problems, but she was just fighting for us so hardly she did not stop, only to fill her mouth with more air for arguings. They did try to take my tools, all my things they did try to take, but she did fight like six dogs for keeping everything, yes my friend!

"After one year and half, when I did become free from
Terry Waite—thanks God for him—she did stay with us
to live, and she did begin making some wine. You know
Khomeini did make wine forbidden: he did close four
wine factories in city and open one million factories in
people's cellars. Really! Now we are all professional
wine-makers, sometimes we have contests, me and my
friends, but even before wine factories closed, Jewish did
make their wine. But you know these Jewish, they are
very careful with their knowledges, they do not give
them to just anyone, they are careful, too careful for
me—*haha!*—so only I did follow our old woman when
she was preparing. I did go with her when she did go to
buy grapes, some of these, some of those, more of those.
I did watch and lift those things into car, but *oooho!* also
I was learning! And later I did watch her in that squishing
of grapes, but she would not tell to me what did she do—
no! This was secret, but even so I did learn. And one year
when she did become heavy with years on this earth, I did
do it alone, but I was not sure! I did buy some of these
grapes and some of those but really I was like blind dog,
only feeling with my feets. After some time, she did insist
to look at my workings, so we did put her in wheelchair
and down into cellar where did we do all of that squishing, and even there—oh, she was fighter! even then she
was telling, oh, and this is wrong and that is wrong, and
do you know? After wine was finished she did die.

"It was big problem to bury her. I did go every day to
offices and I told: I have dead Christian woman in my
house—to say Jewish it will be even bigger problem, so
for this reason I told she was Christian—and what can
I do with her when you close our cemetery? So in that

time I did keep her in cellar with wine, yes! And I think she did like that. It was fine, yes, finally we did get permission to bury her and church it was full full! The peoples they did love her, yes, a good woman." He picks up a dusty green bottle and pours three glasses of wine the colour of old blood. "For you, you have it everywhere, so it is nothing for you, but for us, it is gold, yes, gold. My friend, will you be kind and sharing my wine to drink to this good woman?"

The wine is nutmeggy and has the texture of tanned leather. It is pure ambrosia. I drink it with my eyes closed and think of dead women in basements.

I open my eyes and find them trained on a child's needle-point work on the wall. In the middle of stitched flowers and patterns is the word *Free*.

"My niece did make for me this beautiful thing you are seeing. It was for celebrating my freedom from prison, we did celebrate like this, with friends and family."

"Very difficult time," he says after swallowing hurriedly and tucking his glass under his chair. "Such problems we did have, there were executions in street! Oh it was time of blood. Before they did take me, we were helping many peoples to leave. Every week I was hiding people in my car and driving them, foreign peoples, missionaries, sisters, hiding them in my car and taking them to Tehran airport, so many peoples! It was dangerous time. Bishop did leave after they did kill his son, bishop's secretary they did kill also, then another minister did have some knife in his throat—actually they were crazies who did this, not government peoples, we don't know who was it, but we have some guessings. Such bad times! For days I was hiding these poor peoples and driving to airport until everyone was gone. This is how did we become keepers of this church, because I am not minister, oh my friend, no! I am farming man and my wife, she is nurse. But only we did promise to take care of church until our friends return, and now it is more than fifteen years, and we are still here and we are doing service every Friday, whole service, even if there is only eight peoples as this morning!

"But in this time they did arrest me—for what? Haha! It is still question for me! Year and half they did keep me, and still I do not know what did I do! Only they did ask to me to come to Tehran for collecting some papers for two of my workers, but from moment of my arriving, I knew it was trouble for me. They did put me in one car, BMW, and drive to outside of Tehran for switching cars and driving to prison, and there they did accuse me of everything! Spying for CIA and for British and having five passports—my friend, I do not even have one! Oh, it was very bad joke. So they put me to prison and for year and half I did stay there. For sure they will kill us, I did have such negative thinkings and was maybe little bit depressed. We were nine of us, like one group, some of them I was knowing from long time, some were strangers. One was doctor from England near to my cell and he was very clever man, we did become friends, and after some months we did become friendly also with some of guards. Even they did let us to have one small transistor radio, and I did ask to them to give to my friend one Bible, and they did do it. Nice mans. Yes, everywhere are nice peoples, believe me, my friend.

"And so we were listening always to BBC about this man, Terry Waite, and how he was fighting for us. We did listen about his trips and learn about our situation and do you know? These revolution mens did accuse us to be spyings for CIA and told they did find some documents about us in American embassy, but they did forge them so badly, full with spelling mistakes! Imagine! And these supposedly spying documents were in so poor English that Mr. Terry Waite just told, you cannot be serious with such accusations, it is joke. And he did fly back to Europe.

"After this time our situation did improve, and for Christmas, they told we could call to our families, just to tell we were alive. Karen was pregnant with this son," he says with one hand on Karen's stomach and the other pointing to the older boy reading in his bedroom. "I did call to them, ohooo! and we were very happy for having these voices in our ears again." Karen laughs and falls into the back of her chair, shaking her head.

"Then English doctor was also permitted, but of course he did need to call to England, so they were discussing this, and we were feeling so terrible because we did have chance to talk with our families and poor doctor maybe not, but finally they permitted, and he did call first to house of his oldest son, but no answer, then to second son and there he did find whole family. Oh, he was very happy and sick for home, and I was feeling sad for him.

"We did return to our prison cells and, well, we did wash our faces with tears, very clean cheeks we did have. Then we did listen to BBC and do you know? They told everything on radio! They were talking about us and about our prison and our telephone calls to our families! Ooooh! We were so nervous we did not sleep until morning! Now they will be certain of our spyings or at least connectings with important peoples! Imagine: we do one phone call to England, and it is reported by BBC! No, we did not sleep, only talking and talking about how to save our poor doctor, we knew they could kill him so easy and they were putting peoples on Zoroastrian grave all together for birds to eat, so no one will find us ever.

"Next morning they did come very angry about this BBC reporting, but our doctor he was such clever man, he told to those angry mans that he did ask to his second son to call BBC with information about us, to show us how nice were they, good treating us, all of these things he told, and after long time and with red cheeks from angriness, they did forgive him. Hahaha. Such clever one.

"Some months after, they did move us from this prison to old palace in Tehran, and this was of course much better conditions, and we did become happy, because certainly they will free us. It was same place where were American hostages, you know those poor guys, I did pray for them many times. Never did I see them, but one time guards did put us in one room for questioning, and I did find small paper stuck in back of chair. It had some English, score of some game, and we did think it must be those Americans who were playing with each other. They were very bored. Imagine 444 days just waiting for going home. And so this was good feeling, to know we were in same building with them because we knew they will not kill Americans, they were of course making some deal with American government, and we were eating good food at this time, so our spirits were like that candy that you are blowing—yes, bubble gums," he repeats after Karen's prompt. "We did feel like bubble gums. After Americans, we were first group free, two weeks after. Terry Waite did make us free—thanks God for him."

I never imagined the British hostage negotiator would have such immediacy for me, but in this moment I can imagine Terry Waite sitting in this room with us, sharing this wine. I remember watching him on television news reports, dashing from one Middle Eastern country to the next, seemingly impervious to the political chess game around him. Until he, too, was kidnapped during a meeting with Islamic Jihad, an underground group of Shi'ite extremists, and held captive for five years.

Karen rises from her chair and says a few words in Farsi. She smiles and winks at me, tousles her husband's hair on her way out of the room. He lights up again and announces, "We will have our bread now. Will you be kind and sharing our bread with my family?"

Our wine is topped up before we move into the kitchen, where the three children have assembled around the table, and Karen is heaving pots from the stove. "Sorry 'bout the food. If we'd known you were comin', I would've made ya somethin' real nice."

When Karen speaks in Farsi, which she does even with her children, the tone of her Southern drawl colours the language in a strange and inimitable way. I listen for several minutes and decide that Farsi is, by nature, a language of deep greens and browns, and that Karen speaks it in bright red swaths. At the moment, she is encouraging her children to address us in English, but they blush and look down at their plates instead, whispering to each other behind nervous grins and sitting on their hands.

"So you did meet my childrens," he says, arriving in the kitchen with two extra chairs. "Are they speaking to you in English? They are learning it now in school and becoming angry to their mother because of speaking to them always in Farsi. English class is very difficult for them, and so they tell it is fault of mother who speaks all their lifes in my language."

Karen shrugs and throws her eyes to the ceiling. "He was the one that started speakin' Farsi to me——"

"Oh, my friend, of course! I must do this! I was liking her very much, but when she did speak with her crazy English, I was understanding only some small words for example, *the*, and such small small words like this! No my friend, I did want to use more bigger words, and so I did give to her some words from my language, and this was more easier for me to understand. Now——ooooh!——she speaks Farsi more better than me. So beautiful things she builds with this language, I am smiling every day from these buildings."

The telephone rings, he lifts his eyebrows until the room becomes silent, then answers. It is a short conversation. It ends with a standard greeting and replacement of the receiver, then sighs and smiles all around.

"Our telephones, they are listening them, you know. As for me, I do not believe I am so interesting like they are thinking, so always I am disappointing their spyings. Sometimes even I am hearing their breathings during my conversation, and they think I am not noticing——haha! One time was I speaking with one friend and in middle of conversation one spying did ask to other spying, *What did he say?* so loudly my friend and I, we did begin to laugh. Imagine! Spyings whispering so loudly we are hearing what are they saying! Oh my friend, so many stories I can tell to you!"

Karen urges us to begin before the meal cools, but not before a recital of "For what we are about to receive. . . ," in English.

"I'm awful sorry 'bout the food, there's all kinds of garlic and no meat."

"I love garlic!" I say, to which my host pushes back his chair, raises his hands to the sky and yells, "Even she likes garlic—praise the Lord!" He bounces out of his chair and into a cupboard just behind him, rummages for several seconds and does an *abracadabra* sort of appearance with a bud of garlic cupped in his hands. The same way he might hold a communion wafer. He pushes his plate of rice and eggplant into the centre of the table and begins peeling the garlic. After the eighth or ninth clove, Karen suggests that perhaps that it is enough, but he waves her away and continues, dropping the naked cloves into a bowl and plucking the skin from the rest of the bud.

"Please to eat! This telephone, it was friend calling to me about some business I must do today. Yesterday I did go to court to fix some papers, but mollahs, you know, Muslim religious mans, told, no it is impossible, and so I did go to one friend, only to ask how much were they wanting. I know it was money they were wanting, but I did not know how much! I am not so good at this, you call it bribering, and so I ask to my friends how much should I give! Oh not all, some are good, but so many mollahs they are very bad, they are taking everything for their own hands, and peoples are becoming unhappy with them. Mollahs are like Mafia, they are controlling everything from their behinds." He leans across the table and places a bowl of fresh garlic in front of me. I thank him and begin popping the cloves like candy. He takes one bite of his meal and explodes again.

"Do you know story of our Supreme Leader, Spiritual Leader Kha'menei, how did he become Grand Ayatollah?

Oh, I am joking with my Muslim friends about this, and we are laughing together, because even they know it is little bit stupid. It was when old Supreme Spiritual Leader Khomeini—I think he is famous in your countries?—well, he was dying, and they did need to replace him, but it must be Grand Ayatollah who replace him, and of course the politic people were wanting one of their mans, not just anyone, so what did they do? They told, hello, friend, we are wanting you being our new Spiritual Leader so today you are Grand Ayatollah—just like this! And so I am joking with my Muslim friends, asking, what do you need to become Grand Ayatollah: many years of difficult studying and spiritual developing? No—only you need to go to bed one night and, if you are lucky, you will wake up and your friends will tell you are Grand Ayatollah! Hahahahaha." He takes two bites and a sip of wine.

"They think I have five passports! But I have none, not one! They are thinking I am wanting to leave this country, but I do not want to go out, this is my box where I put my two feets, so I am not taking any passport from any embassy. Only they did call to me last week to tell that I can get passport, after only fifteen years asking! But I did not go! And now they are sitting in office asking to each other, *Why that crazy Christian guy is not coming to take his passport, finally now we give him one?* I am making them confusing! Maybe one day I will take it, but first I will let my son and daughter to go to America for studying, maybe then I will take it. But I am not so wanting to leave as they are thinking."

The two older children address their father as they scoop last spoonfuls of rice into their mouths and clear their plates. They smile to each other, and to me, and urge their mother to translate.

"They're just sayin' they're *real* anxious to leave," Karen says, spooning more rice onto her youngest son's plate. "They're talkin' 'bout leavin' for America and never comin' back after college."

"Maybe yes! Of course they are liking to live in this famous place, America, but maybe they will miss their home—I do not know! Maybe they will find some things in America they do not like—"

He is cut off by his daughter, who tosses her head back in the air and *tsks*. She rises from her chair and begins stacking dirty dishes, then motions to her older brother to carry them over to the sink. The youngest boy swallows his last mouthful of rice, slides off his chair and waddles over to the sink balancing his cutlery on his plate. One by one they kiss their mother and thank her for lunch, kiss their father on the forehead, shake my hand, then race back outside into the sun.

"It's not because of persecution," Karen explains once the front door closes. "It's just they visited my family often enough to see it all. They're not unhappy here, but they sure know there's more, and that's enough to make anyone wanna leave, far as I'm concerned."

"Did you ever want to leave?"

She laughs and trades smiles with her husband, who claps his hands and rises from his chair, fills the sink with water and begins doing the dishes. "My family thought I was crazy to stay, but honestly, I never even thought about goin' back. My life was here, ya know, people needed me here, I was meant to be here. I just never thought about leavin', this is my home. But I understand my kids wantin' to leave, we just gotta let 'em go, and pray they wanna come back is all."

"Important thing is they are happy. Of course I am wishing them to be happy here, but OK, if they are wanting to study in America, and we have such possibility, so they can do that. We trust in God, that he will guide them. And maybe one day I will go down to that office with those confusing peoples and take my passport and we will visit our childrens in America!"

We spend the next few hours around the table, talking, drinking tea, laughing, telling stories. When I pull back and listen to the voices, I feel as though I am somewhere between the Deep South and Siberia. Which I suppose I am. The air is a thick canvas of tales: landscapes of politics and ghosts, portraits of inspiration.

The stories stop at the gates, where I cover myself and prepare for the outside. Karen lifts the deep lock from the earth and kisses me on both cheeks. Her husband takes my hand and shakes it with affection and excitement.

"Goodbye, my friend. We will not forget you. You are good person for coming to see my country. I am thanking for this. God bless you! You did bring to us many smilings!"

I have a grin on my face that will stay for hours, feel my arms swinging at my sides as though I were dancing. I am lighter than I have been for months, buoyed by the spirit and beauty of these people. By the side of a river I stop and close my eyes, laugh as I recall the day's stories. Then I bow my head and mouth the word, *thank you*. And feel I've been lifted ever so slightly from the earth.

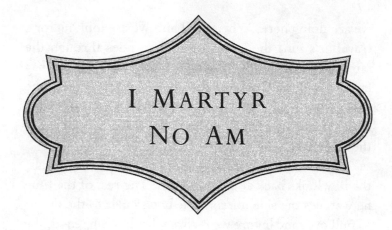

I MARTYR
NO AM

FOR HOURS WE ROLL and dip through the countryside. We descend to this country's lowest, hottest and driest point, then gradually resurface among gentle green hills.

The minibus drops us by the side of the road, in Sanandaj. Ian rustles around in his bag for a map, and I begin sounding out the street sign in front of us. *En-ghe-la-be. An-ghe-lab.* Ian has not even got the map out before we are approached by a teenaged boy wearing a wool jumpsuit tied at the waist with a thick brown sash. His eyes are the colour of the lowest notes on a cello. His eyelashes are so long, I feel them brush against my face as he blinks.

He shakes Ian's hand, puts a hand over his heart and bows to me.

"Canada," Ian answers. "We are from Canada."

At this news, the boy's expression contorts. It goes from shock to delight to confusion to worry, back briefly to shock, pausing again on delight, and ending on confusion.

He moves his right hand in such a way that he looks like he is jiggling an imaginary doorknob and asks us what we are doing here. When I tell him we are looking for a traveller's inn, the boy smiles, then goes through the same series of facial contortions again. He takes my bag in one hand, Ian's hand in the other and brings us to the side of the road. He flags down a taxi, opens the back door for me, pats Ian on the back as he gets in, and sits in the front seat.

We drive for about ten minutes. At regular intervals, the boy looks back at us and smiles. The rest of the time he watches the side mirror. The boy signals to the driver to pull over and before we realize what has happened, the driver is accepting money from the boy and stuffing it into a pouch on the dashboard. When we try to offer some money to the driver, he refuses and points to the boy, so we get out of the taxi, thank the boy very much very very much, we are very grateful, but no no, we'll pay, and try to offer the money to him. He smiles, raises his hands in the air, showing us his palms, and puts both hands over his heart. Our bags are scooped off the side-walk and brought to the door of the hotel. The boy puts them on the landing and bows deeply to me. He takes Ian's head in his hands, stands on his tiptoes, and kisses him on both cheeks.

We call to him as he skips back down the stairs and into the street. He doesn't turn around. We watch him drift into the crowded sidewalk, and we wave when he turns off the street. He doesn't see us. We stand on the landing and continue watching until the faces on the street grow shadows. Eventually, a man comes out of the hotel and hands us two glasses of cardamom tea.

❧

The samosas are piping hot and served to us by a prepubescent boy who looks like a zoo animal. He is thin, listless. He moves slowly, carelessly, inured to the life around him. The sound of our language elicits nothing in him. There seems no point in having interest. As he cooks the pastries, a drop of hot oil spits up from the pan onto his arm. His eyes wince only slightly, then drop back into the cave of his body. He hands us our samosas. We hand him money. He accepts it and throws it under a cloth. Says nothing. We thank him several times. He says nothing. His eyes never leave his work. He flicks grit around the pan; the oil crackles, sends heat and fumes into his face. He doesn't react. He is a child but has already died of old age.

Further down the road are two little boys—teeny—selling flatbread at the side of the road. An older boy helps a younger one with basic sales techniques, arranging the younger boy's stack of breads so the torn ones aren't visible on top. Ten flatbreads sit on filthy tattered fabric and are tended by a filthy tattered five-year-old. Beside them is a girl with no front teeth and hazelnut curls knotted by the wind. She smiles at me, pushes her hair from her face with the palm of her hand, fingers outstretched. She is carrying a basket of what look like dried berries. She tells me they are "toot" and offers me one to try. Blackberry raisins. I buy two handfuls and pay her the price she has come up with after counting on both hands, twice. She puts the money in her basket, gives me a smile that shows all of her no teeth, and winks at me with both eyes.

Ian nudges me awake. "We're almost there."

The bus is lurching through the outskirts of Qom, Iran's holiest city. Its soul, some say. This is the heart of Shi'a fundamentalism, Khomeini's learning, teaching and preaching ground. His disciples walk here, holding his words in their hearts, living his message. The Islamic Revolution was born here. This is the blood source, still.

"The guy across the aisle wants to take us home for the night," Ian whispers. "But there's *no way* I'm going to spend the evening with him. He's been asking a million questions, he's driving me crazy."

I lean forward and look across the aisle. A young bearded man smiles, a huge goofy smile. I smile back.

"Don't talk to him. He's a weirdo," Ian whispers. "We're not staying with him. We're not—fucking—staying— with—him."

The bus stops at the base of a thick, stone bridge. Across the dry carcass of a river is a magnificent shrine, Hazrat-é Masumeh: the burial place of Fatima, sister of Iman Reza. Its golden dome rises out of the haze and bursts with sunlight. Amid the dust and heat and drab surroundings, the building looks magical.

"This Hazrat-é Masumeh is," says the man from across the aisle. He has followed us off the bus and skipped ahead to join us. "I very grateful am. My home like your home is this night."

Ian huffs and looks away. "Thank you, but my wife and I are looking for a *mosaferkhané*. We don't need your help."

The man smiles and closes his eyes. Offers to help us in our search. Introduces himself—Ali—and bows. Extends his arm out to the side—this way, please—and smiles. Ian locks his jaw and folds his arms across his chest.

At this moment, after months of Pablum and nothing ever being *quite* right, I have had enough of Ian's persnickety whining. I turn to Ali and smile. "We would be honoured to be guests in your home."

Ali bites his lip with excitement. His eyes double in size, and he makes a funny choking sound. He confirms several times that we have agreed to be his guests, and every time I say yes, I become more and more convinced that Ian is right. This guy is a lunatic.

But cancelling now is unthinkable.

He is the quintessential host, carrying our bags, checking every two or three minutes to be sure that we are happy and have everything we need. He walks ahead of us like a bodyguard, clearing a path through crowds, nodding and explaining to other pedestrians that they should mind his foreign guests. Canadians. Tourists. Visitors to our country.

The odd person smiles. Most look away. Just as Khomeini averted his eyes during the drive to his home-in-exile outside Paris, lest he be polluted by the sight of Western values. Outside the shrine, a mollah holds the hand of his daughter, a tiny girl of four or five who wears a miniature chaador, holding it tightly beneath her chin. As he passes me, the turbaned man mutters something I do not understand.

"This man say about your nakedness," Ali explains. "He is man holy, no like cloth Western."

I look down at myself. At my floor-length black manteau that cloaks everything but a teensy view of my dark socks and black shoes. I feel the edges of my black scarf for recalcitrant curls, but they are all tucked away out of sight. "My nakedness?"

Ali smiles. "God want that woman has cover not like Western, but in Islam. Your cloth has Western style. Islamic cloth is chaador, separate from Western."

Suddenly I notice that not a single woman or girl is without a chaador in addition to her other covering. That I am, by comparison, quite nattily attired. And that the overwhelming difference in our outfits is the posture they afford us. My scarf is clipped, my coat buttoned, my hands free; I am able to stand with my head up, free to move around. The most difficult thing about a chaador is keeping it on. To stand upright with hands free is to have it fall off.

Many of the men are cloaked as well, in the earth-coloured *aba* that shows modesty and simplicity; their hair is often covered by a turban: white, to show themselves as learned scholars of Islam, or black, the sign of a direct descendant of the Prophet.

Ali takes us through the narrow paths of the bazaar to his home, a small, flat-roofed building at the end of a dusty street. He lopes up the steps and announces our arrival, seats us on the floor in the main room and excuses himself. Disappears into the back of the house. Women's voices, the sound of cooking. Ali reappears. Smiling. He has the largest teeth I have ever seen, more like tusks than teeth, really, so his smile takes up most of his face. And demands a response.

I smile back.

We sit together on the floor, smiling at each other, until there comes a *psssst* sound from the back room. Ali leaps to his feet, smiles, apologizes, leaves, and returns with tea.

We drink.

A few minutes later, there is more whispering from the back room. Ali apologizes again, gets up and returns with a tray of nuts and fruit.

We eat.

When we have finished, Ali calls over his shoulder. There is a whispered response, some faint giggling, then a young woman appears, wrapped in a length of white cotton patterned with clusters of pink and blue flowers. She wraps it well across her face so that only one eye is visible.

"My sister," says Ali. "She pull shy from visitor."

I stand to greet her, as does Ian, and she shakes my hand—*salaam*—hides her face and retreats to the kitchen.

Ali smiles. "I am very happy!" he declares. "I am very happy that you eat tea in home my, eat in home my! God is great! Everything God bring very wonderful is!" He seems overcome with emotion. Holds a hand over his heart as he delivers his creed. "God is One! I am very happy!"

He stands up and goes to a cupboard, pulls out a tattered photo album and lays it on the floor in front of us. They are photos of him as a young man, maybe six or eight years younger than he is now. Photos of young Ali with a white bandana around his head, shouting with his fist raised in the air; photos of young Ali and a group of boys around a tank; of young Ali with a machine gun; of young Ali and a group of boys in a trench; of young Ali standing next to a bazooka, helping to load it.

"Do you know about war with Iraq?" Ali asks, smiling. Genuinely smiling. "War in way God, will from God." He turns to the front of the album and has us go through the photos again. And with what can only be described as war glee, he recounts his tales of the front.

"I want so much fight in war!" His eyes widen with excitement. "War in way God! I only fourteen year was and soldier must eighteen be. It very difficult for me was!" He points to the picture of himself with the bandana, smiles and shakes his head in recollection. "Here I *basiji* am. I cannot soldier be, so I must as *basiji* fight."

"The volunteer brigades?"

He doesn't understand. "I soldier no am, soldier eighteen year is. For *basiji*, sixteen."

"And how old are you there?"

Ali smiles. "Fourteen. But I say that I sixteen year am for fight in way God." He turns to the next page. "Here it is time of prepare build. This one—" he points to a boy who looks even younger "—this one *shaheed* is."

"Martyr."

"Yes, martyr." He smiles, very deeply. "And this one—" he points to a scrawny blond boy with a mischievous smile "—also martyr." Ali smiles and grows more enthusiastic. Begins flipping through the pages more quickly. "He, also martyr. Also he. And he. And he. Maybe twenty or forty my friends, martyr are." He sighs. "I want that I martyr became."

"You wanted to die?"

Ali points to the ceiling. "Have life much better, forever with God."

I flip through the photos a third time, staring into each face, each young, fearless, committed face.

"It war with America was, this is truth. Saddam Hussein only . . ." He lays his hand over his face.

"A mask."

"Yes, mask for government America. They say no, but I know they to Iraq very much money give, and weapon. Even they fight with airplane America. I see them in east part Iraq. Soldier Iraqi come in front us, then I airplane did see—" he looks up at the ceiling as if he were reliving the moment "—and I letters did see: 'US' on airplane. It fell bomb *behind* me on bridge. Then go back to Iraq." He looks at us and insists. "I with my eye it *see*."

He pauses, then smiles. "After from forty month war I return to my family."

"Forty months! I thought men only served for two years. Why did you stay for forty months?"

Ali shrugs, looks sad for the first time all day. "War finish. I want fight, but I must home go."

"Because you weren't a martyr."

He lowers his head. "No, I martyr no am."

ಬಿ

Ali has decided that we should spend the night at the home of one his sisters. She is recently married and has a much nicer house. And a television. We will be happier there.

We take a bus to a new housing development on the outskirts of Qom. It is austere desert landscape: harsh, bitter dust and a heat that feels metallic.

Walking towards us are two girls in simple manteaux and scarves, leaning into each other and giggling. One is wearing something very strange on her face.

Sunglasses.

When the girls pass us, Ali puts a hand over his heart and sighs. "I sorry for her am. She want shape Western."

We turn in at the next gate.

Ali's sister, Khawla, is bright, cheerful, full of humour and youthful energy. Which makes sense, because she is fourteen years old.

Her chaador (which she wears even indoors, just like her sister), is of light floral cotton. She wears it open at the front and thrown over her arm, a bit like an Indian sari. She fiddles with it almost constantly, ensuring that her hair is kept out of sight, but seems unconcerned that her tight yellow T-shirt gives such an unimpeded view of her breasts that even I find myself sneaking peeks.

Khawla gives me a tour of the house (bathroom, sewing room, kitchen), then guides me through her kitchen cupboards, one by one. Pots and pans and plates and a variety of floor cloths, each one unfolded for my viewing pleasure.

Hearing footsteps in the stairwell, she looks up and beams. Takes my hand and leads me back out to the main room, where her husband is being introduced to Ian. *Salaam*. And to me.

He is shy and soft-spoken, seems thrilled but embarrassed to be our host. He speaks not a word of English, so invites us to watch television. Ali smiles and settles us in the living room. Though now that I think of it, I'm not sure he has stopped smiling since we met him this afternoon.

We sit on a carpet in the corner of the room, lean against thick pillows and watch television, while Khawla goes off to make dinner. The program is the trial of three women accused of setting bombs at the Shrine of Imam Reza in Mashhad and Khomeini's Shrine near Qom. "These women in Germany live did," Ali explains. "They thing bad learn." And what will happen to them if they are found guilty? Ali discusses this with his brother-in-law. "We know they guilty become, they kill, so they hang. In Western, if man rich is, he can without problem kill. Money law is."

Ian pipes up. "Actually, it's a lot more complicated than—"

"Newspaper write about it."

"Well, you should see what our newspapers say about Iran," Ian counters.

"But newspaper Western belong people rich. You cannot believe. They speak from place rich. It is not place truth. Some senator America want war in Gulf state. They want control Gulf state because of oil. They very afraid from Islam is, but we no afraid are. We know is right, because at end Islam is God. At end America only is money."

Dinner is served when Ali's family arrives. His father brings fresh bread from his shift at the bake shop and looks as exhausted as I would expect someone to look after a day of leaning in and out of those huge open ovens, tending the coals and throwing thin strips of dough onto the stones, dragging the flatbreads out with a poker and tossing them onto a cooling rack by the street, where people wait in the open air where it is cooler. Only forty degrees or so.

He sits down and calls to Khawla to turn on the air conditioner, a Russian-made contraption in the window that blows air through a layer of wet straw. Ali's mother and sister have arrived too, though they are so shy and covered, it is like sitting among heaps of laundry. Khawla runs in and out of the kitchen bringing plates and platters and bowls. Every time she lays something onto the dining cloth, her chaador slips back on her head, so the order of events is this: carry, set dish down, rush hands to head and cover hair, stand, readjust chaador across the rest of body, throw tail ends over arm, go back for more food. She does all of this at least ten times.

Throughout the meal, Ali's father continues to complain of the heat in the house, but he does it in a way that makes everyone laugh, smiling and yelling into the air, shaking a hand at Khawla. Each time, she doubles over giggling, then jumps up and fiddles with the air conditioner, shaking her hand at it and repeating her father's words to the machine.

After dinner, Ali's father has some questions. He knows that the West has many problems, but what do we think are the worst ones? He read an article in the newspaper about teenage pregnancy. What is our opinion about that?

"Your daughter is married at fourteen, so presumably she'll be pregnant as a teenager herself."

All three men smile. This is something completely different, they explain. She is married, so she will have children with her husband and both of their families. In the West, these girls are unmarried. Their children grow up without fathers or families. Therefore they have problems with drugs and crime.

According to Ali's father, the West's biggest problem is that there is no religious leadership in government. If there is no God in government, there is no God in the people. And then there are drugs and crime and babies without love of their families. Who are the leaders of our country? Are they simple, poor men who live by the word of God?

"Uh, they're mostly lawyers."

"My father one other question has," Ali tells us. "In newspaper is one article about people America, it tell many people must eat pill for sadness. My father ask, reason sadness what is?"

"It depends."

"Newspaper write that people America very much work, like sickness. It sadness is for people that work, also their family. My father make question, America country very rich is. Why this much work?"

Ali has stayed behind and will spend the night with us here. Before rolling out the sleeping mats, Ali tells us they must pray. Ian and I sit in the corner of the room while Ali, Khawla and her husband turn to face Mecca and prostrate themselves. They stand and kneel and bow, stand and kneel and bow, stand and kneel and bow. And something about this ritual relaxes me. It does precisely the opposite to Ian, who is so annoyed by the evening that he feels compelled to go over and over, in a low voice, all of the reasons why all of Ali's father's comments were wrong, misguided, misinformed, and lacking in perspective and empirical data. I listen with one ear and try to find silence with the other.

Khawla and I sleep fully clothed (I have still not been asked to remove my manteau) on one side of the room. Ali, Khawla's husband and Ian lie on the other.

When I wake up, Ian is still asleep and everyone else is gone. On my way to the toilet, I see Ali and Khawla squatting on the kitchen floor. Ali leaps up.

"Good morning! I very happy am!"

Khawla smiles and begins heating water for tea. Once Ian is awake and washed, we eat breakfast. Ali is silent throughout the meal, but the moment he sees that we are finished, he bursts into smile and proud announcement:

"We want go to Imam Khomeini!"

"Isn't he dead?"

Ali laughs, then looks ashamed. "Yes, my friend car has. We will go to . . ." He searches for the word.

"To the shrine? The place where he is buried?"

"Yes! Yes yes! You ready are?"

A car waits in front of the house. Its driver, Mahmoud, gets out and bows, shakes Ian's hand, opens the back door for us. Opens it again when we reach the Shrine of Imam Khomeini.

It is not at all what I expected. Not nearly as ornate, as extravagant, as large, though it is still under construction, so all of that could change. From the outside, it could be anything, even a factory. There is a small pool by the entrance where naked children are wading and laughing. We pass through segregated doors, leave our shoes at a counter and duck under velvet curtains.

Inside, the place looks like an upscale rollerskating arena. The walls and ceilings are bare, the floors are of bright marble. There is one sound: screaming. The screams of children, of kids tearing around and around the building, sliding along the slick floors in their stocking feet, having the time of their lives. There is a gang of five-year-olds playing tag. A little boy in front of us is dragging his shrieking brother around by his ankles.

At the centre of the room is an austere, plain yoghurt-and-rice sort of coffin. Ali is so moved by his proximity to the Father of the Revolution that he must hold Mahmoud's hand to steady himself.

Next to Khomeini's coffin is an even simpler, plain wooden box.

"Ahmad." Ali explains, fighting tears. Khomeini's son, nicknamed "Crying Ahmad" by the less devoted, was known for sitting next to his father while the Imam gave speeches, weeping at the beauty of his father's words. They rest together now.

We collect our shoes and exit the shrine the way Khomeini would have liked: separately. When we meet up again outside, Ali is back to his old self. "I am sorry I no with Imam am, but I must here be." He gestures to the ground. Smiles. "Now we go to place martyr."

As we are pulling out of the shrine's parking lot, an open-topped jeep drives past us at full speed. The young woman driving has her red scarf so far back on her head that it sits practically on her shoulders. She is the proud owner of big hair—*big* hair—jangly jewellery and lipstick so bright I can see it clearly from the other side of the street. There are two other women in the jeep, all in a similar get-up. The one in the back seat is leaning forward between her two friends, laughing and singing along to the sound that beats from their speakers and trails into the air behind them. The music of U2.

Ali mutters to Mahmoud, then turns to us. "Do not worry. These women satanic are," he explains.

The Martyrs' Cemetery is the largest I have ever seen. Row upon row upon row upon row upon row. As far as the eye can see, on all sides. A stone orchard. It grows legends of martyrdom.

We walk through aisles of gravestones. Almost every one is crowned with a framed photograph. Faces fading from the earth's heat. On the backs of many headstones is a picture of Khomeini, stolid and determined. The owner of these lives.

I stray away from the group, begin wandering the rows by myself, watching the blur of faces as I walk. There are photos of boys with big ears, some with wide collars and mirthful smiles, some with their heads tilted to the side the way the school photographer used to tell us to pose, one of a boy talking excitedly on a telephone. Thick curly hair, an open-mouthed smile that shows that he is laughing. I stare at these photos, these men, these boys, and begin to build lives behind their eyes. Their hollow, anonymous eyes. The eyes of something called *casualties*.

An old man comes into the row where I am standing. He squats beside one of the stones and begins to speak, whisper. He tells his son what, I wonder. That he loves him? Misses him? That he still thinks of him, the way his face came alive when he smiled? That he still hears his voice sometimes in his mind? Still feels he's just gone away for a while, that he'll be back sometime, and then they will be able to talk about everything that's happened. Oh, your mother will be so happy when she sees you . . .

The man rises. Squints, rolls his lips together and rests his face in his hand. Turns and sees me, a fellow mourner, he assumes. He bows his head. Lays a hand over his heart.

I do the same. An utterly empty gesture. I keep my hand to my heart long after the man leaves. Hold it there, blankly, until my hand feels cold against my chest.

Today's issue of *Iran News*, one of the country's two English-language dailies, has a special section on Canada: three articles, each one carefully researched and well written. The first is titled, "Yet Another Human Rights Violation in Colonial Canada" and reports on NATO low-level flights over Innu communities and traditional hunting grounds in Labrador. The second, under the headline "Drugs, Prostitution and Crime," is full of statistics about increases in all three, particularly among teenagers. The last article, untitled, is a discreet discussion about Canadian women's inability to walk unchaperoned after dark, their fears of assault and rape, and their consequent lack of freedom.

In the entertainment section of the newspaper, the day's television programs are listed.

> *National Network, Channel One:*
>
> 12:30   Focus on Family
> 13:01   Call to Prayer
> 13:06   Focus on Family
> 14:00   News
> 14:30   Focus on Family

જ

None of the three employees at the counter seems to know when the next train leaves for Tehran. One of them has been looking for a schedule for the last twenty minutes. The other two left the station after walking with us to the edge of the tracks, looking in both directions and shrugging.

I am too exhausted to find this funny. Too exhausted to try any more. I slouch around the empty, dilapidated station and collapse on a broken bench outside. My hair is showing, but I make no move to cover it. I sit like a jock. Hook my arms over the back of the bench. Stare at a man hanging around the entrance to the station. Stare at him. Until he disappears.

Ian slumps down beside me with bad news. The first train is in three days. Maybe. No one seems to know for sure. There is one train leaving tonight, but it's only for military people and families of martyrs. "Can I just remind you that it was your idea to come to this fucking country?" he snarls.

I don't react. Don't have the energy. Between the bedbugs and the traffic and the mosquitoes and the windows that wouldn't close, the damp mattresses that felt like they were full of snakes, and the group of women making tea in the middle of the hallway at three o'clock in the morning, neither of us slept last night. It's the middle of a forty-degree afternoon, and we haven't eaten since yesterday. And I have my period. Am, in fact, staining this bench with a crimson hue as I sit here.

I don't even react when the man I stared down a few minutes ago reappears and begins walking towards us. Don't straighten up and close my legs, don't adjust my scarf, don't stop tugging at my lip and snapping it against my teeth.

The man stands before us and bows, one hand over his heart, the other hand holding two tinfoil containers covered with paper. He gives the containers to Ian, bows again, turns, and heads back down the street.

Ian lifts up the paper and looks inside. "Who was that guy?"

"Dunno. I just saw him in the station."

Ian passes me one of the containers. It is warm. And jammed to the rim with rice, lentils, meat and French fries.

"Merci!" we call.

The man turns around and bows. Hand over his heart.

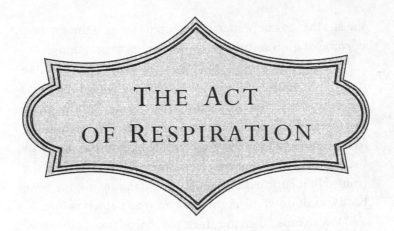

THE ACT
OF RESPIRATION

TEHRAN ISN'T NEARLY as awful a city as it is reputed to be. Unless you insist on breathing, in which case it is an urban nightmare.

The City of Tehran has strict traffic controls to combat congestion, issuing travel permits for certain districts at certain times and placing heavy restrictions on travel during peak hours.

It's not working.

I cannot imagine a more difficult way to acquire oxygen than to stand on a street corner in south Tehran and engage in the act of respiration. Particularly if you're asthmatic.

I am. And my inhaler—my nerd gas, as Ian so respectfully calls it—dried up weeks ago. Inhaling without it is next to impossible as there is practically nothing, beyond ozone, carbon monoxide, lead, cadmium, nitrous oxide, to inhale. I sit, therefore, with my face in the crook of my elbow, gasping, coughing, retching. Ian sits beside me with his legs crossed, one leg swinging around like a manic crane. Oblivious. Excited to be in a big city. Happy to overlook the fact that cosmopolitan living often comes at the expense of some of life's simpler pleasures. Such as breathing.

Tehran's number 32 bus becomes visible through the haze. I am about to climb on behind Ian when someone takes my arm. "You're back here with me," the woman says (in English) and pulls me to the end of the platform. We get onto the bus through the back door and stand by the metal bar that separates the sexes. Ian waves from the front. He is jammed into an aisle of standing men. I wave back and sit down next the woman who helped me on.

"We've only taken minibuses or shared taxis until now," I explain. "I didn't know—"

"—didn't know you were like an animal they keep in the back?" she says, staring out the window.

She's German. Thick accent. Her eyes are a washed-out blue and her skin fair; fairer than most. No smile.

"Do you work here?" I ask.

She looks away from the window, but not at me. "No. I can't work. My husband doesn't let me. I only live here. Since ten years I am here. I can't leave and my children, *ach* that's again something . . ."

"How old are your children?"

"Two sons, one eight and one five. But since two years I don't see them, only in the park where they go from time to time, and in the school sometimes, because I know one of their teachers and she helps. They live with their father. He doesn't permit me to see them." She squints and looks back out the window, but doesn't look, really: she stares at nothing.

I cannot help noticing the two men leaning on the dividing bar in front of us. They fawn over each other like lovers, whispering, giggling, holding hands, tousling hair, running their hands along the arms and chest of the other. No one pays them any attention. Except me, until the German woman speaks again.

"My husband has a new wife, but he doesn't give me any divorce, so it is necessary for him to sign something that allows me to work. But he refuses to sign. And so my relatives in Germany send me some money, but still I can't do anything."

"Can't you go back to Germany?"

She looks at me for the first time. "I can go back, but I cannot take my children. I go back to Germany for some visits, but then I want to see my children, I want them to see me, and so I must come back to this place." She looks into the men's car. "Your friend tries to call you."

I look up and see Ian waving and pointing outside. Our stop is next. I gather myself and prepare to stand. Can think of absolutely nothing to say.

I wait for the doors to open, then hold the woman's thin arm. "Children never forget their mother," I say and wince to myself. Trite. Sterile. The best I can come up with.

She doesn't move. Her face twitches a slight smile, and she looks away.

ಬಿ

There is an Indian restaurant just down the street from the Centre for Sale of US Den of Espionage Documents (the former US embassy). It's pricey, about three dollars for the two of us, but we're in a splurgy sort of mood.

It's a gorgeous evening, cool and breezy, and we are sitting at one of the tables in the back courtyard. I close my eyes and lean my head back, listen to leaves shiver against the wind. My body twitches. Aches suddenly.

The trees carry the sound of home.

I straighten up when the waiter arrives, and we order everything on the menu. Samosas, mulligatawny, sag paneer, daal, bhanji bharta, aloo gobi, chicken dhansak, pulao, nan, raita, mango chutney, lime pickle. And chai. The waiter smiles and collects our menus.

The tables are close together. Close enough that any conversation is easily overheard, but the clientele looks relaxed and insouciant. This place is part of the Tehran that does not seem to be part of Iran. It is the Tehran of make-up and designer manteaux, lots of visible pouffed-up hair, nail polish, jewellery, and groups of young people obviously out on dates. It is also the Tehran of trees and greenery, large houses behind high stone walls, wide streets with few cars—but nice cars—and a sense of relative peace. Breathable air.

There is a man a few tables over who keeps looking at me. Us, I suppose, though I'm the one facing him, so it feels like he's looking at me. And it feels strange. To feel watched. He has a graceful manner about him: calm focus and energy. And he is striking. Chocolatey Indian skin and a clipped beard, round black glasses and lips that he keeps wetting before he speaks. Arabic. He and his table of friends (three men) are speaking Arabic.

I turn back to Ian, who has fallen asleep with his head back and his mouth open. Looking at him, at his wan complexion and the texture of his skin, I can't help but notice how much he resembles a cheese curd. Our soup arrives. Ian revives. We vacuum the entire bowl into our mouths in a matter of seconds. Start in on the samosas.

The breeze picks up and blows my scarf off my head. I lunge for it on the ground and stop. Close my eyes. Feel the wind tease through my hair for the first time in months. I sit up and toss the scarf on again, lightly, open at the front. So that I can sit here and feel the wind-breaths on my neck. My chocolate man is watching me. He smiles.

We are eating with our hands, rice and spinach and cheese and eggplant and chicken and yogurt wrapped into folds of buttery roasted bread, when he stands up and leaves with his friends. And then returns. Walks straight to our table.

"Excuse me, you aren't foreigners by any chance, are you?"

British accent. Chalky voice.

"I thought I heard you speaking English. Do you mind if I join you? It's been so long since I've spoken English—oh, no, thank you. I've just had a full meal myself—I only speak Farsi and Arabic these days . . ."

The chicken and lentils arrive, along with rice.

"I'm a student in Qom. I'm studying Islam, though it's primarily language studies at this stage: Farsi, of course, and Arabic, because as you know, the Koran must be read in the original language. Are you Muslims? No, I didn't think so. How are you doing with your hejab? Is it difficult for you, or are you able to find the freedom in it? Gosh, it feels good to speak my own language again . . ."

Eggplant, potatoes and chutney.

"I've only been a Muslim for about a year. I used to be a musician. Played keyboards in a band. We were into warehouse parties and the like. Sex, drugs and rock and roll—you know how it is. Well, after a while, I really felt my life was missing something. So I became a Nazi."

Lime pickle.

"You see, I joined this group, we were concerned primarily with issues of morality, and we decided to focus on one of those Asian pornography shops. There was one on my street. But instead of doing the intelligent thing and simply talking to the owner and asking him to remove it, we decided to burn the shop down. I was one of the main thinkers in the group, so it was my order to do it. There was a court case and everything, the man was quite badly burned, but the thing that did it for me was a letter I received from this man's eight year-old-daughter. It just had one word: *why*? Just that, why? Well, that just destroyed me, everything I believed in. After that, I became a communist."

Spinach mush and cheese chunks.

"By that time I was in university, and I began to read all kinds of books on the subject. Parts of it really appealed to me, but still I felt there was something missing. Then one of my professors showed me Imam Khomeini's letter to Gorbachev. I don't know if you've ever read it, but I read it that day, and it really blew me away. I just thought, how could this little old man sitting in Qom know so much about world politics? There's a line where he talks about hearing the bones of communism breaking, and this was even before the Berlin Wall came down."

Greenish yoghurt.

"So I went to talk to a mollah in London, and he explained a few things to me, but mostly he told me to just go back and read and think about it all myself. I respected that. In my experience, there are a lot of people who would be happy to tell you exactly what to think, but he encouraged me to think for myself. After that I left university and just began reading heaps of books by Islamic scholars, and then one day I decided, bang! just like that, decided to visit Qom on the fifth anniversary of Imam Khomeini's death. And that was it. That was a year ago, and I'm just about ready to go home for a visit now.

"I have about nine more years of study. There are Islamic scholars who devote their entire lives to the study of Islam. Not me, though. I'll probably go back to computers. I'm a computer programmer by profession."

A pause. And my first question.

"Would I ever consider living here? Christ, no! I grew up in England, not the bloody Third World."

He stands.

"I should be off. My friends are waiting for me inside. Don't like to keep them standing too long. Listen, it was lovely to chat with you, really great. Enjoy the rest of your stay, and if you get a chance, I recommend the trip to Qom. Could turn your life around." He shakes Ian's hand and nods to me.

"We've already been," Ian says in a monotone.

"Ah well, it's not for everybody." He walks across the courtyard and turns around. "Cheer up, then."

Tea.

రావ్

The Canadian embassy is one of the ugliest buildings imaginable. It is surrounded on all sides by equally ugly buildings, and thus blends in.

Ian hands over a wad of bills and the cabbie looks insulted. Rolls his eyes and shrugs, then asks for double what Ian is offering. We compare the ride to others we have taken in the city and stick to our price. The cabbie is angry. So are we. It's the first time someone has tried to scam us since we arrived. Ian offers the money a third time and is refused. Frustrated, we perform a cultural faux pas and climb out of the cab before an agreement has been reached, prompting the cabbie to follow us outside and call to several people on the sidewalk for their opinions. He gathers a quorum of four disinterested bystanders, and our situation is discussed. Two men seem to think that our original offer was on the low side of reasonable. The other two think we are right on and should stick to our guns. As for the cabbie's offer, all four men insist that he come down a few tomans. He protests, calls over a few more people and explains the disagreement all over again.

At this point, I cease to give a damn whether this guy is trying to scam us or not. If it means that much to him, I decide, then the twelve cents we are niggling over is rightfully his, not mine. Because I don't care about it. All I care about at the moment is a stack of envelopes inside this hideous building. Blue striped envelopes with my name on them. Maybe a small package. The first mail we've received in five months.

Ian has acclimatized himself to the scale of the economy to such an extent that he really does care about the twelve cents as much as the cabbie. Eventually, I convince him to split the difference and come inside to collect our mail. At the word "mail" his head cocks to one side like a dog whose name has just been called. He pays the cabbie, and we cross the street to the embassy.

"I just didn't want him to think I was some rich Westerner with a lot of dollars," Ian says.

"But you are a rich Westerner with a lot of dollars."

There is a throng of Iranians waiting outside a side window for information on visas and emigration to Canada. Well over fifty people. In half an hour there will be fifty more. The embassy doesn't process applications here any more, just supplies information on the process. A few years ago, it was (falsely) rumoured that a Canadian immigration officer from the Damascus embassy was in Tehran to process requests. So many people turned up, there was a riot outside the building.

Ian and I bypass the crowd and climb the main steps. We show our passports to the armed guard in the doorway and are allowed to pass through the double-locked doors. We announce ourselves to a woman behind bulletproof glass, and she smiles and presses the intercom. "Sit down, please. Someone will be right with you."

I am so excited I am almost incontinent. Preparing myself for possible bad news, possible good news, possible communication from any number of friends and family members. Preparing myself, also, to adore the people who have written and to try not to despise the people who haven't, the ones who don't understand what communication means to the disconnected: that it is the deepest form of nourishment, that it keeps the soul from starving. I will try not to despise the people who don't know this. It's not their fault.

Ian is just as excited, but about something else: news. *Maclean's* magazines, *Globe and Mails*, federal government communiqués about the state of the nation. He is flipping the pages as quickly as he can, to consume as much information as possible. I feel sure that any moment now he will start stuffing the pages into his mouth and swallowing.

A door opens and a woman with a thick American accent yells to us from across the room: "About time you guys showed up. If you didn't come and get your mail soon, we were gonna give you up for dead." She laughs and waves us through. "Come on up. There's a whole whack of stuff for you."

Ian gathers an armful of newspapers to read on the elevator. I ask for the toilet.

"I'm Mary Jo," she says and hands a file folder full of letters over her desk. "We been wondering who in the hell you were. We even got a fax from one of your parents asking us to look out for you. When I saw that one I just looked around the office and said *nope, no sign of 'em*. Better give them a call soon. If they've watched any TV in the last twenty years, they'll think you been kidnapped or something." She laughs a shoulder-shake laugh and offers to get us something to drink.

The moment she is out of the room, we tear at the envelopes like starving cats. Knowing I will reread everything at least ten times before the day is out, I scan each page for important information only. Anything exciting I read out loud. Ian and I are both reading aloud from different letters when Mary Jo returns and calls to a colleague across the hall. "Hey, Chris, get in here! I got some Canadians needing some company."

Chris is nice. Nice nice nice nice nice. I'd forgotten how nice Canadians can be. Leaping into conversation with the greatest enthusiasm, supplying all sorts of encouraging facial expressions and *wows* and *that's greats* until they find a way to drop the conversation or pass you off to someone else so they can get back to what they were doing. "Here, Tony!" Chris calls to a colleague passing in the hall. "Got some travellers here you should talk to." Then to us: "Tony'll take care of you. Great meeting you."

Tony's been here for three years, he tells us. And he's only been to Shiraz and Esfahan. He and his wife have decided to extend their posting for another year. They have a really nice life here: big house, pool, housekeeper. And they're getting hardship pay for being here, so their time is a good investment.

"Okay, enough. You can talk to them tomorrow." Mary Jo ushers Tony out of her office and closes the door. "Asshole," she mutters and shakes her head. "No one's paying *me* any hardship pay for living here . . . Hey, did you guys know it's the first of July tomorrow? There's a big do at the ambassador's place, there'll be booze and people wearing shorts, the whole bit, some real nice Canadians living here, some duds, a couple of bean counters like that guy, but what the hell, you got 'em in every country, anyway your ambassador's a good guy, wife's real nice, too. It'll be fun. Here's directions to my house. Come around three, and my husband and I'll drive you."

ༀ

We take a bus out to North Tehran and follow Mary Jo's directions to her house. She greets us with a standard American greeting—"Did you have any trouble finding the place?"—and shows us into her home. "Here, take off your monkey suit," she says, taking my scarf and cloak. "Come on in."

We step into a spacious living room, where four teenage-ish children are slouched on the sofa watching television. "These are my kids. You want some pistachios? We had the mayor of Rafsanjan here yesterday, and he brought a whole heap of them. Look at this." She brings out a bowl the size of a watermelon. "This is only half."

Ian and I are too shocked to answer. Shocked, horrified, mesmerized, hypnotised. By the women on the television. Stick figures prancing around in their underwear humping the air. It's a music video. I ca-ca-ca-can't believe how, my God, it's not just the clothes or the lack of clothes or the grinding or the gyrating or the pouffed-out hair or the ass out as far as it can go or anything. It's the look on their faces. I had forgotten how women look when they spend their lives trying to be sexy. I had forgotten how lonely it looks. How painful it is to watch.

Mary Jo's kids look bored and unimpressed. One by one they get up, shuffling around the house in tight jeans and football jerseys, mumbling in that aloof, self-conscious series of grunts that kids use when they—to tell you the truth, I'm not sure why they do that.

The youngest boy is hanging around in the doorway trying to get his mother's attention. She ignores him until he begins to whine, at which point she snaps. The boy stomps and groans in a sort of mini-tantrum and Mary Jo tells him off again. Turns to us and apologizes. "He wants money, but I've already given him his allowance. Now I'm pulling the Muslim wife thing and telling him he has to talk to his father."

The language of the house is Farsi, and Mary Jo speaks it the same way she does English: loud and a hundred miles an hour. The first twenty-odd years of her life were spent in Kansas. After meeting her husband at college and following him back to Iran, her next twenty-odd years have been spent here. "And they been twenty *odd* years, lemme tell ya."

Mary Jo shows us around her house, guiding us around each of its very spacious rooms, pointing out the most extraordinary carpets—"In America you'd pay about twenty thousand bucks for that one"—showing us the view of the pool (surrounded by twelve-foot walls) and the satellite dish. When I tell her I thought satellite dishes were illegal, she looks nonchalant. "Oh yeah, but you can't see it from where we've got it on the balcony. Did you wanna watch some TV? We get everything: CNN, BBC, MTV. If you'd've come over earlier we could've watched a video. We got just about everything you'd ever wanna see." She points us back to the living room, and we sit down with another handful of pistachios.

Her oldest son gets up and excuses himself as soon as we sit down. "He's embarrassed that his English isn't perfect," Mary Jo explains. "Lately he's been getting mad at me for always speaking to them in Farsi, but it feels strange to speak to them in English, like I'm not really talking to them. They're Iranian. That's their language.

"Know what his latest thing is?" Mary Jo whispers. "He loves to wear blue jeans, but the kids aren't allowed to wear 'em to school. Last few weeks he's been walking out with his school pants on, then before he goes by the girls' school he puts his jeans on overtop so all the girls can see him, then when he's out of their sight, he pulls off his jeans and walks the rest of the way in his normal pants. It was a friend of mine who first saw him doing that. She came over and told me, and the two of us sat here laughing until our stomachs hurt."

I ask her about the rest of her family.

"When the revolution hit, my parents thought I was completely nuts to live here. They'd turn on their TVs and see a screen full of lunatics, then they'd call me and ask me to come home. I'd tell them: Mom, Dad, I just walked down to the American embassy in my blue jeans and had a look. There might be hostages inside the building, but outside everything's fine, people are all real nice to me.

"It was true. Every Iranian I knew was so grateful I didn't bail out on them. You know, all these Americans lived here when it was easy to make money, but no one stuck around after the Shah left. They just hightailed it out of here and let the Iranians deal with the fallout. It's like all these revolutions. People steamroll through a place sucking out its resources until the natives figure out that 'development' actually means 'freeloading,' then they figure out that they're starving, and the foreigners are even richer than before, and the whole place goes spastic. The moment things get ugly, everyone bails and says it's the natives' problem. As far as I'm concerned, if you're gonna haul out when things get ugly, you shouldn't have been here in the first place."

My eyes keep pulling towards the television. It's a broadcast of a Madonna concert.

"It's hard to believe now, but in the early days of the revolution, no one knew what was going to happen. I mean, the communists thought maybe they'd get something out of the whole thing, the mujahedin were all in there too at the beginning. We were all waiting for some great democracy. No one knew it was going to turn out like this, I sure didn't anyway. At the beginning, they just said women should wear the hejab to show support for the revolution or something. Next thing you know, you have to wear a scarf to get into government buildings. I went back to America for a visit that summer and, by the time I flew back, I had to wear the whole sack just to get out of the airport. I couldn't believe it.

"My family really went bananas after that. They thought for sure we were all starving and when I said, look, Mom, *relax*—we've got everything we need, she thought I was lying to make her feel better. Finally I just opened up my fridge, took a picture and sent it to her."

Mary Jo's husband arrives. He is a slight, soft-spoken man with glistening black eyes and a moustache. He introduces himself, greets each of his children with a touch—hand on a shoulder, pat on the back, tousle of hair—and excuses himself. He must get dressed for the party. He murmurs a few words to Mary Jo and trots upstairs, grinning.

"He says he has to go and make himself look beautiful for Canada." Mary Jo watches him up the stairs and laughs. "A couple of years ago, my family watched some movie on TV about Iran, and after that they were just convinced he was beating me. Can you believe that? I said, Dad, I just watched an American movie about a man who gets drunk and beats up his kids—does that mean every man in America does that? It's nuts, I tell ya."

Mary Jo's husband glides down the stairs and makes a grand theatrical entrance dressed in a tuxedo. Even I, who normally have an allergic reaction to suit-like clothing, am impressed.

"I'm afraid we're going to be pretty underdressed," Ian says. "These are the only clothes we have with us."

"Oh, God, you're fine." Mary Jo waves us away and starts towards the door. "It's supposed to be casual. He's just doing that to show off." Her husband smiles and tries to look innocent. We walk onto the street, and Mary Jo throws her hands up in the air and spins around. "Bathing suits! I bet you guys don't have any with you. I'll grab some of the kids'."

The ambassador's residence is exactly what I'd expected. When I heard the words "ambassador's residence," an image of a place immediately came to mind. And that's exactly what it's like.

High stone walls topped with jagged glass, a wide grand entrance manned by dapper guards. Lots of lawn, lots of trees, lots of garden, the swimming pool, as promised, and even a stone fountain pissing into the wind. The house is the indoor version of what I've just described. Picture-perfect furniture made for looking at, lots of mirrors and pastel pictures made not to look at, lamps and chande-liers, a grand staircase.

The ambassador and his wife are also exactly what I anticipated when I heard the words, "the ambassador and his wife." He is tall and looks like he just walked out of a mail-order catalogue. She is tall and looks like she just walked out of a mail-order catalogue. Blond, both of them. Neither of them naturally. And nice. Nice nice nice nice nice. We are all smiling so hard we're giving each other wrinkles.

We are shown to a powder room that is larger than any apartment I've ever lived in and told to hang up our coats and come outside for a cocktail. We're in Canada now, we are told with a smile.

I hang my cloak on the rack and stare at myself; the image of myself; the wall of full-length mirrors in front of me. I am surprised by what I see, how coarse I look, how worn, how rough. How indelicate. I bring my hands up to my head and pull the elastic out of my hair, pull my braid out, twist by twist, my thick wiry hair—the stuff of horns. I push the skin around on my face, watching my face distort itself, see how horrifying a picture I can make of myself. Splash water on my face. Use the front of my shirt as a towel. Straighten up. Must go.

Cocktails.

Ian is chatting with a group of Canadians on the patio. I spy a table of bottles and guess this must be the bar. The man serving is the darkest man in the gathering, dressed in a white suit, as are all the other servers. I don't think we call them servants any more.

I ask for a beer, and he nods. As he is pouring, I begin to salivate. So much so that I have to swallow several times before he is finished. He places a napkin under the glass, and I thank him in the manner to which I have grown accustomed. Three or four times, with my hand over my heart.

I turn and scan the gathering. Groups of casually well-dressed people are sipping cool drinks and chatting. I snap my toes in my shoes and chew on my lip. Decide to drink a bit of my beer over here before I go and join the party. I bring the glass up to my mouth and take an enormous mouthful, let the liquid play across my tongue and swallow it. In horror. It tastes like apple juice that has been strained through a sock.

I make a sour face and turn back to the server. I tell him I've changed my mind: I think I'll have a glass of wine.

After one mouthful, I decide to switch to vodka tonics. I have one while I'm standing at the bar and take another one with me to a seat in the shade. Another dark man in a white suit approaches me with an enormous tray of something chopped up and squirted onto crackers. I take as many as I can fit onto my napkin, eat all of them without tasting any of them, then look around the grounds for more food.

Ian is waving. He stands with a group of people, who all look in my direction and smile. As I walk towards them, I feel myself sliding into my skin. Conscious of how my breasts jiggle as I move, how my hips move, how aware I am of all of those things.

In the time it takes me to reach the patio I have slowed my pace to half, pulled back my shoulders, raised my chin and remembered how to glide. Gracefully. By the time I reach the group, I've remembered how to smile and say, *Hi, nice to meet you.* Whether it's actually nice or not.

And it is, sometimes. Yes, genuinely. Chit-chat chit-chat chit-chat chit-chat. Perfectly nice people as foreign to me as any others I've met in this country. Except that we're all related by passport, so we have a kinship that comes from voting in the same elections, reading the same textbooks, decorating our houses with the same kinds of Christmas decorations, watching the same television programs. A familiarity that comes from being able to predict entire conversations before they happen.

"It's comforting to be around your own people again, eh?" Ian says as we return to the bar for another refill. I drop back and seek out Mary Jo. Pull on her daughter's bathing suit and spend the rest of the afternoon floating on my back, staring up at the square of sky above this spot of ground called Canada.

IRAN
KHOOB

T HIS IS THE LAST STOP before the border: A
tiny one-road town whose purpose is to facili-
tate the shuttling of people back and forth across
a geopolitical line that separates their state from the next
one. That separates an Islamic government from a secular
one; separates veiling by law from veiling by choice; a
West-friendly government from a West-unfriendly government; Kurds who want a measure of recognition and
self-determination from Kurds who want a measure of
recognition and self-determination; Iranian rials from
Turkish lira.

As we are preparing to leave the town and walk the
last mile to the border, Ian is suddenly overcome with
emotion. Starts approaching every Iranian he can find to
tell them what a wonderful time he had in their country,
how good the people are, how good they have been to
him, how good the country is.

"Iran khoob!" he shouts to everyone he passes. Smiling
and bowing and laying a hand over his heart. *"Iran khoob!
Kheylee-mam-noon! Iran khoob ast!"*

People are smiling and watching him in a way that suggests that they are wondering if it's the heat that's getting to him, or if he is just a raving lunatic. Ian is oblivious to the stares he is receiving and continues to announce his creed at top volume as we walk the dusty road out of town and towards the border. I am yomping along beside him wondering if it's the heat that's getting to him, or if he's just gone stark raving mad. In all the time we've been here he has devoted most of his free time to insulting, judging and despising the place. Yammering. Almost constantly. But now that we are within a mile of the border he actually has tears in his eyes at the thought of leaving.

The border is jammed with buses disgorging luggage in preparation for customs. Seeing the mounds of stuff—carpets, cookware, clothes, clothes, clothes, gifts, more carpets, box upon box upon box, every possible size and shape of bag—it is an exercise in mental agility to try to imagine how it all fitted into the bus in the first place.

We are looking for passage to Syria, and so begin asking around for someone heading in that direction. One of the buses is going all the way to Damascus. Perfect. They'll take us for twenty-five dollars, payable in US cash only. We agree, shake on it, and arrange to meet them on the other side of customs.

It takes us all of two and a half minutes to pass from under Khomeini's portrait to Atatürk's. Ian was still bursting out with his *Iran khoob!* declarations when we handed our passports over, so no doubt this sped up the process somewhat.

It takes our busmates seven and a half hours to meet us on the Turkish side. They are all in good form, though all of the spirited packing it took to squish their belongings into various containers has been destroyed and they are forced to start all over again. And then load it all onto the bus.

This takes another five hours.

Surprisingly, I am still in hejab. After weeks of dreaming of this moment, when I would pass out of the reach of Islamic law and could shed my black skin, I find myself with absolutely no inclination to do so. I had envisioned a celebration of some kind, maybe a furious dance that gradually fed the fetid fabric to the ground. But something is clear to me only now as I stand here: I am out of the country, but my blood is not. It needs a chance to let go of this place and begin to feed itself with the water, the air and the soul of the next. I will shed my skin only when it has had time to separate from me.

The bus is ready to pull out, just before dark. We are introduced to the entire bus, parents of all the children I've been running around with the last several hours, plus two students from China, members of a Shi'ite Chinese minority who've spent the last five years pursuing Islamic studies in Qom. The taller of the two boys, Li, speaks English. This bus is on a pilgrimage to Shi'ite sacred sites in Syria, he explains. Are we pilgrims or simply passengers?

"Passengers. Any idea when we will be arriving in Damascus?"

"Probably after one night," he replies, smiles, and returns to his seat.

The bus heaves out of the parking lot and onto the narrow road to Turkey. I rearrange myself in search of the most comfortable sleeping arrangement and finally settle myself with my knees crammed up against the seat in front and a balled-up shirt between my shoulder and cheek. Am just settling into the soothing rhythm of motion when the bus slows down and wheezes to a halt by the side of the road. People around us stand up and begin filing outside, the driver and several other men begin taking things off the roof, carpets are rolled out on the ground and metal canisters are hauled out from the luggage holds underneath the bus.

"We eat," says Li, smiling, as he walks past us in the aisle.

Ian says a number of things, none of which are suitable to print.

The meal (rice with eggs and potatoes and eggplant), doesn't take all that long to prepare and is delicious. The plates are all collected and wrapped—we will wash them tomorrow when we drive past a river—and water is boiled for tea. In all, Ian tells me, this stop has added almost two hours to our trip so we may not get into Damascus until quite late tomorrow.

The pots are stacked and put away, the carpets rolled up, put back on top of the bus and tied down, all passengers and pilgrims settled back into the bus for a night of travel. We lumber back onto the road and away. I unbutton my manteau, settle back into my shirt-pillow and begin dreaming of Damascus.

We are not on the road an hour before we slow down again. Checkpoint. Turkish soldiers posted in the region to keep the Kurds down; young kids from big cities in the western part of the country bored stiff and full of resentment. A pair of teenaged soldiers climb onto the bus and demand money from the driver. They pocket the bribe, then swagger down the aisle where all the children lie sleeping. The soldiers kick them awake feeling, no doubt for the first time all day, powerful and in control. Just for the hell of it, they ask all of the passengers in the back half of the bus to unpack all of their bags. For hours the soldiers pick through belongings, taking what appeals to them and tossing the rest onto the floor. They manage to get three cartons of cigarettes out of the ordeal and seem satisfied. Laugh their way back out of the bus and let us pass. Passengers at the back almost seem ashamed as they gather their things together quietly, humbly; and the bus moves on.

From the middle of the night and the very deepest sleep, I am nudged awake. Another checkpoint, another kid in green clothes with a gun, this time asking for my passport. He takes it, along with Ian's, and leaves. Is gone long enough that I begin to wonder if we are going to get them back. We do, but not before Ian is called to the front of the bus to help sort out a problem. The soldiers have discovered some alcohol and are about to confiscate it because, they say, Muslims don't drink. Ian is the only non-Muslim on board. If he says it belongs to him, Li explains, maybe they won't take it.

Ian goes to see what he can do. While he is distracted at the front of the bus, one of the soldiers comes back to return our passports. He leans over and tosses the passports in my lap, then plunges his hand between my legs and tries to get as much out of the experience as he can before I pummel him into the aisle.

He laughs, saunters back down the aisle and leaps off the bus.

I rebutton my manteau and call to Ian to just offer them another bribe so that we can get out of here.

He does, we do, and I make another attempt at sleep.

We wake up by the side of the road. It is dawn. Light is beginning to leak through the windows. It is beautiful outside. Green hills and a roaring river.

Passengers slowly wind themselves out of sleep and trudge outside. From my window I see Li, his friend and a handful of men monitoring the sunrise and trying to figure out which way Mecca lies; which way they should pray. There is some discussion, a decision, and one of the men begins his morning ritual. Then more discussion among the remaining men, another decision, and a polite interruption of the man who had started. He stops, listens and agrees. Shifts his position about ten degrees to the east and begins again. The other five join in. The rest of the men are off taking a piss.

I join the women down by the river. Half are washing last night's dishes, the other half are washing their children's faces. I dip my hands into the cool water, hold ice cube pebbles against my cheeks, drench my face again and again and again, sneak water to the back of my neck. A moment of gratitude and peace.

I am here when the yelling starts. Frenzied yelling laced with panic. The women gather themselves up as quickly as possible, yell to their children, husbands, sisters and run back up to the bus where two Turkish tanks stand, their soldiers waving machine guns and urging us back on the bus. Now.

We are packed up and gone within minutes. The panic settles quickly, and before long the atmosphere in the bus is as it ever was. Cheerful.

Li, who seems to have taken us on as his charges, approaches us with handfuls of nuts and dried fruit. He explains that the Turkish soldiers were trying to protect us. We had stopped in a very dangerous area, actually right in the middle of the Kurdish insurrection, where rebel forces, the Kurdish Liberation Army, are fighting Turkish soldiers. Apparently, the area is full of snipers and kidnappers. The soldiers told us not to stop again until we reach the Syrian border. That should be fairly soon, within the next few hours, Ian calculates.

We drive for most of the day. The checkpoints are frequent and lengthy. At one point, the driver stands up and makes an appeal to all passengers. He has used up all of the money he brought for bribes, and there is still the border to cross. Could we all donate some Turkish lira?

We reach the border in the late afternoon. There are dozens of buses ahead of us, and the place doesn't feel like the kind of operation that gets things done in a hurry. My busmates seem to get the same sense, as the first thing they do after we hand over our passports is start pulling the carpets off the top of the bus. Then the cooking equipment, then the food. We all sit, lie, snooze in the middle of the parking lot—no, they don't need any help, the women tell me again and again and again—until the meal is prepared. We eat, tea is made and people begin wandering around the border post. On my wanderings I discover a group of kids from another bus hurling rocks at a litter of small puppies. I scream at the kids (who find my antics hilarious), and stand guard until the mother, a ragged stray who had been out scavenging for food, returns. I am exhausted, frustrated, spent. I hide away behind a crumbling concrete wall and dream of home.

Our passports are returned, and the customs check begins. Everything is taken off the bus and examined, scrutinized and reloaded. We get back on the road at dusk. I hadn't anticipated spending another night on the bus, but am too tired to care. We'll wake up in Damascus and that's enough.

For some reason, we drive for less than an hour before stopping in a sleazy border town and unpacking again.

We'll spend the night here, Li explains. "Better to sleep in hotel than in bus."

Normally I'd agree, but a cursory check of this town's accommodation has me convinced that the bus is the finest place around. And I've never thought my standards to be very high. In the end, Ian and I sleep on the roof of the bus with several other passengers. I'm not sure any of us actually slept, for the street noise—cars, music, talking, laughing, yelling—went on all night without a break.

We are all assembled and on the road by eight. Damascus is an easy drive from here. Should be there by early afternoon at the latest. I settle into my seat and begin to get excited about phone calls home.

We drive for ten minutes before stopping at a roadside stop with running water. Everyone piles out, carpets are pulled off the top of the bus, cooking equipment dragged out from beneath.

Just a quick breakfast.

No one slept well, so after eating the men begin to stretch out on their carpet and doze off. I can't bear to watch. I ask the driver when we'll be leaving, tell him Ian and I definitely need to be in Damascus today, but he gives me the same line he's given every other time I've asked: Soon. Maybe one hour.

I have to walk around. If I sit down, even lie down, I believe there's a danger of spontaneous self-combustion. I get up from the women's carpet and am turned around when it happens. Which is why I only hear the hard cracking *thwack!* but don't see it coming. I spin around immediately and see only the aftermath: my neighbour from across the aisle hunched over holding her head, and her husband walking away with a wooden hairbrush in his hand.

He sits down and laughs with the other men. His wife rocks back and forth holding her head. Eventually she leans to the woman next to her and whispers. This woman peels back the scarf and checks the area. No, she assures her. No blood. My neighbour wipes the tears from her face and straightens up, forces a smile. I sit down beside her and hold her hand, ask her if she is all right. Oh yes, fine, she says and laughs. The other women laugh too, find it funny how seriously I am taking this. Start making jokes about hitting their kids, hitting each other. They can see that I am upset and are determined to calm me down.

Impossible. I stand up and walk to the men's carpet, approach the Thwacker and ask for the hairbrush. Don't know why. Neither does he, but he hands it over and begins the loudest laughter he can manage. Is joined by some of the other men. I grab Ian by the arm and tell him to get on the bus. "You're not sharing a carpet with this asshole," I tell him. "And we're not just going to sit around drinking tea as though nothing's happened."

Ian disagrees. Doesn't want to insult anyone. Make a scene. So I hurl the hairbrush into the dust and stomp off to the bus on my own, knowing on the one hand that I am committing the grand crime of being culturally insensitive, but being unable on the other hand to stop myself.

I sit inside the bus for about five minutes before someone climbs on to talk to me. A girl. Maybe thirteen years old. Sits down beside me and begins to explain that I must have misunderstood. There is no reason to be upset, because that man is *her husband*. She says the words slowly and with emphasis, to be sure I have understood. She is laughing and holding my hand, pointing to my wedding ring and repeating, her *husband*, her *husband*.

The next person to climb on the bus is the woman herself, still holding her head in her hand, but smiling as she walks towards me. The young girl gets up, and the woman sits down beside me. Holds my hand. Brings her tear-stained eyes into view and tells me it's okay. Her husband is a good man. He has given her five children, four of them sons. She pulls back her scarf to show me there is no cut, then smiles again. Everything's fine, she says in a whispery voice. Patting my hand. Everything's fine.

Before too long, the bus is packed up and ready to go. The men are the last to climb back on board, and they linger at the front, talking with Ian and Li. Ian leaves the group and sits down beside me. Silent. Li is the next to approach. "They don't want to leave until you are happy," he explains. "Please tell me what they can do to make you happy."

I am stunned. Dumbstruck.

"Do you want this man to apologize to his wife?" Li asks.

I nod. Yes. That would be fine.

The Thwacker swaggers down the aisle suppressing a smile, like a kid who's been called up by the teacher. Li explains my request to him. The Thwacker laughs and looks back at his friends, then spits out an apology to his wife, who finds this whole thing as amusing as he does. He finishes, addresses a few casual, incomprehensible words to me and returns to the front of the bus. Li asks if this was satisfactory. I say no. I want him to swear on the name of Mohammed that he will never hit his wife again. Li calls this request to the front of the bus and translates the answer: "He cannot do this. He says it is custom for man to hit his wife. He says it is custom."

"Well, it's a terrible custom," I say to Li, who, to my surprise, translates this too.

The bus is absolutely silent. We sit like this for more than a minute before the driver starts the engine and pulls away. I feel numb and heavy, too exhausted to sleep. I sit like a zombie—expressionless—until a man comes up from behind my seat and whispers.

"Please forgive. This man is not good man. I no hit my wife, never, also no my children. It is not custom, as he tell. Please forgive."

We pull into the outskirts of Damascus sooner than I'd expected. I am so relieved that I am sighing audibly. I've said "Thank God" more in the last five minutes than in the last ten years combined. I packed up my things hours ago. All that remains is to get up and walk outside.

Except that this isn't Damascus, Li corrects. It's not even Aleppo, although that is the city *way* off there in the distance. We're going to be stopping here, in the outskirts, in order to visit the head of Imam Hossein (he was decapitated) reputedly buried under a big rock in—*this* place, Li explains, pointing to a modest building on a hill. After that, he assures me, we will go to Damascus.

The bus parks at the side of a fairly busy two-lane street at the base of the shrine. The street is lined with buses, all Iranian it seems, and the place is jammed with chaadored women, their husbands and children. People trickle off the bus and make their way up the stone pathway to the shrine. My neighbour from across the aisle takes my hand and asks me to accompany her. The two of us join the stream of pilgrims and pay our respects to Imam Hossein's head.

On our way back down the hill, I stretch my arms in the air and loosen the scarf under my chin. A single curl has sprung loose and hangs right in the middle of my forehead. I leave it, my second outrageous act of the day, and delight in watching it bounce up and down as I walk.

I am almost smiling when I notice the men on the top of our bus. How they are unloading everything, positively everything, and laying it out on the ground. I hike up my cloak and run to the bus, find the driver and ask what is going on.

"Bazaar," he says and points around him.

I hadn't noticed. That all of these buses had done the same thing: unloaded their contents and spread them on the ground to be sold. There are more Persian carpets and cartons of cigarettes along this stretch of road than I'll bet there are in all of Syria.

These aren't pilgrims, it suddenly dawns on me. They're smugglers.

The moment I figure this out, the whole scene becomes clear. Suddenly I can pick out the Syrian carpet dealers milling around from bus to bus picking out their wares. Suddenly I figure out why the only ones on the bus who seemed like devoted pilgrims and were committed to regular prayer were Li and his friend. Because they are the only two pilgrims on the bus. Suddenly I understand why there was alcohol on our bus that Ian had to claim, why the Turkish soldiers knew they'd be guaranteed at least a few cartons of cigarettes if they gave us a hard time.

Not that it matters.

For no sensible reason, I ask the bus driver how long we will be stopped here before we leave for Damascus.

Maybe one hour, he says, and smiles.

Seven hours have passed, and it is getting dark. I've walked the length of this street sixty-five times and now feel ready to retire. The place is hopping, with hundreds of Iranians selling and an equal number of Syrians buying. Constant car traffic along the street and constant human traffic on the sidewalk. It feels like kicking into an ant hill: the constant to-ing and fro-ing, transporting and shifting. Carpets and cigarettes, trinkets and gold, pistachios and ashtrays. All for sale. Right now. Best price on the block.

Ian is flaked out on a concrete slab outside an abandoned building beside the road. I lie down beside him and am almost asleep when, for some reason, I feel compelled to sit up.

I do. And just as I do, I see three women, three figures in black cloth, starting to make their way across the road. Two go back, but the third continues and just as she steps into the centre of the road, a minivan screeches and hits the black figure broadside. She flies into the air and is hurled farther than I knew a body could fly, then lands—thuds—in a lifeless heap.

Pandemonium.

Screaming. Fast-paced yelling of those who stand nearby. Frantic frantic frantic. The anonymous black-cloaked woman is everyone's wife, mother, daughter, sister, aunt, niece. *Who is she?* Everyone is screaming. She is identified, finally finally finally, and people collapse in heaps. Hysterical sobbing. The woman's husband is found, and he lifts her into the minivan, which inches through the crowd and screams down the street to the hospital. It is over in minutes. There is no sound now but the moans of weeping and the low voices of those who dare to speak.

Our bus is loaded as quickly as possible, and we are out of there before a single policeman arrives. The bus is quiet, cold, hollow. Women clutch their children and cry, softly, stroking their hair and whispering. We are dazed, all of us. So much so that when the bus pulls over an hour later and men begin unloading carpets and cooking equipment, I don't even react. I go outside, sit on the women's carpet, and prepare to eat. It is the middle of the night.

We eat in silence. Spoon the food in mechanically. Stare into space. Then it hits. Another scream. A man's voice howling in pain. Men leap up from the ground and run to investigate. They return dragging the Thwacker, who is clutching his side and wincing. It seems he was out relieving himself behind the bus and didn't notice that the doors to the luggage compartments underneath the bus had been left propped open. He ran at full speed and, blind in this darkness, smacked his ribs right into the door.

Divine retribution, you might say.

Space is cleared on the carpet, and he is laid down on his back. His wife rushes to him and holds his head in her lap. The Thwacker's mother joins them on the carpet and becomes so upset to see her son in such pain that she begins panting strangely until her eyes roll into the back of her head, and she falls into her daughter-in-law's arms. The Thwacker's wife is beside herself with grief. She is wailing, beating her hands to her head and pleading with Allah. Someone rushes into the bus and returns with a vial of pills, places one of them under the mother's tongue and fans her.

She revives quickly, as does her son, who moans and stands up, holding his side, and walks away without a word to either woman. The remains of the meal are packed up, we climb inside the bus for what could only be our last leg of the journey and are almost ready to pull back onto the road, when the engine is turned off, the luggage compartments are reopened, and the cooking equipment pulled out again.

It's the Thwacker. In all the excitement he didn't get to eat. One of the men whips him up a few scrambled eggs and he eats outside, standing up.

This time we get ready to go and actually go. The Thwacker is up at the front of the bus getting a lot of sympathy from his friends. His mother lies sleeping in the arms of another elderly woman. And his wife, my neighbour from across the aisle, is trembling and whimpering like a puppy. She is comforted by some of her friends, given some pills, and quickly falls asleep.

I've never been more exhausted and more unable to sleep in my life. Ian and I spend a bit of the night talking, agreeing to split up when we reach the city, wishing each other well. It has been a long, hard haul together. We're both in need of some solitude, time to let the last few months soak into our skin, to forget the stresses of the trip and the constant companionship; to remember the poetry of our friendship.

I spend the rest of the night listening to the bus sleep, passing my mind over the country, face by face by face. Trying to imagine how I will remember this place. I think of Hamid greeting us in the middle of the road in his pyjamas, Abbas's smile, ping pong and the Six Million Dollar Man, an irrepressible Anglican minister, an angel at an airport. I think of Esperanza's spirit, a German mother's despair, an interminable trip into the desert, a young drug dealer, bodies in prayer, a boy by the sea, and a hundred people who have given me their heart.

Then I watch as the sky reddens over Damascus.

There is a fierce wind. It stirs up the air into cones and blows sheets of dust down the street. Ian and I say our goodbyes through squints and coughs and hands shielding faces. I secure my scarf under my chin and heave my bag over my shoulder. The wind is blowing my cloak up and around my legs, making it difficult to walk.

Once I am around a corner, out of sight, I throw my bag on the ground and unbutton the cloak, slowly, deliberately. I ease my arms out and feel the wind on my back, my stomach, my breasts. Smile. Laugh at how simply a pleasure can be found.

I wait for the next big gust to launch the fabric into the sky. It swoops up like a kite and hovers. A ghostly figure. It swims along currents of air, then drifts, drifts,

drifts. I am leaping up and down on the sidewalk, trying to keep it in sight. My arms flying high above my head. Waving. Watching the air make light of weight. Watching the shape of a darkness that dances.

The sky holds my prayer.

ACKNOWLEDGMENTS

All the people of Iran, all those who welcomed me, helped me and met me with such generosity that I have never looked at the world the same way since.

Joan Harcourt and the *Queen's Quarterly*, for plucking me from obscurity and insisting that my words mattered; Maryam Labib, for your good-humoured help "Farsifying" my English; Diane Martin, for your editorial wisdom and your knack for titles; Anne McDermid, for being the sort of agent everyone dreams of having; Stephanie Aykroyd, for your artistry.

Stephen Brown and Champlain College at Trent University, Franca Cerretti, Virginia Rogers and Harvey Sachs, for so generously providing retreats and workspaces in Peterborough, Montreal, Bronte and Loro Ciuffenna; Emile, Nicole and Yann Martel, for all your help with and understanding of the practical and impractical aspects of this journey.

The Canada Council, the Ontario Arts Council and the late Marjorie Eleanor Wearing, for financial assistance.

Denise Della Rossa, David Glassco, Alison Gzowski, Eva Houskova, Megan Laughton, Kim McKellar, Brinda Narayan, Natasha Pairaudeau, Harvey Sachs and especially Susan Roxborough, for the magic of your friendship.

Dad, for your inspiration and faith in my ability to do

anything I set my mind to; Michael Johnson, for always taking the time to send me letters that made me laugh; Peter and Timothy Wearing, for ensuring that I never took myself too seriously, and for being serious enough when it mattered.

Mom, for your kindness, your grace, your home, for all the things I cannot possibly even list; Sally Soanes, for the Scrabble breaks; Gramps, for your spirit; and Jarmo and Noah, for putting the whole thing into perspective.

I thank you all.